Entrepreneurship, Universities & Resources

Entrepreneurship, Universities & Resources

Frontiers in European Entrepreneurship Research

Edited by

Ulla Hytti
University of Turku, Finland

Robert Blackburn
Kingston University, UK

Denise Fletcher
University of Luxembourg, Luxembourg

Friederike Welter
IfM Bonn and University of Siegen, Germany

IN ASSOCIATION WITH THE ECSB

 Edward Elgar
PUBLISHING

Cheltenham, UK • Northampton, MA, USA

Published by
Edward Elgar Publishing Limited
The Lypiatts
15 Lansdown Road
Cheltenham
Glos GL50 2JA
UK

Edward Elgar Publishing, Inc.
William Pratt House
9 Dewey Court
Northampton
Massachusetts 01060
USA

A catalogue record for this book
is available from the British Library

Library of Congress Control Number: 2016942193

This book is available electronically in the **Elgar**online
Business subject collection
DOI 10.4337/9781786432544

ISBN 978 1 78643 253 7 (cased)
ISBN 978 1 78643 254 4 (eBook)

Typeset by Columns Design XML Ltd, Reading

Printed and bound in Great Britain by TJ International Ltd, Padstow

Contents

List of tables		vi
List of contributors		vii
Preface		viii
Acknowledgements		x

1	Introduction: focusing on the role of resources and universities in entrepreneurship *Ulla Hytti, Robert Blackburn, Denise Fletcher and Friederike Welter*	1
2	Exploring processes and structures in social entrepreneuring: a practice-theory approach *Bengt Johannisson, Jan Alpenberg and Pär Strandberg*	6
3	Entrepreneurship and equity crowdfunding: a research agenda *Thanh Huynh*	30
4	How business angels found a way to contribute non-financially: a processual approach *Olli-Matti Nevalainen and Päivi Eriksson*	49
5	Resource flexibility, early internationalization and performance *R. Isil Yavuz, Harry Sapienza and Youngeun Chu*	70
6	Overcoming the 'smallness challenge' in asymmetrical alliances *Krister Salamonsen*	94
7	Evolution of the scientrepreneur? Role identity construction of science-based entrepreneurs in Finland and in Russia *Päivi Karhunen and Irina Olimpieva*	117
8	The intention–behaviour link of higher education graduates *Elina Varamäki, Sanna Joensuu-Salo and Anmari Viljamaa*	146
9	'Made in Liverpool': exploring the contribution of a university–industry research partnership to innovation and entrepreneurship *Sam Horner and Benito Giordano*	168

Index	195

Tables

5.1	Variable definitions	79
5.2	Descriptive statistics and pairwise correlations for the full sample (H1)	81
5.3	Logistic estimate of the likelihood of early internationalization as a function of resource flexibility	82
5.4	Descriptive statistics and pairwise correlations for the international sample (H2a, H2b, H2c)	83
5.5	Logistic estimate of the international sales intensity, short-term survival, and short-term sales growth as a function of resource flexibility	85
6.1	Geographical, organizational and technological proximity	98
6.2	Small firm characteristics	101
6.3	Quotes illustrating asymmetry dynamics	103
6.4	Quotes illustrating the level of proximity	106
7.1	Finland and Russia as institutional contexts for science-based entrepreneurship	124
7A.1	Profiles of science-based entrepreneurs in Finland and in Tomsk Province, Russia	138
7A.2	Examples of interview codes	140
8.1	Level of intention during studies and entrepreneurial behaviour after graduation	155
8.2	Logistic regression, variables in equation	155
8A.1	Variables and their items	164
8A.2	Correlations among studied variables	166

Contributors

Jan Alpenberg, Linnaeus University, Sweden

Robert Blackburn, Kingston University, UK

Youngeun Chu, State University of New York at Buffalo, USA

Päivi Eriksson, University of Eastern Finland, Finland

Denise Fletcher, University of Luxembourg, Luxembourg

Benito Giordano, University of Liverpool Management School, UK

Sam Horner, University of Liverpool Management School, UK

Thanh Huynh, Bournemouth University, UK

Ulla Hytti, University of Turku, Finland

Sanna Joensuu-Salo, Seinäjoki University of Applied Sciences, Finland

Bengt Johannisson, Linnaeus University, Sweden

Päivi Karhunen, Aalto University School of Business, Finland

Olli-Matti Nevalainen, University of Eastern Finland, Finland

Irina Olimpieva, Centre for Independent Social Research, Russia

Krister Salamonsen, Nord University Business School, Norway

Harry Sapienza, University of Minnesota, USA

Pär Strandberg, Linnaeus University, Sweden

Elina Varamäki, Seinäjoki University of Applied Sciences, Finland

Anmari Viljamaa, Seinäjoki University of Applied Sciences, Finland

Friederike Welter, IfM Bonn and University of Siegen, Germany

R. Isil Yavuz, Ozyegin University, Turkey

Preface

Dear Reader

As President of the European Council for Small Business (ECSB), I am delighted to introduce the 11th volume in the 'Frontiers in European Entrepreneurship Research' series. This latest volume contains chapters developed from among the 113 papers presented at the 28th Research in Entrepreneurship and Small Business (RENT) conference held in Luxembourg in 2014. The RENT conference, which is jointly organized by ECSB and the European Institute for Advanced Studies in Management (EIASM), is the most important pan-European conference for entrepreneurship scholars and experts. We are very proud of how ECSB and EIASM have been able to develop this event into one of the most influential entrepreneurship conferences worldwide. The RENT conference provides a wonderful opportunity for researchers to come together, share ideas and make new friends. Whilst the ECSB also runs the 3E Conference (the ECSB Entrepreneurship Education Conference) and co-brands numerous other activities all year round, the life of our association still culminates in our annual meeting at the RENT conference, which is also the ECSB signature event running successfully for almost 30 years. The ECSB is a non-profit organization that strives to contribute to developing an understanding of entrepreneurship and consequently to improve the competitiveness of European small and medium-sized enterprises. With around 400 full members and a growing network in excess of 2000 friends from 38 European countries, ECSB remains the largest European association of researchers, educators and practitioners in entrepreneurship. It is this strong membership base that provides the backbone of the ECSB and helps drive forward the frontiers of research in this significant field of human endeavour.

The Board of ECSB works hard at making the RENT conference more attractive to its members. The conference is supplemented by several pre-conference activities including a doctoral and a post-doctoral workshop, the former assisting doctoral students to improve their research, the latter providing post-docs with an opportunity to strengthen their publications and dissemination activities. In 2015, we launched a new initiative in the form of Professional Development Workshops, designed to share expertise and foster the broader intellectual skills of members: one on peer-reviewing and another on a wonder-lab in entrepreneurship. We also continue to offer the policy forum themes around topical issues and linking up with the local organizers of the conference. In addition we offer special interest groups (SIGs) for our members and a mentoring programme to assist in career development, which links up seasoned scholars with junior members who can benefit from the experience and advice of their peers.

The RENT Frontiers series is an important means of acknowledging the scientific achievements of our community and of leaving a tangible legacy for our current and future members. The Frontiers series offers a selected overview of the latest and cutting-edge developments in entrepreneurship and small business research in Europe. The chapters presented in this book were selected from the best papers presented at the conference upon nomination from the Scientific Committee and the session chairs. The chosen papers then go through a review process of a minimum of two stages until they have achieved the high-quality standard required to be included in the final publication. I would like to thank those authors and reviewers who have contributed to this volume.

The aim of the series is to disseminate the latest research insights to the benefit of a large community of stakeholders that extends well beyond the academic network. The Frontiers series has become a key resource for all those interested in understanding entrepreneurship and how this knowledge can be exploited to create a more entrepreneurial and sustainable Europe. I encourage you to visit our website for the most up-to-date developments and initiatives from the ECSB, www.ecsb.org. In the meantime, I do hope that you find this latest volume stimulating and useful.

Robert Blackburn
ECSB President
2016

Acknowledgements

We would like to thank Edward Elgar Publishing for their encouragement and support in the development of this book. We are also grateful for the administrative assistance provided by Valerie Thorne, Kingston University. Finally, we are grateful for the reviewers listed below who helped in the selection and development of the chapters:

List of reviewers
Rocky Adiguna, University of Luxembourg, Luxembourg
Alexander Chepurenko, Higher School of Economics, Russia
Dirk de Clercq, Brock University, Canada
Allan Discua Cruz, University of Lancaster, UK
Hang Do, Kingston University, UK
Josefina Fernández Guadaño, Universidad Complutense de Madrid, Spain
Lene Foss, UiT The Arctic University of Norway
Audley Genus, Kingston University, UK
Mickael Geraudel, University of Luxembourg, Luxembourg
Oswald Jones, University of Liverpool, UK
John Kitching, Kingston University, UK
Steffen Korsgaard, University of Aarhus, Denmark
Josip Kotlar, University of Lancaster, UK
Sascha Kraus, University of Liechtenstein, Liechtenstein
Hans Landström, Lund University, Sweden
Boyi Li, University of Exeter Business School, UK
Magdalena Markowska, Jönköping University, Sweden
Alexandra Moritz, IP Concept, Luxembourg
Colm O'Gorman, Dublin City University, Ireland
Rauno Rusko, University of Lapland, Finland
Arnis Sauka, SSE Riga, Latvia
Nadine Schlömer-Laufen, IfM Bonn, Germany
Jens Schüler, Technische Universität Kaiserslautern, Germany
Armin Schwienbacher, SKEMA Business School, France
Sanna Suomalainen, University of Turku, Finland
Sara Thorgren, Luleå University of Technology, Sweden
Anne Trybe, University of Luxembourg, Luxembourg

Sirje Ustav, Tallinn University of Technology, Estonia
Karen Verduijn, Vrije University, the Netherlands
Markku Virtanen, Aalto University, Finland
Thomas Wainwright, Royal Holloway, University of London, UK
Arndt Werner, University of Siegen, Germany

1. Introduction: focusing on the role of resources and universities in entrepreneurship

Ulla Hytti, Robert Blackburn, Denise Fletcher and Friederike Welter

INTRODUCING THE CHAPTERS

Research on social entrepreneurship has been booming in recent years. In Chapter 2, Johannisson, Alpenberg and Strandberg aim to contribute to this area by recognizing its processual character through the new concept of 'social entrepreneuring'. Through an interactive, in-depth case study of two social enterprises and by drawing on practice theory, the authors investigate the practices of social entrepreneuring to identify their structural and processual features. The chapter suggests three conceptual dualities as structural cornerstones in social entrepreneuring: the individual and the collective as subject/actor; personal and institutional rules of action; and self-identity and social identity. In terms of processual features, six practices are identified: social bricolaging, amplified immediacy, dynamic involvement, ambiguous legitimacy, self-enforced heterogeneity and urgency for financial viability. The chapter concludes by emphasizing the importance of collective effort and local adaptation in social enterprises compared with commercial businesses. Interestingly, however, the need for financial capital is considered no less important in social than commercial enterprises and considered much more important than the role of social capital.

Accessing external finance is challenging particularly for new ventures. Thus, the role of online social networks, providing access to a new funding stream referred to as 'crowdsourcing', has raised a great deal of interest recently. In Chapter 3 Huynh discusses one particular form of crowdfunding, namely equity crowdfunding. The chapter conceptualizes this new phenomenon, reviews past research in this field and suggests an agenda for further research in equity crowdfunding in the entrepreneurship context. It points towards three perspectives: crowd-funders, entrepreneurs and government. First, there is a need to under-stand the decision-making of funders in equity crowdfunding, including motives, incentives and processes. Second, more research is needed on successful crowdfunding plans, proposals and processes that are attract-ive to investors as well as the risk management that is needed to help entrepreneurs in obtaining and managing equity crowdfunding. Finally, further research should inform policy of the regulatory environment for equity crowdfunding.

While finance is important for new ventures, the non-financial resources of investors such as business angels and venture capital firms have been highlighted in the literature. Based on a longitudinal, intensive case study by Nevalainen and Eriksson, Chapter 4 investigates how the role and non-financial contributions of a group of business angels change over time as their experience of the business, as well as their cooperation with the business, evolves. The chapter highlights the dynamic and interactive nature of the relationship by suggesting that it is not only the contributions that change over time but also the ways in which the business angels provide their input. The research shows that entre-preneurs also have an influence over the contributions the business angels provide. Thus, the contributions of both parties change as the business angels and the entrepreneurs interact and interpret the situation at hand.

Internationalization is an important growth strategy for new and small ventures. However, internationalization requires resources. In Chapter 5, Yavuz, Sapienza and Chu discuss how resources impact on inter-nationalization. More specifically they investigate how resource flexibil-ity can facilitate and enhance internationalization in start-ups. The chapter finds that a greater degree of flexibility in new ventures facilitates their identification of international opportunities earlier in their life cycles and also improves their performance after the entry into the new markets. Consequently, the authors suggest that resources are an important ele-ment distinguishing internationalization of new ventures from more established firms, and resource allocation decisions are the most critical decisions for entrepreneurs for success in early internationalization.

Alliances represent one potential strategy for overcoming resource constraints in small firms. However, research evidence suggests that the size asymmetries between large and small firms can undermine the role of the small firm and represent a 'smallness challenge'. In Chapter 6, Salamonsen addresses alliances between large and small firms to inves-tigate how geographical, organizational and technological proximity influence small firms' relationships with large partners. Drawing from case studies conducted from small firms in five asymmetrically sized alliances in the Norwegian oil and gas industry, the author suggests that the non-spatial dimensions of proximity can mitigate the smallness challenge. Personal relationships, common industry experience, shared understanding of technology and mutual dependence were identified in this chapter as central elements in those small firms that succeeded in their collaboration with large partners. Hence, the findings suggest that in small firms, managers should form social relationships and legitimacy in the industry before entering into alliances.

Academic entrepreneurship and the role of universities in entrepreneurship is an important contemporary research theme. Based on biographical data of 12 Finnish and 11 Russian science-based entrepreneurs, Karhunen and Olimpieva investigate the role identities of science-based entrepreneurs in two different institutional contexts in Chapter 7. The authors suggest an emergence of new hybrid role identity, that of the 'scientrepreneur'. The chapter identifies the ways in which context and institutions influence role identity construction. In Finland, the two identities seem to be mutually supportive and the two roles cannot be separated. The commercialization of research is viewed as an integral part of the work as a scientist and parallels are drawn between the science and entrepreneurship. On the other hand, in Russia the role of the scientist is placed at the core, and in need of protection from entrepreneurial role demands. Hence, the entrepreneurial role is that of forced identity. Thus, the chapter illustrates the role of institutional context as an important factor.

The study of entrepreneurial intentions is one of the enduring themes in entrepreneurship research as shown in past Frontier volumes. However, longitudinal studies and investigations addressing the link between intentions and actual start-up behaviour have been few. In Chapter 8, Varamäki, Joensuu-Salo and Viljamaa address this gap by examining the realization of students' entrepreneurial intentions in entrepreneurial behaviour after graduation. The chapter finds that entrepreneurial intentions measured during education explain the graduates' entrepreneurial behaviour. The chapter also indicates that perceived behavioural control is more important in actual behaviour than in intentions. This suggests that cultivating students' capabilities and their perceptions of their own capabilities in entrepreneurship are important tasks for entrepreneurship educators. Additionally, the chapter suggests that entrepreneurship educators should tailor their efforts to different groups: those who start their ventures while in education and those with high and low entrepreneurship intentions.

University–industry cooperation is increasingly regarded as an important mechanism for local and regional economic development. In Chapter 9,

Horner and Giordano discuss the ways in which a university–industry partnership can play a role in enhancing open innovation efforts and capabilities at the regional level. Based on a social constructivist analysis of a single case study the chapter suggests that geography and physical space play an important role in the formation and functioning of the open innovation partnership. Geographic proximity facilitates the formation of trust and personal relationships and transfer of tacit knowledge and ease in making contacts. Funding, other forms of public support and creation of a common technology platform also play an important role in forming research partnerships. In addition to these institutional arrangements, individuals and individual agency are important to the establishment and functioning of open innovation partnerships. The chapter suggests that universities can impact entrepreneurship and innovation beyond the formal transfer of intellectual property by providing tacit know-how, technological capabilities and open access facilities.

INTRODUCING RENT XXVIII IN LUXEMBOURG

This volume presents a selection of significant chapters developed from the 113 papers presented at the RENT Conference XXVIII hosted by the University of Luxembourg in November 2014. The RENT Conference is one of the key entrepreneurship research conferences in the world, attended by 170 delegates. The anthology reflects the variety of contemporary topics and approaches that researchers of entrepreneurship are focusing on today. The selection of the chapters for the anthology is based on a peer-review evaluation of the conference papers and their contributions to the knowledge, theory and practice. The Frontiers in European Entrepreneurship Research anthology series aims to contribute to and extend discussions in entrepreneurship research with the idea of consolidating knowledge. But the ambition is also to offer room for new ideas and concepts to help the entrepreneurship research field evolve into new directions. This volume is not an exception in this respect.

First, the concept of 'social entrepreneuring' is presented (Chapter 2) and discussed in this volume as a new opening. Second, the resource-based view has been influential in entrepreneurship research to highlight first that resources are important for the success of new and small ventures and second that most new and small firms face resource constraints. Four chapters (3–6) in this volume draw upon this concept to answer specific questions. Third, from the societal perspective, there is an expectation that universities, with their knowledge base, represent an important resource for promoting entrepreneurship and innovation in the region or society at large. Universities are increasingly considered sources of entrepreneurship, in terms of new entrepreneurs from faculty members and from the pool of graduates. Universities are also seen to contribute to entrepreneurship and innovation by cooperating with businesses. Three chapters (7–9) in this volume address the role of universities in entrepreneurship.

OUTLOOK

Overall, this anthology offers varied and novel insights to our understanding of financial, knowledge and other resources in developing and sustaining entrepreneurship and innovation. The chapters offer new insights, conceptual and empirical, into the ways of overcoming resource constraints typical for new and small ventures, for example by relying on new forms of funding, interacting with investors or by developing strategic alliances in ways that are beneficial also for small firms. They also emphasize the crucial importance of resource allocation. Universities are increasingly seen as important for innovation and entrepreneurship either directly by contributing to the entrepreneur population or by indirectly serving as engines for growth and innovation by cooperating with the business and regions. The chapters also provide new information of these processes. The chapters illustrate the variety of research methods in the field, including the much called for longitudinal research settings both in qualitative and quantitative studies.

2. Exploring processes and structures in social entrepreneuring: a practice-theory approach

Bengt Johannisson, Jan Alpenberg and Pär Strandberg*

INTRODUCTION

Since the turn of the millennium there has been a plethora of research on social entrepreneurship (see, for example, Ziegler, 2009; Fayolle and Matlay, 2010; Berglund et al., 2012; Massetti, 2013). The majority of this literature positions social entrepreneurship against the established frameworks and methodologies in the field of entrepreneurship. However, juxtaposing such approaches runs the risk of not paying enough attention to the unique structural and processual features of social entrepreneurship when identified on their own terms. The notion of 'social enterprise' and recognizing its processual character, social entrepreneuring (see Steyaert, 2007) is still an emerging concept with, accordingly, a broad range of operational definitions and interpretations (Lyon and Sepulveda, 2009; Lyon and Fernandez, 2012). A common definition used by the UK government appears in the *Social Enterprise: A Strategy for Success* document, which states that a social enterprise is 'a business with primarily social objectives, whose surpluses are principally reinvested for that purpose in the business or in the community, rather than being driven by the need to maximise profits for shareholders' (DTI, 2002). Mair and Marti (2006, p. 37) define social entrepreneurship 'as a process involving the innovative use and combination of resources to pursue opportunities to catalyse social change and/or address social needs'. In order to make sense of the way social enterprises operate, these general descriptions have to be considerably qualified.

A social enterprise as a work organization differs in a number of ways from a commercial firm. First, a commercial firm is usually an outcome of a discrete entrepreneurial initiative, originating in an innovation or a distinct market demand that triggers the establishment of an appropriate and stable organizational structure that supports a focused production. In a social enterprise the demand for ongoing creative organizing is constant since new challenges linked to social needs arrive constantly, which creates a centrifugal pressure for increased diversity with regard to offered products that ultimately may make the organization disintegrate, gradually or through an 'explosion'. Second, social enterprises are often 'work integrating', which means that they are staffed with people who themselves are physically, mentally or socially disadvantaged. The workforce often also includes volunteers who, however committed and well meaning, contribute on terms that originate in personal priorities, which makes management control difficult. Third, while business firms acquire resources on commercial markets alone, social enterprises also penetrate public and private subsidy and grant markets. This trisected resource market means that social enterprises in their everyday practices have to accommodate three rationales in parallel. These originate in the different logics that characterize the private, public and non-profit/voluntary sector (see Berglund et al., 2012).

The unique features of social enterprises are best reflected in the way they practise entrepreneuring as a processual phenomenon (Steyaert, 2007). Schumpeter (1943 [1987], p. 132) underlined that entrepreneurship is about concrete action – 'getting things done' – and later, Drucker (1985) claimed the need for a practice perspective on entrepreneurship. However, the notions of 'practice' and 'process' are seldom related in the academic literature on (social) entrepreneurship/-ing. The practice perspective in received models of organizational behaviour is mainly concerned with patterns of activities that sediment soon enough into routines and standards, which reveals a bias towards structural stability that is challenged by genuinely processual approaches (Helin et al., 2014) that recognize the ongoing change that we associate with (social) entrepreneuring. Therefore, close-up studies are necessary that will make it possible to reveal such entrepreneurial practices. In this study the aim is to make inquiries into the practices of social entrepreneuring in order to identify their structural and processual features through an interactive in-depth study of two social enterprises that are linked in a franchisor–franchisee relationship.

Drawing upon previous research we first present conceptual pillars that frame the field research reported in the next section. The qualitative methodology adopted when studying the evolving practices in the franchisor and its franchisee is presented in the third. The fourth section reports our findings in terms of identified structural and processual features of social entrepreneuring. In the last section of the chapter we reflect upon our findings and need for further research. We also indicate some implications for policy-making in the field of social entrepreneurship.

CONCEPTUAL PILLARS AND OUR PREVIOUS RESEARCH

In this section we discuss in detail the phenomenon of social entrepreneuring, its core features and how they may be disclosed. Then we present the conceptual framework that we use to inquire into social entrepreneuring – practice theory. We also summarize the main findings in a previous study of the franchisor in the social franchising system that the present empirical inquiry concerns.

Featuring Social Entrepreneurship

The field of social entrepreneurship/-ing has become recognized as being of social and economic importance but also as a cultural phenomenon (Pless, 2012). Kraus et al. (2014) point out that there is a need for a wider scope in future research into social entrepreneurship since the present research agenda only focuses on definitions and conceptual approaches, impetus, personality and impact and performance.

Governments and public organizations across the world have revealed that they are not able to fight the growing gaps in welfare economies between the wealthy and the poor, as well as other pressing social challenges like unemployment and immigration (Bornstein, 2004; Chell et al., 2010). Dedicated and visionary entrepreneurs who want to 'change the world' therefore have designed new ways to deal with urgent social needs.

Emerging academic literature reports how social issues are effectively addressed by innovative and entrepreneurial social organizations (Zahra et al., 2009; Estrin et al., 2013). A new challenge for social enterprises is to transform from small-scale social initiatives into financially sustainable enterprises (Bradach, 2003; Dees and Anderson, 2003; Lyon and Fernandez, 2012). It is then common to use commercial expansion strategies as models for this transformation (Mort et al., 2003; Weerawardena and Mort, 2012). One of those strategies is franchising, which can be viewed as a way of organizing expansion in order to attain primarily financial goals in a commercial market (Dant et al., 2009). Social franchising departs from the business perspective as a way of expansion, but puts strong emphasis on the creation of societal change through the creation of social values

(Tracey and Jarvis, 2007; Zafeiropoulou and Koufopoulos, 2013). Social franchising illustrates a general trend towards more management in public sectors, a phenomenon known as New Public Management (NPM) (Christensen and Laegreid, 2002). However, there is a risk of tension between social and commercial goals/demands in a social franchising structure, therefore, insight into the nature and management of these tensions is needed (Smith et al., 2013).

There are several reasons why franchising is considered a feasible way to accelerate the diffusion of learning and growth in the context of social entrepreneuring. First, the operational performance of a social enterprise may improve performance by adapting commercially viable strategies such as franchising (Dees and Anderson, 2003). Second, social goals add legitimacy to the commercial operations of an enterprise and this legitimacy in itself could be used to substitute accumulated social capital with financial capital (Dart, 2004). More generally, some argue that social franchising is a useful model for mobilizing different forms of capital in social enterprises: human, financial and social (Mair and Marti, 2006).

Despite the growing popularity of the field, social entrepreneuring research is still in a formative stage and a unified definition is missing (Moss et al., 2009). Many scholars argue that only a broad definition is feasible considering the cross-sectoral nature of social entrepreneuring. The definitions provided in the introductory section thus move beyond the research that focuses on social entrepreneurs and their personalities, qualities, values and visions (Bornstein, 2004; Pless, 2012). Research in social entrepreneuring according to Dacin et al. (2011) thus includes: (1) the characteristics of individual social entrepreneurs; (2) their sphere of operation and the social needs and constituencies targeted; (3) the processes and resources used (it is in this area where core research questions are identified); and (4) the mission of the social entrepreneur/ enterprise. Furthermore, Dacin and his colleagues point towards the importance of gaining understanding of the organizing processes that are fundamental when researching social entrepreneuring and argue that there is a need for additional studies like the current study.

There is a critical dividing line between commercial and social enterprises. The majority of commercial ventures are started and run as family enterprises mainly for benefit of the owners and the employees. Hence, commitment and involvement are centripetal and aim at consolidating the firm rather than triggering growth. Social enterprises that focus on work integration are primarily concerned with the well-being of their own staff, who often consist of people who are marginalized in society. At the same time there are general concerns about social challenges in society, not the least in their own local community, and this concern puts a constant pressure on the organization. Although it is important to the social enterprise to keep a balance between centripetal and centrifugal forces, the latter often dominates and new social problems appear incessantly in welfare economies. However, uncontrolled ambitions to create a better world may cause the organization to disintegrate or 'explode'.

The risk of 'exploding' may be dealt with in several ways by the social enterprise, but only three of them are commented on in this chapter. One strategy is to introduce a professional management approach that would focus on key markets and products. However, the professional management approach may gradually jeopardize the social mission of the organization to serve the community. A second strategy to deal with the risk of exploding from within is to establish or join a collaborative network of social enterprises where interaction and self-organizing organically will help the individual network members to focus their operations. The collaborative network approach is inspired by cooperation in localized small firm clusters where collaboration and competition trigger alertness (Becattini et al., 2009). The challenge then is to use the shared values and the trust they generate to reduce the risk of spending too much time and resources on coordinating the activities within the network.[1]

A third strategy to control the dissipative pressures is the creation of a franchised structure. The case of social franchising has been discussed above. An additional argument is that a social enterprise, by taking on the role of a franchisor, presumably as a role model for its franchisees, itself becomes more focused in its operations and tightens its own administration as well. Research into small, growing commercial firms suggests that these organizations combine spontaneous and planned strategies (Brytting, 1990). Instead of expanding by internal growth the social enterprise may grow externally by mentoring new ventures through franchisees. On the one hand, the franchisor will create additional social value by caring for other social enterprises and simultaneously creating intellectual capital by enforcing its trademark. On the other hand, the franchisor has to control its own embedded pressures for diversification.

Introducing Practice Theory

A general concern with practice theories has increased over the last few decades (see, for example, Bourdieu, 1990; Nonaka and Takeuchi, 1995; Schatzki, 1996, 2001). Scholars have also become more concerned with the processes in organizations – see, for example, Chia and Holt (2006,

2009). Although the entrepreneurial phenomenon has not yet been discussed much from a practice perspective, strategy has (for a comprehensive overview, see Vaara and Whittington, 2012). Approaches inspired by chaos and complexity theories (see Chia and Holt, 2009), conclude that more detailed observations of the contemporary world will reveal that it is unknowable to a large extent, which implies that any attempt to foresee future events, whether guided by rational plans or strongly believed visions, is futile. Such an ambiguous world instead provides a potential space for those who can mobilize concerted and dedicated (inter)action in order to actualize ideas. The belief that the environment is enacted and ventures are enactable is what we associate with entrepreneuring as practice.

Schatzki (1996) addresses the generic features of the practice approach. Reflecting upon previous writers, such as Pierre Bourdieu and Anthony Giddens, Schatzki sees 'practice [as] a temporally unfolding and spatially dispersed nexus of doings and sayings' (p. 89) that puts 'the doing, the actual activity and energization, at the heart of action' (p. 90). Elsewhere, Schatzki argues that a practice 'embodies materially mediated arrays of human activity centrally organized around shared practical understandings' (Schatzki et al., 2001, p. 2). Schatzki's image of practice is appealing when applied to entrepreneuring, whether commercial or social. First, it makes action rationality rule over decision rationality (Brunsson, 1989). Second, the notion of practice underlines the importance of hands-on (inter)action. We know that entrepreneurial venturing becomes more action oriented as the future becomes increasingly unknowable (Johannisson, 2008). This insight is also shared by strategy scholars (Johnson et al., 2007; Demir, 2010; Golsorkhi et al., 2010). Third, the practice approach involves all human faculties in the crafting of the venture, or as Reckwitz (2002, p. 249) puts it:

> A 'practice' ... is a routinized type of behaviour which consists of several elements, interconnected to one another: forms of bodily activities, forms of mental activities, 'things' and their use, a background knowledge of understanding, know-how, states of emotion and motivational knowledge.

Schatzki et al. (2001) argue that many researchers focus on 'the routine and repeatable actions of daily life' because practices are the source and carrier of meaning, and they are almost always social in the sense of involving interacting participants, meaning and language. Yet Reckwitz and others' view is insufficient, if not misleading, when applied to entrepreneurial phenomena in ambiguous environments. Routinization is insufficient when spontaneity and improvisation are called for.

Adopting a practice approach in order to understand social activities, which can be associated with commercial and social entrepreneuring, has considerable face validity (Johannisson, 2011, 2012). Knowledge is embodied, thus intuitive and tacit, which means that action is as much guided by emotion and conation as by cognition (Snow et al., 1996). Personal networking, communicative action, handling scarce resources, and passion are crucial to social entrepreneuring. Timing in changing environments calls for belief in serendipity and alertness, meaning that embodied actionable knowledge (Jarzabkowski and Wilson, 2006) is used and social capabilities mobilized to build the 'swift trust' (Meyerson et al., 1996) that makes it possible to judiciously turn coincidences into opportunities and attract needed resources accordingly. Practices are lived out and communicated in everyday language, which eliminates the translation from/into a management vocabulary, which in turn enhances sense-making and speeds up action. Entrepreneuring calls for what Aristotle addressed as *metis* or 'cunning intelligence'.

Previous Own Research in the Setting

In this section we elaborate on previous research reported by Johannisson (2012). Interactive empirical research into a small work-integrating social enterprise, Macken, disclosed three generic processual practices in mobilizing cunning intelligence for social entrepreneuring: social bricolage, amplified immediacy and dynamic involvement:

- *Social bricolage* is an organizing mode that orchestrates an assemblage of loosely coupled concrete moves and activities. Vagueness, with regard to both output and means in the social venture, paves the way for unconventional activities when it comes to resourcing the operations. Challenges are dealt with as they arrive by adjusting the organizational boundary so that further resources can be acquired or connected to according to underlying need. An increasing demand for standardization and routinization within organizations in both the private and the public sectors in combination with an increasingly ambiguous world accelerates the need for social ventures that offer flexible organizing.
- *Amplified immediacy* captures the genuinely processual, dynamic features of social entrepreneuring as reflected in the doings and interactions in venturing processes. The stabilizing and institutionalized forces in the environment of the social enterprise and the struggle for survival and recognition generate a dynamic tension, which in turn produces what can be considered a basic rhythm in

the practice of social entrepreneuring (cf. Bourdieu, 1990). Amplified immediacy can be seen through features linked to spontaneity, which is based on the belief that every moment can, balancing intentional synchronization and coincidental serendipity, be made into the 'right' one. Hence, timing and intuition guide action. Intense collective involvement is mobilized, including a feeling of shared ownership and a perceived joint responsibility to complete projects that have been initiated.

- *Dynamic involvement* elaborates on the centripetal and centrifugal forces in social entrepreneuring mentioned above. The core members of the organization may look upon their involvement as a duty, while marginal members may argue that they commit themselves for the fun of it. In both groups the commitment being demonstrated is constantly open to new challenges. Johannisson (2012) found that members who once entered the social enterprise as marginal members over time either became more involved or exited, which suggests that involvement in social entrepreneurial processes either completely absorbs contributors or repels them.

In summary, practice theory provides a magnifying lens to further understand the challenges that sustainable social entrepreneuring has to cope with. In the next section we present the design of the field research for the present study and how we went about identifying further practices in the context of franchised social entrepreneuring.

THE FIELD RESEARCH

In the following section we present the background and the design of the study. Additionally, the adopted methodology is presented.

Background and Design

The field research concerns Macken, a social enterprise that started in Växjö, a university town in southern Sweden. Växjö is internationally recognized as a 'green city', but it also presents itself as a multicultural town with a significant number of new immigrants. Several other social enterprises also operate in Växjö but the majority of them organize a considerably narrower range of activities than Macken. A journalist and environmental activist launched Macken in 2005; its mission is to integrate citizens into society.

In Macken, user value is created by reconditioning used objects such as furniture, bikes, electronic devices and clothes in 'language workshops'. These workshops are staffed by individuals with physical and mental disabilities, socially marginalized native Swedes and not yet integrated 'new' Swedes. The latter are introduced to the Swedish language in a working context that is familiar to them and the native Swedes can use their knowledge about the trade and Sweden in the workshops. Macken's products are distributed through its own second-hand outlets and the enterprise also provides services such as courses in Swedish to immigrants. Since 2012 Macken has also run a business development centre that offers a start-your-own-business programme and operates as a social incubator.

In 2012 the social franchising concept was broadly introduced in Sweden through an EU-financed national project entitled 'Explosion'. With three other social enterprises, Macken Växjö joined the project in order to enact a social franchising structure. Its original franchisee, Macken Högsby, is located in a small town about 100 kilometres from Växjö. However, Macken Högsby initially emerged as a spin-off from the municipal administration and we studied their work practices and collaboration with Macken Växjö and interacted closely with both organizations throughout 2013.

In Macken Växjö our involvement concerned both the social enterprise itself and its local context. The study also included the national project 'Explosion'. The 'process leaders' supporting the Macken franchise constellation were interviewed and we participated in meetings arranged for all franchise systems that were launched within 'Explosion'. In this chapter we do not elaborate further on this.

Adopted Methodology

Our practice approach calls for interactive research that goes beyond 'engaged scholarship' (Van de Ven, 2007) and aims for joint knowledge creation between researchers and practitioners (Aagaard Nielsen and Svensson, 2006). The researcher gets insight into detailed processes, and acquires 'tacit knowledge' by contributing to the actions and interactions that construct the emerging practices. Such qualitative research calls for 'indwelling' (Polanyi, 1966 [1983], p. 17; cf. Chia and Rasche, 2010). Elsewhere we argue that only if the researcher is familiar with the context of the phenomenon/practices studied will it be possible to make sense out of the experiences gained as an interactive researcher (see Johannisson, 2014).

The original interactive research in Macken Växjö, to achieve familiarity and track processes, is reported in detail in Johannisson (2012). The research behind the findings of the three processual practices in Johannisson (2012) built the trust needed for further inquiry into both Macken Växjö and Macken Högsby and their structural and processual practices. As much as organizations reveal themselves when changes in the establishment occur, the adoption of a franchise system in Macken appeared as a critical incident, a 'disjuncture' (Levinsohn, 2015) that uncovered further practices.

All three authors have been involved in different roles at Macken Växjö – one as an activist with operative responsibilities in the organization and also previously as a researcher, another as a teacher in Macken Växjö's programme on how to start your own business, and the third as a consultant on financial issues. These involvements also opened doors at Macken Högsby. Our involvement created familiarity with not just the two social enterprises themselves but also with further stakeholders. The parallel empirical case study of Macken Växjö and Macken Högsby has made it possible to compare and reflect upon adopted practices at both the franchisor and the franchisee. In this way they could be analysed both as members of the same franchise system and as parallel social enterprises.

Altogether, 37 individuals were interviewed in this study, some of them several times, including the social entrepreneurs, local politicians, employees at both sites and representatives from a regionalized public organization called Coompanion, which supports cooperatives. Coompanion was the leading organizer of the national project 'Explosion'. The interviews lasted from 15 minutes up to 90 minutes and averaging close to an hour. All the interviews were audio-taped and transcribed. The interactive approach meant that the research team spent considerably more time on site than the interviewing time indicates. Also, observations were made not only in conjunction with the interviews, but also while being involved in concrete activities and 'hanging around' in the social enterprises.

The empirical data have been analysed systematically by all three authors in order to identify structural and processual practices in use. If compared with Eisenhardt's (1989) rationale for constructing theory from case study research, our approach stands out in three respects. First, our study is explorative even if it is a continuation of the Johannisson (2012) research and accordingly not as 'complete' as Eisenhardt's modelling. Second, the interactive method used has made a more holistic approach possible concerning the social enterprises and their contexts, and both structured and casual data collection. Third, although it is difficult in any case study to link accounts and conclusions (Eisenhardt, 1989, p. 39) it is especially challenging in interactive research in as much as the presence of the researchers makes them co-producers of the same accounts that they interpret. This calls for further reflection and makes teamwork essential.

PROPOSED PRACTICES IN SOCIAL ENTREPRENEURING

As an outcome of the empirical research, a set of structural and processual practices found in Macken Växjö and Macken Högsby have been identified and are presented below. Adopting a weaving metaphor (cf. Bouwen and Steyaert, 1990), we see the structural features as the 'weft' and the processual practices, the (inter)activities that constitute them, as the 'warp'. Below we first present three structural dualities that our research has disclosed and then six processual practices. The three practices originally tracked down in Macken Växjö were followed up while the continued study presented here also includes the franchising relationship between Macken Växjö as the franchisor and its first franchisee, Macken Högsby. Excerpts from interviews with the entrepreneurs in two social enterprises illustrate the processual practices while the structural practices emerged from our overall interpretation of our relations with the enterprises.

Identified Structural Practices

As much as the interactive research into social entrepreneuring has furthered our understanding of entrepreneuring as a processual phenomenon in particular, the inquiry into the relationship between the franchisor and its (first) franchisee has revealed structural characteristics of social entrepreneuring as a practice. As indicated, classic research in organizational behaviour associates practices with routines and standards. When these studies were published, entrepreneuring was not yet recognized as an organizational phenomenon and process theories were not that well developed. Drawing upon seminal organizational research and our overall accounts, we propose three conceptual dualities as structural cornerstones in an adequate practice theory of social entrepreneuring. A duality provides a constructive tension between two coexisting and contrasting forces that condition each other (Achtenhagen and Melin, 2003). We identify three closely related dualities capturing the structural characteristics of social entrepreneuring, namely:

- the individual and the collective as subject/actor;
- personal and institutional rules of action;
- self-identity and social identity.

Each of these dualities will first be anchored to receive conceptual frameworks and then validated against our empirical accounts.

The individual and the collective as subject/actor

Giddens's (1984) structuration theory appears as a cornerstone in frameworks that juxtapose the freedom-loving actor and the sometimes restricting, sometimes enabling, externally imposed structures. Researchers who in the 1960s argued in favour of bounded rationality as a norm for decision and action, among them Cyert and March (1963), presented practices as standardized routines sedimented out of collective action. Nelson and Winter (1982) from a technical/economic angle elaborate on the importance of routines to get things done. Some scholars such as Callon and Law (1997) argue that the individual/collective duality dissolves if it is recognized that people never act on their own since they use tools provided by other actors. Challenging the received image of the independent entrepreneur we argue that entrepreneuring is genuinely collective in as much as the enactment of a venture emerges organically out of the personal network of the entrepreneur (Johannisson, 2003).

With regard to their staffing, as work-integrating organizations neither Macken Växjö nor Macken Högsby could be considered efficiently managed organizations. Even if their customers excused incomplete deliveries of services the social entrepreneurs personally often had to make up for absent personnel or mistakes made by the employees. On one hand, Macken Växjö's entrepreneur desperately tried to get more people involved in emerging new projects in order to reduce the pressure on himself as a figurehead. On the other hand, his fellow organization members as well as the majority of the external stakeholders expected him to epitomize the organization. In Macken Högsby the entrepreneur was equally committed and therefore both practically and symbolically crucial to the viability of the social enterprise. Based on his prior managerial experience as a municipal employee the entrepreneur realized that he could not be made personally responsible for every action taken by the staff in the social enterprise. In order to maintain his freedom of action the social entrepreneur manoeuvred skilfully on the indistinct boundary between the enterprise and the municipality not the least when dealing with the expectations that the initiative 'Explosion' had on its operations.

Nurturing personal and institutional rules of action

Drawing upon Wittgenstein, Schatzki (1996) provides a philosophical platform for a discourse on how practices and associated rule systems vary with respect to how local/personal vs institutional adopted rules of action are. Polanyi (1974) argues that knowledge appropriate for action in concrete settings, 'actionable knowledge' (Jarzabkowski and Wilson, 2006) is personal and is closely related to the individual's own experience. Argyris and Schön's (1974) concern is the set of rules that individuals possess as professionals that make them able to cope with situated challenges. Wenger (1998) proposes the notion of 'communities of practice' as the outcome of common sense-making in an organization.

The embedding of Macken Växjö in a franchising structure paved the way for more institutionalized rules of action with the ambition to enhance both the social and commercial viability of the social enterprise. However, the strong democratic culture in the social enterprise made the organization eagerly defend its bottom-up collective procedures. The process consultants representing the national 'Explosion' project were also impressed by how Macken Växjö materialized the cooperative ideals they shared. In Macken Högsby, the entrepreneur nurtured the personal and the institutional duality by keeping the number of members of the local organization very small (the cooperative only had three members).

Manifestation of self-identity and social identity

A distinct and strong self-identity, the product and origin of self-confidence, is fundamental when pursuing unique projects. Many researchers in entrepreneurship associate practising entrepreneuring with identity construction (see, for example, Sarasvathy, 2008). After all, practising entrepreneuring is an existential challenge. A person also has to be aware of his or her social identity, how he or she is perceived by others in order to gain legitimacy. This awareness is enhanced through membership in interest groups. Forester (1999), for example, considers the exchange of experiences between practitioners as crucial in the crafting of a professional identity. Schön (1983) explains how training by and inclusion in a professional community is a way to create a social identity.

Macken Växjö was recognized early on as a role model for social enterprising because of its committed leader and its ability to incessantly launch new social activities. This intensity was as much created from inside the organization as from forces in its context outside. Those involved felt a strong responsibility to compensate for deficiencies in the private and public sectors and it was taken for granted by external stakeholders that the social enterprise could manage where no actor in the public or private sector would succeed. Entering the role as a franchisor helped Macken Växjö to deal with this self-imposed pressure to contribute to society. The entrepreneur at Macken Högsby used his involvement in the social enterprise to personally facilitate and publicly confirm his changed identity from that of a commercial agent to that of a social leader who is strongly aware of the need to stay above the double bottom-line.

Processual Practices

The inquiry into entrepreneuring as it appears in two social enterprises, Macken Växjö and Macken Högsby, highlights six generic practices. The first three practices were initially disclosed in a prior study of Macken Växjö (Johannisson, 2012) while the other three practices were identified in the present study of social enterprising in a franchised setting. Here we report how the original three practices were confirmed in the later study of Macken Växjö and then also identified in Macken Högsby. These practices concerned are:

- social bricolaging;
- amplified immediacy;
- dynamic involvement;
- ambiguous legitimacy;
- self-enforced heterogeneity;
- urgency for financial viability.

Social bricolaging
Lévi-Strauss (1962 [1966]) brought up the notion of 'bricolage', meaning the recycling of artefacts at hand to suit a new need or demand. It has later been rediscovered by, for example, Baker and Nelson (2005). In this study we argue that social venturing has to be qualified as social bricolaging. First, it appears as an ongoing process, rightly addressed as 'bricolaging', and not a final product. Second, the aim of 'bricolaging', that is, 'making do', is not just meant to instrumentally solve a problem involving artefacts or, as elaborated upon by Sarasvathy (2001, 2008), to enter a journey with unclear ends and stretchable means to cover the entrepreneur's needs. It is also addressed as social bricolaging because it is about social value creation, which is especially challenging considering the staff involved. Third, it is social, because it is about bringing people into new constellations (often across sectoral borders).

The variety in terms of objectives, projects and membership in the social enterprise enforces the processual features of social bricolaging.

The development of Macken Högsby illustrates this. A café was one of the first materialized operations. The social entrepreneur identified the business potential of the café after screening the local market, visiting local supermarkets and bakeries proposing collaboration. The common factor directing the development has generally been the capacity, skills and experiences of the individuals enrolled in the social enterprise. The following excerpt illustrates the perceived difficulties in aligning the planned approach promoted by 'Explosion' with the entrepreneur's own 'organic' view on how to develop a social enterprise:

> I choose to not focus on those parts [details, future goals and planning ahead], since there are a number of strings to pull and we continue to work on what is in our hands at the moment … It'll work out, we'll manage, find a way for that [details and planning ahead] as well. (Entrepreneur, Macken Högsby, 4 March 2013)

The entrepreneur at Macken Växjö also recognizes the complexity and challenges of relating quantitative goals such as number of start-ups in the new-venture programme within a given period of time, and the social implications for the would-be entrepreneurs. The different views on the value output created by Macken Växjö in their programme funded by Växjö municipality created tensions:

> Yes, I've told the [Växjö] municipality! You can't see ten companies. What is interesting for you is the number of people who stop living on the welfare system – that is what should be of interest to you. (Entrepreneur, Macken Växjö, 21 March 2013)

Amplified immediacy
Amplified immediacy is a practice that concerns the constant need for prompt action. At Macken Högsby, reflection takes place parallel to all daily activities, mixing administrative assignments with hands-on practical tasks. As indicated earlier, three parties put pressure on the organization: Macken Växjö as the franchisor, Högsby municipality as a collaborator and 'Explosion' as the organizer of the overall social franchising project. A sense of urgency is constantly present in both social enterprises, not least because short-term projects are financing the operations. During one of our conversations with the entrepreneur in Macken Växjö he reflects on how decisions are made in the two social enterprises, under pressure from multiple stakeholders:

> He [referring to the entrepreneur in Högsby] makes the calls … how it is supposed to be and he makes that in a calm and confident way and I see how he is respected for that and they do what he tells them, and I see how well

that turns out in comparison to our relatively democratic process. (Entrepreneur, Macken Växjö, 9 September 2013)

The entrepreneur in Högsby reflects on the same topic:

> We have had a different approach to this [including the will of every stakeholder in the decision-making process] and no one has said we're doing it in the wrong way. Therefore we have followed our own ideas and claimed that we're doing it in the right way. (Entrepreneur, Macken Högsby, 21 September 2013)

Dynamic involvement

Dynamic involvement is a practice that reflects that personal commitment is difficult to regulate rationally. An intended outcome of the creation of the Macken franchising system was the production of a handbook for potential franchisees, using Macken Högsby as a pilot project. The handbook was seen as a key building block in the making of the standardized franchise system that would make further diffusion more efficient. However, the production of the handbook was delayed again and again and not completed when our study ended in December 2013. The 'liabilities' of democratic organizing was one possible explanation for the sluggishness of the production process:

> Every chapter has to be revised by everyone, and everybody is given the opportunity to have their say – it is a really tough process. (Entrepreneur, Macken Växjö, 9 September 2013)

In Macken Högsby the ongoing talk about the handbook functioned as a 'parking lot' for operational problems that might have slowed down, even hindered, the organic process developing the social enterprise. The absence of formalized operations, however, enabled the entrepreneur at Macken Högsby to act at will and improvise successfully, unrestrained by imposed routines:

> I want to keep an open mind, and if it [the diffusion process] moves in one direction, I move in the same direction. I'm not worried for more control through the franchise agreement. I do as I please anyway. (Entrepreneur, Macken Högsby, 23 March 2013)

Ambiguous legitimacy, self-enforced heterogeneity and urgency for financial viability

We now turn to the three processual practices that were identified in the daily operations of both the franchisor and the franchisee of the present study.

The fourth proposed practice is ambiguous legitimacy. On one hand legitimacy contributes to the institutionalization and visibility of the social enterprise on relevant markets; on the other it threatens the much needed plasticity of its operations since new needs arrive unannounced and then call for immediate and unconventional action. Any sustainable social entrepreneurial enterprise must stand out as a respected actor whose existence and behaviour is taken for granted. On the other hand it must appear as truly innovative. The franchisor entrepreneur pointed out that flexibility is the key to a successful enactment:

> The methodology of Macken is to get things done, find solutions, unusual solutions, just to get it done the best possible way. (Entrepreneur, Macken Växjö, 21 March 2013)

Macken Högsby instead crafted its own legitimacy by leaning against the municipal political system and its administration rather than against a non-existent handbook:

> I feel, or want to believe that, this [the establishment of Macken in Högsby] is something that engages the municipality. If it would turn out that they are totally uninterested it would reduce the chances to continue the project. (Entrepreneur, Macken Högsby, 4 March 2013)

The fifth proposed processual practice of social entrepreneuring that was disclosed in the field research was self-enforced heterogeneity. The mission of a social enterprise is to satisfy emerging needs in society, not to become successful by 'sticking to one's last'. This pushes the social enterprise into a 'state of heterogeneity' because of an incessant and uncontrolled inflow of needs. Another pressure towards heterogeneity is the composition of its staff. What challenges can be taken on are limited to the competencies of these people. A third dissipating force is the external stakeholders who control financial and physical resources but lack ideas or the capability to enact them, or both, and therefore want to team up with the social enterprise. Self-imposed pressure towards heterogeneity was especially strong in Macken Växjö because of the entrepreneur's background as an activist and his habit of acting with spontaneity when new options surfaced. This was highlighted in a discussion with the entrepreneur concerning his view on getting things done:

> Well, if [the social entrepreneur] is under pressure he likes to work around the clock. That's not ideal, but I want results and maybe this is just what it takes at the moment. (Entrepreneur, Macken Växjö, 21 March 2013)

In Macken Högsby the entrepreneur (as a former salesperson) limited launched projects to those that appeared financially sound, arguing as follows:

> It has from the start been important for me to think commercially, and try to think profitability before thinking about municipal contracts and subsidies. (Entrepreneur, Macken Högsby, 29 August 2013)

The sixth proposed processual practice that emerged during the interviews, observations and interactions with the entrepreneurs and other interviewees from both Macken Växjö and Macken Högsby is the urgency for financial viability. A reason for this 'urgency' is a constant concern by the staff in the social enterprise that a lack of financial resources will jeopardize the entire operation. The risk of not being able to pay the employees' salaries forces them to scramble for resources on a daily basis and it often becomes some kind of ad hoc matching of resources and needs. Also, concern for their reputation is forcing the staff at the social enterprise to look for projects that can generate cash, either through commercial activities like running a thrift shop/second-hand store or by applying for grants and public subsidies in order to 'fill the holes'. How this urgency plays out is somewhat different in Macken Växjö and Macken Högsby. In Macken Växjö the entrepreneur jumps from 'one cash-generating project turf to another' without any focus. He reflects on the possibility for the social enterprise to become a financially viable business:

> I think so. I think so, but one must understand that our financial situation is very fragile. We have generated a small profit every year, modest though, but we are a small social enterprise with scarce resources and we have no ambitions like other companies in terms of growth ... With poor terms of agreement [with customers] we are very fragile here in Växjö; if we, however, were bigger, we might win better terms. (Entrepreneur, Macken Växjö, 9 September 2013)

Macken Växjö relies on commissions from the municipality as well as grants and funds from a variety of public organizations. The social entrepreneur at Macken Växjö proudly states that he 'is pretty good at getting money from the public sector' and his background as a journalist helps him write convincing grant proposals. Macken Högsby on the other hand is less inclined to become dependent on public funds. Instead, there is a strong drive from the entrepreneur to create a sustainable cash flow through business activities. This desire for financial independence has triggered him to launch several ventures, which offer services and products on the open market in competition with private firms. Reflecting upon the differences between himself and the entrepreneur at Macken Växjö he points out:

> I can feel that ... when we meet, the Växjö crew and us talk about different things. I have great use for my commercial background in sales and trading, because I see the need for structure. (Entrepreneur, Macken Högsby, 24 May 2013)

CONCLUSIONS AND IMPLICATIONS FOR FURTHER RESEARCH AND POLICY-MAKING

Our empirical research demonstrates that in a social franchising structure, the practices of social entrepreneuring are quite similar in the franchisor and the franchisee organizations. Neither the differences in origin of the two social enterprises, nor the hierarchical order between them made process practices significantly different. We see three major reasons for this finding. First, franchising as a management model has not been studied from a practice-theoretical perspective that pays attention to unique features in contrast to generalizing normative models. Second, the everyday doings of social entrepreneuring are much more influenced by the local context and its many stakeholders than by imposed organizational structures. Third, in a socially intense setting of the social enterprise, personal leadership is much more important than formal management tools. This explains the surprising finding that feasible process practices turn out to be similar because of the absence, not presence, of a streamlining franchising handbook.

Although all entrepreneuring is the outcome of collective efforts, joint efforts and local adaptation are explicitly emphasized in social enterprises where both means and ends are more diverse than in commercial enterprises. Profit-seeking ventures operating on input and output markets can easily identify feasible strategies while social enterprises aiming at social, or cultural or environmental, value creation have to constantly reflect upon how to combine available resources and potential contributions to the (local) community. From this perspective, what remains in terms of leadership for the franchisor is to legitimize the franchisee.

Another lesson from the empirical research is that financial capital remains as important in the social enterprise as in any market-oriented business operation. The main reason is that the social enterprise must also be financially sustainable, which implies that the social enterprise has to be able to operate successfully on the 'market for subsidies' as well. The market for subsidies is mainly populated by public authorities and private funds but to an increasing extent by crowdfunding initiatives. This may explain why, in contrast to what may have been expected, social capital does not appear to be a very important resource for social enterprises. Another possible explanation is that involvement in social enterprises is based on shared values rather than on mutual emotional commitment. Shared values may enforce solidarity and create sympathy but not preparedness for taking action. Although the image of social capital as founded in social relations certainly varies from very rational-istic information models to highly personalized exchange (see, for example, Castiglione et al., 2008), neither interpretation of social capital is present in the empirical research reported above.

In order to create a more definitive practice-based theory of social entrepreneuring of the kind that Eisenhardt (1989) proposes, further empirical research and conceptual elaboration are needed. Preferably this should be done in parallel with elaboration of practice-theoretical approaches to entrepreneuring in general. We then hope that our explora-tive study can inspire further research.

Some practical implications of the research reported here is that individual social enterprises should try to carefully balance their profes-sional and voluntary staff. They should also build supportive contextual networks including friends but possibly also partners in spontaneous clusters of social business and/or formally organized (regional) innov-ation systems and thereby learn to mobilize social capital. Listening to the message from the research reported here, which is that work-integrating social enterprises should aim at territorial – rather than functional – integration with other social enterprises, cf. Johannisson and Lindholm Dahlstrand (2009). Accordingly, policy-makers on the local, regional or national levels should consider supporting collectives of social businesses rather than individual enterprises, which is in line with Levinsohn (2015), not because it is unfair to support individual social enterprises but because they need help to see the potential of collabor-ation for their mutual benefit.

NOTES

* We would like to thank Erik Rosell and Mathias Karlsson for valuable comments in the research seminar at Linnaeus University. We also would like to express our thanks to the participants in our seminar at the RENT XXVIII conference in Luxembourg in 2014 for useful comments and also to the two anonymous reviewers who gave us valuable comments during the review process. Also, we would like to express our thanks to the Family Kamprad Foundation for funding this research.
1. In 2014 the social enterprise Macken Växjö became a member of such a localized network.

REFERENCES

Aagaard Nielsen, K. and L. Svensson (eds) (2006), *Action and Interactive Research. Beyond Practice and Theory*, Maastricht: Shaker Publishing.

Achtenhagen, L. and L. Melin (2003), 'Managing the homogeneity–heterogeneity duality', in A. Pettigrew, R. Whittington and L. Melin et al. (eds), *Innovative Forms of Organizing: An International Perspective*, London: Sage, pp. 301–28.

Argyris, C. and D.A. Schön (1974), *Theory in Practice, Increasing Professional Effectiveness*, San Francisco, CA: Jossey-Bass.

Baker, T. and R. Nelson (2005), 'Creating something from nothing: resource construction through entrepreneurial bricolage', *Administrative Science Quarterly*, **50** (3), 329–66.

Becattini, G., M. Bellandi and L. de Propris (eds) (2009), *A Handbook of Industrial Districts*, Cheltenham, UK and Northampton, MA, USA: Edward Elgar Publishing.

Berglund, K., B. Johannisson and B. Schwartz (eds) (2012), *Societal Entrepreneurship – Positioning, Penetrating, Promoting*, Cheltenham, UK and Northampton, MA, USA: Edward Elgar Publishing.

Bornstein, D. (2004), *How to Change the World: Social Entrepreneurs and the Power of New Ideas*, New York: Oxford University Press.

Bourdieu, P. (1990), *The Logic of Practice*, Cambridge, UK: Polity Press.

Bouwen, R. and C. Steyaert (1990), 'Construing organizational texture in young entrepreneurial firms', *Journal of Management Studies*, **26** (6), 637–49.

Bradach, J. (2003), 'Going to scale: the challenge of replicating social programs', *Stanford Social Innovation Review*, Spring, 19–25.

Brunsson, N. (1989), *The Organization of Hypocrisy. Talk, Decisions and Actions in Organizations*, Chichester, UK: John Wiley and Sons.

Brytting, T. (1990), 'Spontaneity and systematic planning in small firms – a grounded theory', *International Small Business Journal*, **9** (1), 45–63.

Callon, M. and J. Law (1997), 'After the individual in society: lessons on collectivity from science, technology and society', *The Canadian Journal of Sociology*, **22** (2), 165–82.

Castiglione, D., J.W. van Deth and G. Wolleb (eds) (2008), *The Handbook of Social Capital*, Oxford: Oxford University Press.

Chell, E., K. Nicolopoulou and M. Karatas-Özkan (2010), 'Social entrepreneurship and enterprise: international and innovation perspectives', *Entrepreneurship & Regional Development*, **22** (6), 485–3.

Chia, R.C.H. and R. Holt (2006), 'Strategy as practical coping: a Heideggerian perspective', *Organization Studies*, **27** (5), 635–55.

Chia, R.C.H. and R. Holt (2009), *Strategy without Design. The Silent Efficacy of Indirect Action*, Cambridge, UK: Cambridge University Press.

Chia, R.C.H. and A. Rasche (2010), 'Epistemological alternatives for researching strategy as practice: building and dwelling worldviews', in D. Golsorkhi, L. Rouleau, D. Seidl and E. Vaara (eds), *Cambridge Handbook of Strategy as Practice*, Cambridge, UK: Cambridge University Press, pp. 34–46.

Christensen, T. and P. Laegreid (eds) (2002), *New Public Management. The Transformation of Ideas and Practice*, Burlington, VT: Ashgate.

Cyert, R.M. and J. March (1963), 'A behavioral theory of the firm', *University of Illinois at Urbana-Champaign's Academy for Entrepreneurial Leadership Historical Research Reference in Entrepreneurship*.

Dacin, M.T., P.A. Dacin and P. Tracey (2011), 'Social entrepreneurship: a critique and future directions', *Organization Science*, **22** (5), 1203–13.

Dant, R.P., M. Grünhagen and J. Windsperger (2011), 'Franchising research frontiers for the twenty-first century', *Journal of Retailing*, **87** (3), 253–68.

Dart, R. (2004), 'The legitimacy of social enterprise', *Nonprofit Management and Leadership*, **14** (4), 411–24.

Dees, J.G. and B.B. Anderson (2003), 'Sector-bending: blurring lines between nonprofit and for profit', *Society*, **40** (4), 16–27.

Demir, R. (2010), 'Strategy as sociomaterial practices: planning, decision-making, and responsiveness in corporate lending', dissertation, School of Business, Stockholm University Press.

Drucker, P. (1985), *Innovation and Entrepreneurship*, New York: Harper & Row.

DTI (2002), *Social Enterprise: A Strategy for Success*, London: Social Enterprise Unit, Department of Trade and Industry.

Eisenhardt, K. (1989), 'Building theories from case study research', *Academy of Management Review*, **14** (4), 532–50.

Estrin, S., T. Mickiewicz and U. Stephan (2013), 'Entrepreneurship, social capital, and institutions: social and commercial entrepreneurship across nations', *Entrepreneurship Theory and Practice*, **37** (3), 479–504.

Fayolle, A. and H. Matlay (eds) (2010), *Handbook of Research on Social Entrepreneurship*, Cheltenham, UK and Northampton, MA, USA: Edward Elgar Publishing.

Forester, J. (1999), *The Deliberative Practitioner*, Cambridge, MA: MIT Press.

Giddens, A. (1984), *The Constitution of Society*, Cambridge, UK: Polity Press.

Golsorkhi, D., L. Rouleau, D. Seidl and E. Vaara (2010), *Cambridge Handbook of Strategy as Practice*, Cambridge, UK: Cambridge University Press.

Helin, J., T. Hernes, D. Hjorth and R. Holt (eds) (2014), *The Oxford Handbook of Process Philosophy and Organization Studies*, Oxford: Oxford University Press.

Jarzabkowski, P. and D.C. Wilson (2006), 'Actionable strategy knowledge. A practice perspective', *European Management Journal*, **24** (5), 348–67.

Johannisson, B. (2003), 'Entrepreneurship as a collective phenomenon', in E. Genescà, D. Urbano and J. Capelleras et al. (eds), *Creación de Empresas – Entrepreneurship*, Barcelona: Servei de Publicacions de la Universitat Autònoma de Barcelona, pp. 87–109.

Johannisson, B. (2008), 'The social construction of the disabled and unfashionable family business', in V. Gupta, N. Levenburg and L.L. Moore et al. (eds), *Culturally-Sensitive Models of Family Business in Nordic Europe: A Compendium Using the Globe Paradigm*, Hyderabad: ICFAI University, pp. 125–44.

Johannisson, B. (2011), 'Towards a practice theory of entrepreneuring', *Small Business Economics*, **36** (2), 135–50.

Johannisson, B. (2012), 'Tracking the everyday practices of societal entrepreneuring', in K. Berglund, B. Johannisson and B. Schwartz (eds), *Societal*

Entrepreneurship – Positioning, Penetrating, Promoting, Cheltenham, UK and Northampton, MA, USA: Edward Elgar Publishing, pp. 60–88.

Johannisson, B. (2014), 'The practice approach and interactive research in entrepreneurship and small-scale venturing', in A. Carsrud and M. Brännback (eds), *Handbook of Research*, Cheltenham, UK and Northampton, MA, USA: Edward Elgar Publishing, pp. 228–58.

Johannisson, B. and Å. Lindholm Dahlstrand (2009), 'Bridging the functional and territorial rationales – proposing an integrating framework for regional dynamics', *European Planning Studies*, **17** (8), 1117–34.

Johnson, G., A. Langley, L. Melin and R. Whittington (2007), *Strategy as Practice. Research Directions and Resources*, Cambridge, UK: Cambridge University Press.

Kraus, S., M. Filser, M. O'Dwyer and E. Shaw (2014), 'Social entrepreneurship: an exploratory citation analysis', *Review of Managerial Science*, **8** (2), 275–92.

Levinsohn, D.S. (2015), 'No entrepreneur is an island. An exploration of social entrepreneurial learning in accelerators', doctoral dissertation, Jönköping: Jönköping University.

Lévi-Strauss, C. (1962 [1966]), *The Savage Mind*, Chicago, IL: University of Chicago Press.

Lyon, F. and H. Fernandez (2012), 'Strategies for scaling up social enterprise: lessons from early years providers', *Social Enterprise Journal*, **8** (1), 63–77.

Lyon, F. and L. Sepulveda (2009), 'Mapping social enterprises: past approaches, challenges and future directions', *Social Enterprise Journal*, **5** (1), 83–94.

Mair, J. and I. Marti (2006), 'Entrepreneurship in and around institutional voids: a case study from Bangladesh', *Journal of World Business*, **41** (1), 36–44.

Massetti, B. (2013), 'The duality of social enterprise: a framework for social action', *Review of Business*, **33** (1), 50–64.

Meyerson, D., E.K. Weick and M.R. Kramer (1996), 'Swift trust and temporary groups', in M.R. Kramer and T.R. Tyler (eds), *Trust in Organizations*, London: Sage, pp. 166–95.

Mort, G., J. Weerawardena and K. Carnegie (2003), 'Social entrepreneurship: towards conceptualization', *International Journal of Nonprofit and Voluntary Sector Marketing*, **8** (1), 76–88.

Moss, T.W., J. Short, G. Tyge Payne and G. Lumpkin (2009), 'Dual identities in social ventures: an exploratory study', *Entrepreneurship: Theory and Practice*, **35** (4), 805–30.

Nonaka, I. and H. Takeuchi (1995), *The Knowledge-Creating Company*, Oxford: Oxford University Press.

Nelson, R.R. and S.G. Winter (1982), *An Evolutionary Theory of Economic Change*, Cambridge, MA: Harvard University Press.

Pless, N. (2012), 'Social entrepreneurship in theory and practice – an introduction', *Journal of Business Ethics*, **111** (3), 317–20.

Polanyi, M. (1966 [1983]), *The Tacit Dimension*, reprint, Gloucester, MA: Peter Smith.

Polanyi, M. (1974), *Personal Knowledge, Towards a Post-Critical Philosophy*, Chicago, IL: The University of Chicago Press.

Reckwitz, A. (2002), 'Toward a theory of social practices – a development in culturalist theorizing', *European Journal of Social Theory*, **5** (2), 243–63.

Sarasvathy, S.D. (2001), 'Causation and effectuation: toward a theoretical shift from economic inevitability to entrepreneurial contingency', *Academy of Management Review*, **26** (2), 243–63.

Sarasvathy, S.D. (2008), *Effectuation. Elements of Entrepreneurial Expertise*, Cheltenham, UK and Northampton, MA, USA: Edward Elgar Publishing.

Schatzki, T.R. (1996), *Social Practices. A Wittgensteinian Approach to Human Activity and the Social*, Cambridge, UK: Cambridge University Press.

Schatzki, T.R. (2001), 'Introduction: Practice theory', in T.R. Schatzki, C.K. Knorr and E. von Savigny (eds), *The Practice Turn in Contemporary Theory*, London: Routledge, pp. 1–14.

Schön, D.A. (1983), *The Reflective Practitioner. How Professionals Think in Action*, New York: Basic Books.

Schumpeter, J.A. (1943 [1987]), *Capitalism, Socialism and Democracy*, 6th edition, London: Unwin.

Smith, W.K., M. Gonin and M.L. Besharov (2013), 'Managing social–business tensions: a review and research agenda for social enterprise', *Business Ethics Quarterly*, **23** (3), 407–42.

Snow, R.E., L. Corno and D. Jackson III (1996), 'Individual differences in affective and conative functions', in D.C. Berliner and R.C. Calfee (1996) (eds), *Handbook of Educational Psychology*, New York: Simon and Schuster MacMillan, pp. 243–310.

Steyaert, C. (2007), 'Entrepreneuring as a conceptual attractor? A review of process theories in 20 years of entrepreneurship studies', *Entrepreneurship & Regional Development*, **19** (6), 453–77.

Tracey, P. and O. Jarvis (2007), 'Toward a theory of social venture franchising', *Entrepreneurship Theory and Practice*, **31** (5), 667–85.

Vaara, E. and R. Whittington (2012), 'Strategy-as-practice: taking social practices seriously', *The Academy of Management Annals*, **6** (1), 285–336.

Van de Ven, A.H. (2007), *Engaged Scholarship. A Guide to Organizational and Social Research*, New York: Oxford University Press.

Weerawardena, J. and G. Mort (2012), 'Competitive strategy in socially entrepreneurial nonprofit organizations: innovation and differentiation', *Journal of Public Policy & Marketing*, **31** (1), 91–101.

Wenger, E. (1998), *Communities of Practice: Learning, Meaning, and Identity*, Cambridge, UK: Cambridge University Press.

Zafeiropoulou, F.A. and D.N. Koufopoulos (2013), 'The influence of relational embeddedness on the formation and performance of social franchising', *Journal of Marketing Channels*, **20** (1–2), 73–98.

Zahra, S.A., E. Gedajlovic, D. Neubaum and J. Shulman (2009), 'A typology of social entrepreneurs: motives, search processes and ethical challenges', *Journal of Business Venturing*, **24** (5), 519–32.

Ziegler, R. (eds) (2009), *An Introduction to Social Entrepreneurship: Voices, Preconditions, Contexts*, Cheltenham, UK and Northampton, MA, USA: Edward Elgar Publishing.

3. Entrepreneurship and equity crowdfunding: a research agenda

Thanh Huynh

INTRODUCTION

The imperfections of the capital market caused by the uncertainty of investment returns, the asymmetric information between entrepreneurs and potential investors, and the lack of collateral available to entrepreneurs create financial constraints and funding gaps for new ventures (Carpenter and Petersen, 2002; Hellmann, 2007; Chen et al., 2009; Kirsch et al., 2009). Such imperfections have a negative impact on the provision of early-stage finance and limit the ability of new ventures to develop their inventions and knowledge into practical commercial applications (Lindstrom and Olofsson, 2001; Widding et al., 2009). It is, therefore, difficult for new ventures to gain access to external finance in the early stages of development because traditional investors (e.g., banks, business angels and venture capitalists) are attracted to the more cost-effective and less risky investments available in established firms. Thus, entrepreneurs usually utilize their own capital or that from family and friends to finance proof-of-concept and other early start-up costs (Dushnitsky and Shapira, 2010).

Within the context of start-up finance, Shane and Cable (2002) and Zhang and Wong (2008) have suggested that social networks may provide a solution to early-stage finance gaps, leading to an assumption that online social networks could provide access to a new funding stream referred to as crowdsourcing. Latterly, Shiller (2013) indicated that resources dispersed over millions of people must be activated to successfully grow an economy and crowdsourcing is one means by which this can be achieved.

A great deal of interest has recently been paid to crowdsourcing among scholars in management and entrepreneurship studies. While most early contributions focused on crowd resources (Hempel, 2006; Howe, 2006), more recent works have focused upon the contribution a crowd can make to 'open innovation', a combination of open resources and innovation concepts (Gruber and Henkel, 2006), and the ability of the crowd to collate financial resources (Cumming and MacIntosh, 2006; Ordanini et al., 2011). Moreover, the rising interest in crowdfunding is evidenced by the increasing number of refereed journal articles being published that cover a diverse range of themes, including process, platforms, the dynamics of operation (Ordanini et al., 2011; Wieck et al., 2013; Mollick, 2014), and regulations that manipulate the relations between financial receivers and crowd funders (Bradford, 2012; Lehner, 2013; Stemler, 2013).

Crowdfunding, therefore, seeks to overcome the problems faced by new ventures by utilizing a large, dispersed audience, 'the crowd', to contribute relatively small sums of money by using an open call, commonly through the Internet (Sigar, 2012; Lehner, 2013; Belleflamme et al., 2014). Crowdfunding has been used for various purposes, for example to fund research projects (Cameron et al., 2013; Loucks, 2013), film, music and game projects (Sorensen, 2012; Weigmann, 2013), and new firm start-ups (Ibrahim and Verliyantina, 2012; Lehner, 2013).

Shiller (2013) has suggested that the funding issues faced by start-ups can, potentially, be resolved by an innovative method of securitization, namely equity crowdfunding. This is because the process has the opportunity to increase the number of investors and the amount invested, and also change the investor/investees' relationship due to changes in investor objectives and investor interference. This is emphasized by a comment made by President Obama, 'for start-ups and small businesses, this bill is a potential game changer', upon signing the JOBS [Jumpstart Our Business Startups] Act, also known as the Crowdfund Act, in 2012 (Mollick, 2014). However, being a new phenomenon, our understanding about the nature of equity crowdfunding and its contributions to entrepreneurial activities are explorative. Thus, this study attempts to survey and draw together the equity crowdfunding element of entrepreneurship studies, to review the past research in this field, and to outline opportunities for potential further research in equity crowdfunding within the entrepreneurship context.

In doing so, a systematic review (Tranfield et al., 2003) and a 'fit-for-purpose' methodology (Macpherson and Jones, 2010) are adopted to categorize and classify the existing literature in order to collate a knowledge base that summarizes our current understanding of the crowdfunding phenomenon. This chapter then reviews the diffusion of equity crowdfunding in entrepreneurship studies that have been published in the Social Sciences Citation Index (SSCI) and elsewhere up to

December 2014. To undertake the research, 'protocol-driven' and 'snow-balling' methods (Greenhalgh and Peacock, 2005) have been employed. Because crowdfunding is a new research domain and only a minority of academic articles specify equity crowdfunding, this chapter will collect all papers with titles, abstracts or keywords containing the expression 'crowdfunding' published in the SSCI and Business Source Complete databases. These papers have been systematically reviewed to construct a knowledge base of equity crowdfunding. An initial set of 77 papers was obtained; however, 38 papers were excluded from the study as they were either short essays or represented personal reflections. Thus, in total, this study reviews 39 papers published by the end of 2014.

All collected literature was read to identify the core themes of research in relation to equity crowdfunding; these were identified as equity crowdfunding within an entrepreneurial context, fund receivers (entre-preneurs), crowdfunders, and regulatory environment (the government). To present the findings of this study, the chapter first describes how crowdfunding was conceptualized in management studies before explor-ing the notion of equity crowdfunding as an alternative source of funding for early-stage firms. This will be undertaken through an analytical comparison between equity crowdfunding and other, more established sources of funds. The chapter will scrutinize equity crowdfunding within the context of early-stage firms from the perspective of the investor, entrepreneur and government to highlight the contribution made by equity crowdfunding and possible gaps in the literature. Finally, the chapter suggests a research agenda that is based upon the adoption of agency theory (Arthurs and Busenitz, 2003), signalling theory (Connelly et al., 2011), and behaviour theory (Connelly et al., 2010) to explore, investigate and further develop our understanding about equity crowd-funding and how it contributes to enterprises.

CROWDFUNDING CONCEPTUALIZATION

The concept of crowdfunding originates from the disciplines of micro-finance and crowdsourcing, but contains unique features facilitated by the rapid growth of the Internet (Poetz and Schreier, 2012; Sorensen, 2012; Mollick, 2014). Crowdsourcing relates to activities in which a large group of participants (i.e., individuals, institutions, non-profit organ-izations, or companies) respond to a flexible open call by undertaking voluntary tasks (Howe, 2006; Brabham, 2009; Bayus, 2013; Schwartz, 2013; Belleflamme et al., 2014). Crowdsourcing can benefit participants by creating a context in which ideas can be generated and, through the creation of networks, provide feedback on those ideas, facilitate product development via the testing of early prototypes, through to the funding of the process (Brabham, 2009). It also triggers a new model of business development in which the crowd is mobilized to support a new venture as active customers, investors or both (Belleflamme et al., 2014).

External investment is often the catalyst that transforms an idea into a commercial offering; however, entrepreneurs often find that investors, either through equity or debt, are very circumspect about the risks associated with new ventures (Riedl, 2013). As a consequence, informal external investment associated with the friends and family of the founder, or other high net worth individuals (business angels) is already far more important than other forms of funding, and crowdfunding has the potential to enhance this form of investment (Lehner, 2013). Crowd-funding, as a part of crowdsourcing, is to raise capital directly through investments from large groups of interested people either as a donation or in consideration of some reward (Ordanini et al., 2011; Schwartz, 2013).

In fact, the crowdfunding model has been historically utilized to collect small amounts of money from many people for charitable purposes and social cooperation (Ordanini et al., 2011). The successful services of intermediaries (e.g., Kickstarter, Indiegogo and Crowdcube) in organizing crowdfunding activities attest to the viability of this vehicle of attracting investment (Ordanini et al., 2011). In addition, the levels of investment from crowdfunding platforms have significantly increased, suggesting that the new method of mobilizing informal investment has considerable scope in the future (Belleflamme et al., 2013).

From Crowdfunding to Equity Crowdfunding

Crowdfunding has been classified into various models. For example, Larralde and Schewienbacher (2012) identify three crowdfunding models: donation, passive and active investments. The donation crowdfunding model in which the crowd does not receive any kind of return has been used for a long time for charitable purposes or non-profit institutions (Lehner, 2013). The passive crowdfunding model involves some rewards for investors, such as products, honorary recognition or other forms of revenue shares, while the investors in the active crowdfunding models not only provide money but also bring the best manner of open sources. Other authors (Wieck et al., 2013; Belleflamme et al., 2014; Mollick, 2014) have categorized crowdfunding into four types: donation (patronage), reward, lending and equity models and this approach seems to be most popular with scholars, governments and practitioners. The reward model in which entrepreneurs offer different non-financial rewards, for example acknowledgements, products, services, or creative rewards in return for investments is the most prevalent. In this model, crowdfunders are often treated as early customers, able to access products at an earlier date and offered better prices and/or other special benefits. This kind of pre-selling product model is a common choice of entrepreneurs who are producing novel software, hardware, or consumer products. The lending (debt) model allows crowdfunders to lend money and receive interest or the returns of the principal loans after some fixed terms. Finally, start-ups or SMEs utilize equity to offer part ownerships and shares of any future profits made by the new venture to third parties in exchange for a cash injection (Schwartz, 2013; Mollick, 2014).

However, Lehner (2013) believes that donation is saturated because the number of crowdfunding initiatives and platforms for this funding market increase rapidly, and when the crowd can actually become shareholders of new ventures donation becomes a less important alternative market. Additionally, studying individual crowdfunding practices, Belleflamme et al. (2013) find that the donation-based crowdfunding model has become less common in practice, and most crowdfunding projects offer either non-financial rewards (final products or tokens of appreciation) or financial compensation (equity or profit-share arrangements). In the pre-order model, when the amount of capital required is significant, the entrepreneur will reduce the offering prices to attract more participants. However, when the distortion is too large, the pre-order model is unlikely to be the best choice (Belleflamme et al., 2014).

According to Belleflamme et al. (2014), for larger capital needs, entrepreneurs prefer investments from investors rather than through pre-sales or reward in returns. It is because the rewarding function in the reward (pre-order) model limits the interaction between a new venture and its investors (Lehner, 2013). In such cases, the profit-share model, thus, seems to generate more benefits to crowdfunders. The choice between debt and equity finance of investors and entrepreneurs is influenced by the stage and phase of ventures, aspects of risk dispersion, legal regulations, cooperate governance and reputation (Kreiser et al., 2010).

However, the equity model essentially democratizes the financing activities by allowing all kinds of investors with various characteristics and different levels of wealth to become venture capitalists (Shiller, 2013). Thus, it becomes more unavoidable (Larralde and Schewienbacher, 2012) and is one of the current financial innovations that allows simple projects to raise needed capital (Shiller, 2013). However, because the equity model requires high-level regulation (Mollick, 2014) and current regulations in many countries are inadequate, it is less preferred than other models in those countries (Lehner, 2013).

EQUITY CROWDFUNDING VS TRADITIONAL FINANCING METHODS

Traditional finance (provided by banks, business angels and venture capitalists) typically involves only a few experienced people or institutions rather than a large group of individuals. In contrast, because it is Internet based, an equity crowdfunding campaign can more easily and more quickly reach potential investors than traditional methods (Schwartz, 2013). Thus, the costs and risks per investor in equity crowdfunding projects are significantly lower than in public offering, business angel and venture capital models (Ordanini et al., 2011).

Registration requirements and regulations accompanying a public securities offering are too onerous and registration costs for public offerings generated by compliance with the extensive securities laws and regulations are too expensive and disproportionately burdensome on small offerings (Lehner, 2013). Using a public offering of equity also incurs significant costs for entrepreneurs as a consequence of the necessary due diligence (ibid.). Additionally, the promotion costs involved for public relations, catering, travel, printing and many other types of specialists are high.

On the other hand, registration is free and costs are lower to promote an equity crowdfunding project via the Internet. Furthermore, equity crowdfunding issuers can avoid the costs of obligatory quarterly or annual audited reports (Schwartz, 2013). And, although reward crowdfunding has been practised with great success on the Internet since about 2009, equity crowdfunding takes the concept one step further. In the US for example, rather than receive a copy of an author's book participants receive a share in the profits of the book, or some other security. This was previously banned but the Crowdfund Act creates a new exemption to those regulations (ibid.).

In general, the costs may discourage and prevent entrepreneurs from raising capital from public offerings (Cumming and Johan, 2013). Furthermore, the high investment thresholds, inability to diversify portfolio investments, investment costs (Loucks, 2013), the limited number of solicited investors and actual investors, and the minimum wealth requirements of investors preclude many venture capitalists and business angels from investing in emerging growth companies (Cumming and Johan, 2013). Thus, Loucks (2013) suggests a critical need for a bridge to the financial market through the equity crowdfunding model. Equity crowd-funding allows small and high-risk projects to be funded by both small and big investors (Riedl, 2013), and helps entrepreneurs to collaborate with investors to undertake their entrepreneurial projects and manage new ventures (Belleflamme et al., 2014).

The benefits of an equity crowdfunding model are not only the financial aspects but also the additional contributions to production, promotion and distribution made by the crowd (Sorensen, 2012). However, Sigar (2012) indicates that equity crowdfunding projects per se contain high risks with the uncertainties for crowdfunders about the project's legitimacy and development of products or services. They also have a high rate of failure and may face administrative and accounting challenges that require meticulous and laborious bookkeeping of a large number of shareholders.

EQUITY CROWDFUNDING: CROWDFUNDER, FOUNDER AND GOVERNMENT PERSPECTIVES

Crowdfunders

The investment process in an equity crowdfunding model may go through three distinct phases (Ordanini et al., 2011). First, approximately half of the target capital will be obtained quickly by the rapid and significant investments from those have direct links with the projects or their creators, such as friends or family. The second phase is normally a more gradual growth of investment created by the desirability of the pitch and through word of mouth. Many projects fail at this phase primarily because of the inability to trigger the interest of the crowd. Finally, the investments will come from others who can access the called project through the Internet.

Through the conduit of the Internet, equity crowdfunding is able to mobilize social networks in which online participants can share information, knowledge and suggestions, or select initiatives to support and provide financial capital (Ordanini et al., 2011). It is the participation by the crowd that creates the interest in social media that will attract more potential funders to the crowdfunding platform (Belleflamme et al., 2014). It is through these processes that entrepreneurs can have a global reach and access crowdfunders (Zahra et al., 2008, 2009; Lehner, 2013).

In equity crowdfunding, the opportunity of an initiative has to be not only identified by entrepreneurs but also recognized and evaluated by the crowd (Lehner, 2013). Unlike other traditional investors, crowdfunders are unlikely to use any analytic software tool to evaluate the feasibility and commercial potential of projects (Riedl, 2013). Thus, it is suggested that entrepreneurs use various instruments and strategies to communicate with a mass of heterogeneous people who can passively listen to available information or actively look for opportunities to make their commitment decisions (Lehner, 2013).

The involvement of a crowdfunder is based upon his or her own personal motivations (ibid.) and will shift between passive and active depending upon the individual's motivation since, besides providing financial resources, they can contribute ideas, information and solutions, and support the start-up process (Larralde and Schewienbacher, 2012). In an equity crowdfunding project, monetary returns from investments are not the motivation behind a crowdfunder's decision to contribute large amounts of money to early-stage ventures (Ordanini et al., 2011). However, the majority of crowdfunders enjoy the investment experience, which is linked to community benefits generated by the crowdfunding activity (Belleflamme et al., 2014). They enjoy the feeling of belonging to a group of special people, engaging in innovative behaviour, being the first to use highly interactive tools, and helping a friend or someone else to fund a social or personal cause (Ordanini et al., 2011). In general, the participants are more likely to be motivated by the enthusiasm of the group of crowdfunders for the desired outcome of the new venture than ensuring monetary or other tangible incentives (Lehner, 2013).

Ordanini et al. (2011) find that crowdfunders are from groups of people with unforeseen, chaotic and complex behaviours. Thus, a small omission in a firm's action can lead to a hyperbolic response (Lehner, 2013) and negatively influences the belief of potential investors (ibid.). This means that that local investors are likely to invest earlier, with more responsive decisions to projects created by trusted people, even though equity crowdfunding is a global approach (Belleflamme et al., 2014).

Founders

Similar to other traditional funding methods, information asymmetry between entrepreneurs and crowdfunders is a challenge in any equity crowdfunding model (Belleflamme et al., 2014). To mitigate these difficulties, entrepreneurs rely upon the capabilities of the Internet (Lehner, 2013) to establish their connections with the crowd during the funding process (Belleflamme et al., 2014). This process enables the entrepreneur to communicate the potential of the idea and the qualities of the founding teams to a global audience (Lehner, 2013).

Riedl (2013) finds that entrepreneurs who already have large social networks are likely to be more successful in equity crowdfunding than those whose existing social networks are narrow. This is because social networks can help potential investors to access information related to the characteristics and reputation of entrepreneurs, and social information about other crowdfunders' decisions. However, according to Belleflamme et al. (2014), successful equity crowdfunding is likely to rely on the quality and reliability of the start-up in delivering promised products or services rather than the quality of products or services themselves.

To accurately provide credible signals and disclosure information about the quality of start-ups (ibid.), and to ensure that the process of an equity crowdfunding project is appropriately managed, Ley and Weaven (2011) suggest that entrepreneurs have an initial screening criterion, and Weigmann (2013) advises creating a good website with a convincing video. All provided information should show that the project is technically savvy that consumers can appreciate and value (Riedl, 2013), and must contain the start-up's financial roadmap, board structure and risk factors (Cumming and Johan, 2013). Ordanini et al. (2011) also find that a project without a minimum individual investment target is likely to attract more participants with small contributions. In contrast, an equity crowdfunding project is likely to fail if it requires too much funds, or has already received external certifications such as awards and government grants because the crowd assumes that the project is so valuable that they do not need to raise any external equity (ibid.).

Governments

Mollick (2014) finds that there has been a new trend in studying and exploring the potential and risks associated with equity crowdfunding to identify adequate policy action. It is recommended that both intermediaries and policy-makers help entrepreneurs create realistic plans and goals to ensure that their crowdfunding projects are low in fraud and high in growth. Thus, many countries including the United States, European member states, and Australia have introduced equity crowdfunding acts to encourage and stimulate innovation and entrepreneurship. These acts have been established as exemptions to the Securities Acts of many countries, creating a big change in securities regulation in many ways (Schwartz, 2013).

First, a crowdfunding act allows SMEs and start-ups to sell securities to not only business angels and venture capitalists, but also to friends, relations and other investors through the Internet. Second, the act does not require a minimum investment per individual, and there is no limit on the number of investors, leading to the possibility of a huge number of investors involved in a project. However, the regulation limits the maximum amount of money that each individual can invest each year to protect crowdfunders from potential loss, and a start-up can raise as a registration constraint applied to equity crowdfunding (Belleflamme et al., 2014). Finally, crowdfunding intermediaries are required to ensure that each investor understands the risks generally applicable to investment start-ups, the risk of illiquidity and other appropriate matters. Such intermediaries have to check the background of the issuer's directors, officers and substantial investors, provide such disclosures to reduce the risk of fraud, and authorize actions against those who make untrue or omit statements to mislead the investors (Schwartz, 2013).

To leverage the equity crowdfunding activity of new start-ups, the regulation only requires a basic disclosure such as the name, legal status, address, website, the names of directors and officers, business plans and financial conditions. Moreover, successful crowdfunded issuers have to provide annual reports of their financial statements and operational results. Issuers must offer their shares through the registered crowdfunding portal, and self-offerings are prohibited (ibid.). These crowdfunded securities can be transferred between investors after one year or between family members. Thus, the secondary market of crowdfunded securities will be very small because the number of share orders from an equity crowdfunding issuer is smaller than in a registered one (Schwartz, 2013).

Cumming and Johan (2013) find that, in general, crowdfunders require more disclosure information from start-ups, a limitation on the number of entrepreneurs that can raise crowdfunds, and a lower threshold of audited financial statements. Meanwhile, entrepreneurs prefer fewer disclosure requirements and restrictions on the ability to crowdfund, and a free trading of crowdfunded shares as well. Investors and portals are indifferent to crowdfunding laws, but both prefer relaxed regulations in order to maximize the crowdfunded capital and want strict regulations and mechanisms related to risk mitigation.

PROPOSED RESEARCH AGENDA

The results from the literature review have revealed the limits of our understanding about the nature of equity crowdfunding and its contributions to entrepreneurial activities. Thus, this chapter proposes a research agenda for future equity crowdfunding studies in the entrepreneurial context towards three perspectives: crowdfunders, entrepreneurs and government.

Crowdfunders

Equity crowdfunding activities are facilitated by the Internet and involved funders who will be from a group of heterogeneous people. Because each individual has different values, self-images, needs and wants, it is difficult to predict the decision of a large heterogeneous crowd that behaves in unforeseen, chaotic and complex ways (Lehner, 2013). Thus, further research on the individual explanations of funders in equity crowdfunding needs to be undertaken. As a new topic, our understanding about the decisions of crowdfunders to commit financially to start-ups is still limited. Thus, this chapter would suggest that future researchers employ behaviour theory (Connelly et al., 2010) and grounded theory methods to study the decisions and incentives of investors in equity crowdfunding.

Schwartz (2013) indicates that a limited disclosure of an equity crowdfunding project is likely to increase fraud and inaccurate information. Unlike other registered security methods, equity crowdfunders have to make their decisions based upon limited information provided by entrepreneurs through online platforms. It means that either small or high net worth investors (business angels and venture capitalists) cannot apply the normal due diligence process. Thus, a different study on special due diligence process for equity crowdfunders needs to be undertaken to help investors learn how to evaluate the provided data, market risk, people risk, technology risk and monetary risk, and to make the investment decision.

Entrepreneurs

In equity crowdfunding, how to attract crowdfunders is the key element of a project. This depends on the business plan and communication strategy of the entrepreneurs. A business plan can consist of market opportunity, product or service explanations, business model, people involved, financial, strategy and dilution schedules. Although Belleflamme et al. (2014) believe that an equity crowdfunding project per se serves as a signal of high quality, this study proposes future research on how to write a business plan and choose a communication strategy to attract more investors in that Internet platforms normally only allow entrepreneurs to provide limited information.

In entrepreneurship research, the potential investors assess the readiness of new ventures to move to the next level when making an investing decision (Wiltbank et al., 2009). Each investor has different scales and ratings of the new venture's readiness based upon technology, market and management stage (Douglas and Shepherd, 2002), or the business, risk/returns ratio and time to exit (Wiltbank et al., 2009). Additionally, in studying the early-stage financing of new ventures, other scholars have found that the funding decisions depend on the investor's perception of management skills, business model, potential market, growth perspective (Mason and Harrison, 2004), shortcut heuristic (Maxwell et al., 2011), and the presentation of entrepreneurs (Clark, 2008). In general, potential investors tend to look for a signal of future success from the new ventures when making funding decisions (Meseri and Maital, 2001). Thus, this study suggests that future researchers employ investment readiness criteria to study what a good equity crowdfunding proposal should be.

Furthermore, how large are the number of crowdfunders and the amount of capital needed for an equity crowdfunding project are challenging questions. So far, the current literature has not addressed this and the entrepreneurs have to make their own decisions based on their experience or personal advisors. A study of the methods of financial forecasting and assessing financial needs is required to help entrepreneurs to identify a reasonable amount of crowd equity. Moreover, because the shares of firms can be held by strangers, risks and concerns will be raised for entrepreneurs even if it is a single non-voting share (Schwartz, 2013). Thus, risk management for start-ups using the equity crowdfunding method also needs to be studied.

Asymmetric Information, Investment Readiness and Networks

Beside the uncertainty of the investment returns, information asymmetry plays an important role in the financial markets (Leland and Pyle, 1977). Entrepreneurs and investors unequally access the information about the new ventures, leading to the absence of perfect information (Certo, 2003). In fact, entrepreneurs possess more inside information about their true intentions, planned activities and value of the firms than outside investors (Amit et al., 1990; Prasad et al., 2000). This asymmetric information can lead to the rejection of good investment opportunities or underinvestment (Myers and Majluf, 1984). An investment is likely to be undertaken when the financial providers are able to mitigate the risks derived from the information asymmetry problems (Cumming and Johan, 2008). However, in equity crowdfunding, the limited disclosure information seems to aggravate the asymmetric information problem between investors and investees (Belleflamme et al., 2014).

Investors can reduce information asymmetry regarding the intentions and planned activities of entrepreneurial teams, and the value of new ventures through contingency (incentive) contracts and monitors (Kreps, 1997). The asymmetric information can be alleviated via signals (Certo, 2003) conveyed by the knowledgeable parties or/and through screening activities that seek additional information from uninformed parties (Lee and Venkataraman, 2006; Carpentier et al., 2010). These parties can have direct or indirect relationships with entrepreneurs, and they thus can receive relevant information about the entrepreneurial teams.

Nofsinger and Wang (2011) argue that entrepreneurs at early stages may rely on their social networks. Many scholars have proved that social ties provide a potential mechanism to reduce the information asymmetry between potential investors and entrepreneurs (Uzzi, 1996; Freiburg and Grichnik, 2012). Social networks also provide additional information about the values of new ventures (Granovetter, 2005), leverage the trust between entrepreneurs and financial providers (Kautonen et al., 2010) and eventually positively influence the investment decision. Even though Mollick (2014, p. 14) finds that 'threshold funding, active participation by large communities, frequent interaction between founders and potential funders, and the ability of founders to broadcast signals of quality' are likely to help the crowd to identify quality projects and reduce the chance of fraud, our understanding about the roles of social networks in equity crowdfunding is still limited.

Ownership and Control

Equity crowdfunding is not only a means for entrepreneurs to share risks with other investors but also disperses their control and governance in start-ups. Shareholders can gain their control of firms by purchasing shares from other holders (Schwartz, 2013). The increasing dispersion of control may impede the entrepreneurial activities of entrepreneurs, adjusting the business strategy and entrepreneurial innovation. How to balance the benefit of equity crowdfunding with the disadvantages generated by the dispersion of control is a challenging question.

Moreover, in equity crowdfunding, shareholders of start-ups generally have the right to vote and coordinate, and all activities are facilitated through the Internet (ibid.). Agency theory could be adopted to investigate the cost-control mechanisms of the equity crowdfunding model that reflect the likely acceptance of the investor–investee relationships in start-up finance. Future research on how the ownership and control rights of crowdfunders can be managed through the Internet must also be undertaken.

Mollick (2014) finds that large numbers of successful crowdfunding projects fail to deliver their promised products because crowdfunders underestimate the complexity and scope of the project. Thus, several relevant questions need to be answered on how to ensure that initial resource endowments prove adequate to mitigate the risk of delay or failure, how a successful equity crowdfunding project develops and delivers promised products or services, and how entrepreneurs can develop an alternative plan if need be.

Regulatory Environment

The regulation landscape for equity crowdfunding around the world provides a fascinating new financial market (Cumming and Johan, 2013). Although billions of dollars are invested by millions of crowdfunding backers, comprehensive regulations to encourage the equity crowdfunding activity of entrepreneurs and academic knowledge on this domain are still limited (Mollick, 2014). Shiller (2013) believes that equity crowdfunding is not only an exciting concept but also a dangerous innovation because it can be used to abuse people, so it needs to be constantly updated and improved. Similar to a public offering of a company's securities, equity crowdfunding faces multifaceted challenges including regulatory hurdles, governance and control (Lehner, 2013), and requires strict regulation to prevent fraud and ameliorate the crowdfunding market. Moreover, Cumming and Johan (2013) propose that there are potential risks associated with equity crowdfunding, such as entrepreneurs diluting the equity stake held by crowdfunders by issuing more shares to themselves, paying themselves more, and not investing in the project after successfully finishing the crowdfunding campaign. Thus, studying the advantages and disadvantages of the current regulations will help policy-makers improve relevant acts to encourage practical equity crowdfunding activities. Future researchers need to find out how to perfect relevant regulations in the national context, as well as in the international environment because equity crowdfunding is a global financing method.

CONCLUSION

This chapter provides a theoretical review of the extant literature and from that review develops an agenda for future research. The study identifies the core themes of research in relation to equity crowdfunding. These were identified as equity crowdfunding in the entrepreneurship context, fund receivers (entrepreneurs), crowdfunders and regulatory environment (the government). The chapter describes how crowdfunding was conceptualized in management studies and how the notion of equity crowdfunding as an alternative source of funding for early-stage firms emerged. The chapter also scrutinized the equity crowdfunding within the context of early-stage firms from the perspectives of the investor, entrepreneur and government to highlight the contributions made by equity crowdfunding and possible gaps in the literature that could help inform future research. Based upon the findings of the theoretical review, the chapter suggests research directions in which future researchers can employ behaviour theory (Connelly et al., 2010), agency theory (Arthurs and Busenitz, 2003), and signalling theory (Connelly et al., 2011) to explore, investigate and achieve our understanding of equity crowdfunding in the entrepreneurial context.

While the findings from the review are robust, it is acknowledged that there are areas within the research process that could impinge upon the strength of the work. In comparing the requirements of a systematic review, the number of collected articles was restricted because of the limited number of published papers on equity crowdfunding. Moreover, some of those articles were written a few years before publication in the top journals. Thus, this suggests reviewing more working papers on the SSRN or elsewhere to capture more up-to-date discussions in relation to research topics in equity crowdfunding.

REFERENCES

Amit, R., L. Glosten and E. Muller (1990), 'Entrepreneurial ability, venture investments, and risk sharing', *Management Science*, **36** (10), 1232–45.

Arthurs, J.D. and L.W. Busenitz (2003), 'The boundaries and limitations of agency theory and stewardship theory in the venture capitalist/entrepreneur relationship', *Entrepreneurship Theory and Practice*, **28** (2), 145–62.

Bayus, B.L. (2013), 'Crowdsourcing new product ideas over time: an analysis of the Dell IdeaStorm Community', *Management Science*, **59** (1), 226–44.

Belleflamme, P., T. Lambert and A. Schwienbacher (2013), 'Individual crowdfunding practices', *Venture Capital*, **15** (4), 313–33.

Belleflamme, P., T. Lambert and A. Schwienbacher (2014), 'Crowdfunding: tapping the right crowd', *Journal of Business Venturing*, **29** (5), 585–609.

Brabham, D.C. (2009), 'Crowdsourcing the public participation process for planning projects', *Planning Theory*, **8** (3), 242–62.

Bradford, C.S. (2012), 'The new federal crowdfunding exemption: promise unfulfilled', *Securities Regulation Law Journal*, **40** (3), 195–249.

Cameron, P., D.W. Corne, C.E. Mason and J. Rosenfeld (2013), 'Crowdfunding genomics and bioinformatics', *Genome Biology*, **14** (9).

Carpenter, R.E. and B.C. Petersen. (2002), 'Capital market imperfections, high-tech investment, and new equity financing', *The Economic Journal*, **112** (477), F54–F72.

Carpentier, C., J.-F. L'Her and J.-M. Suret (2010), 'Stock exchange markets for new ventures', *Journal of Business Venturing*, **25** (4), 403–22.

Certo, S.T. (2003), 'Influencing initial public offering investors with prestige: signaling with board structures', *Academy of Management Review*, **28** (3), 432–46.

Chen, X.P., X. Yao and S. Kotha (2009), 'Entrepreneur passion and preparedness in business plan presentations: a persuasion analysis of venture capitalists' funding decisions', *Academy of Management Journal*, **52** (1), 199–214.

Clark, C. (2008), 'The impact of entrepreneurs' oral "pitch" presentation skills on business angels' initial screening investment decisions', *Venture Capital*, **10** (3), 257–79.

Connelly, B.L., S.T. Certo, R.D. Ireland and C.R. Reutzel (2011), 'Signaling theory: a review and assessment', *Journal of Management*, **37** (1), 39–67.

Connelly, B.L., R.D. Ireland, C.R. Reutzel and J.E. Coombs (2010), 'The power and effects of entrepreneurship research', *Entrepreneurship: Theory and Practice*, **34** (1), 131–49.

Cumming, D. and S. Johan (2008), 'Information asymmetries, agency costs and venture capital exit outcomes', *Venture Capital*, **10** (3), 197–231.

Cumming, D. and S. Johan (2013), 'Demand-driven securities regulation: evidence from crowdfunding', *Venture Capital*, **15** (4), 361–79.

Cumming, D. and J.G. MacIntosh (2006), 'Crowding out private equity: Canadian evidence', *Journal of Business Venturing*, **21** (5), 569–609.

Douglas, E.J. and D. Shepherd (2002), 'Exploring investor readiness: assessments by entrepreneurs and investors in Australia', *Venture Capital*, **4** (3), 219–36.

Dushnitsky, G. and Z. Shapira (2010), 'Entrepreneurial finance meets organizational reality: comparing investment practices and performance of corporate and independent venture capitalists', *Strategic Management Journal*, **31** (9), 990–1017.

Freiburg, M. and D. Grichnik (2012), 'Institutional investments in private equity funds: social ties and the reduction of information asymmetry', *Venture Capital*, **14** (1), 1–26.

Granovetter, M. (2005), 'The impact of social structure on economic outcomes', *Journal of Economic Perspectives*, **19** (1), 33–50.

Greenhalgh, T. and R. Peacock (2005), 'Effectiveness and efficiency of search methods in systematic reviews of complex evidence: audit of primary sources', *British Medical Journal*, **331** (7524), 1064–5.

Gruber, M. and J. Henkel (2006), 'New ventures based on open innovation – an empirical analysis of start-up firms in embedded Linux', *International Journal of Technology Management*, **33** (4), 356–72.

Hellmann, T. (2007), 'Entrepreneurs and the process of obtaining resources', *Journal of Economics and Management Strategy*, **16** (1), 81–109.

Hempel, J. (2006), 'Crowdsourcing', *BusinessWeek*, 1 September, 38–9.

Howe, J. (2006), 'The rise of crowdsourcing', accessed 24 May 2016 at http://www.wired.com/wired/archive/14.06/crowds.html.

Ibrahim, N. and Verliyantina (2012), 'The model of crowdfunding to support small and micro businesses in Indonesia through a web-based platform', *International Conference on Small and Medium Enterprises Development with a Theme 'Innovation and Sustainability in SME Development' (ICSMED 2012)*, **4**, 390–97.

Kautonen, T., R. Zolin, A. Kuckertz and A. Viljamaa (2010), 'Ties that blind? How strong ties affect small business owner-managers' perceived trustworthiness of their advisors', *Entrepreneurship and Regional Development*, **22** (2), 189–209.

Kirsch, D., B. Goldfarb and A. Gera (2009), 'Form or substance: the role of business plans in venture capital decision making', *Strategic Management Journal*, **30** (5), 487–515.

Kreiser, P.M., L.D. Marino, P. Dickson and M.K. Weaver (2010), 'Cultural influences on entrepreneurial orientation: the impact of national culture on risk taking and proactiveness in SMEs', *Entrepreneurship: Theory and Practice*, **34** (5), 959–83.

Kreps, D.M. (1997), 'Intrinsic motivation and extrinsic incentives', *American Economic Review*, **87** (2), 359–64.

Larralde, B. and A. Schewienbacher (2012), 'Crowdfunding of small entrepreneurial ventures', in D. Cumming (ed.), *The Oxford Handbook of Entrepreneurial Finance*, New York: Oxford University Press.

Lee, J.H. and S. Venkataraman (2006), 'Aspirations, market offerings, and the pursuit of entrepreneurial opportunities', *Journal of Business Venturing*, **21** (1), 107–23.

Lehner, O.M. (2013), 'Crowdfunding social ventures: a model and research agenda', *Venture Capital*, **15** (4), 289–311.

Leland, H.E. and D.H. Pyle (1977), 'Informational asymmetries, financial structure, and financial intermediation', *Journal of Finance*, **32** (2), 371–87.

Ley, A. and S. Weaven (2011), 'Exploring agency dynamics of crowdfunding in start-up capital financing', *Academy of Entrepreneurship Journal*, **17** (1), 85–110.

Lindstrom, G. and C. Olofsson (2001), 'Early stage financing of NTBFs: an analysis of contributions from support actors', *Venture Capital*, **3** (2), 151–68.

Loucks, D. (2013), 'Will crowdfunding and general solicitation spur orphan drug development for biotechs?', *Formulary*, **48** (10), 343–4.

Macpherson, A. and O. Jones (2010), 'Editorial: strategies for the development of International Journal of Management Reviews', *International Journal of Management Reviews*, **12** (2), 107–13.

Mason, C.M. and R.T. Harrison (2004), 'Does investing in technology-based firms involve higher risk? An exploratory study of the performance of technology and non-technology investments by business angels', *Venture Capital*, **6** (4), 313–32.

Maxwell, A.L., S.A. Jeffrey and M. Lévesque (2011), 'Business angel early stage decision making', *Journal of Business Venturing*, **26** (2), 212–25.

Meseri, O. and S. Maital (2001), 'A survey analysis of university-technology transfer in Israel: evaluation of projects and determinants of success', *The Journal of Technology Transfer*, **26** (1–2), 115–25.

Mollick, E. (2014), 'The dynamics of crowdfunding: an exploratory study', *Journal of Business Venturing*, **29** (1), 1–16.

Myers, S.C. and N.S. Majluf (1984), 'Corporate financing and investment decisions when firms have information that investors do not have', *Journal of Financial Economics*, **13** (2), 187–221.

Nofsinger, J.R. and W. Wang (2011), 'Determinants of start-up firm external financing worldwide', *Journal of Banking and Finance*, **35** (9), 2282–94.

Ordanini, A., L. Miceli, M. Pizzetti and A. Parasuraman (2011), 'Crowd-funding: transforming customers into investors through innovative service platforms', *Journal of Service Management*, **22** (4), 443–70.

Poetz, M.K. and M. Schreier (2012), 'The value of crowdsourcing: can users really compete with professionals in generating new product ideas?', *Journal of Product Innovation Management*, **29** (2), 245–56.

Prasad, D., G.D. Bruton and G. Vozikis (2000), 'Signaling value to business angels: the proportion of the entrepreneur's net worth invested in a new venture as a decision signal', *Venture Capital*, **2** (3), 167–82.

Riedl, J. (2013), 'Crowdfunding technology innovation', *Computer*, **46** (3), 100–103.

Schwartz, A.A. (2013), 'Crowdfunding securities', *Notre Dame Law Review*, **88** (3), 1457–90.

Shane, S. and D. Cable (2002), 'Network ties, reputation, and the financing of new ventures', *Management Science*, **48** (3), 364–81.

Shiller, R.J. (2013), 'Capitalism and financial innovation', *Financial Analysts Journal*, **69** (1), 21–5.

Sigar, K. (2012), 'Fret no more: inapplicability of crowdfunding concerns in the Internet age and the JOBS Act's safeguards', *Administrative Law Review*, **64** (2), 473–506.

Sorensen, I.E. (2012), 'Crowdsourcing and outsourcing: the impact of online funding and distribution on the documentary film industry in the UK', *Media Culture and Society*, **34** (6), 726–43.

Stemler, A.R. (2013), 'The JOBS Act and crowdfunding: harnessing the power – and money – of the masses', *Business Horizons*, **56** (3), 271–5.

Tranfield, D., D. Denyer and P. Smart (2003), 'Towards a methodology for developing evidence-informed management knowledge by means of systematic review', *British Journal of Management*, **14** (3), 207–22.

Uzzi, B. (1996), 'The sources and consequences of embeddedness for the economic performance of organizations: the network effect', *American Sociological Review*, **61** (4), 674–98.

Weigmann, K. (2013), 'Tapping the crowds for research funding – crowdfunding, a common practice to support projects in the arts, music or gaming, has also attracted the attention of scientists', *Embo Reports*, **14** (12), 1043–6.

Widding, L.O., M.T. Mathisen and O. Madsen (2009), 'University-affiliated venture capital funds: funding of university spin-off companies', *International Journal of Technology Transfer and Commercialisation*, **8** (2/3), 229–45.

Wieck, E., U. Bretschneider and J.M. Leimeister (2013), 'Funding from the crowd: an Internet-based crowdfunding platform to support business set-ups from universities', *International Journal of Cooperative Information Systems*, **22** (3).

Wiltbank, R., S. Read, N. Dew and S.D. Sarasvathy (2009), 'Prediction and control under uncertainty: outcomes in angel investing', *Journal of Business Venturing*, **24** (2), 116–33.

Zahra, S.A., E. Gedajlovic, D.O. Neubaum and J.M. Shulman (2009), 'A typology of social entrepreneurs: motives, search processes and ethical challenges', *Journal of Business Venturing*, **24** (5), 519–32.

Zahra, S.A., H.N. Rawhouser and N. Bhawe et al. (2008), 'Globalization of social entrepreneurship opportunities', *Strategic Entrepreneurship Journal*, **2** (2), 117–31.

Zhang, J. and P.-K. Wong (2008), 'Networks vs. market methods in high-tech venture fundraising: the impact of institutional environment', *Entrepreneurship and Regional Development*, **20** (5), 409–30.

4. How business angels found a way to contribute non-financially: a processual approach

Olli-Matti Nevalainen and Päivi Eriksson

INTRODUCTION

This chapter focuses on the cooperation between entrepreneurs and angel investors that extends over several years. More specifically, we investigate the non-financial contributions that a group of business angels (BAs) provide to a group of entrepreneurs. BAs are private individuals who use their personal wealth to directly invest in business ventures. The value that a BA can add is not limited to finances; investees also appreciate non-financial contributions.

The contribution of our study lies in the processual approach we use to study the cooperative relationship between a group of BAs and entrepreneurs. As noted by Avdeitchikova et al. (2008), previous studies on angel investing have mostly been quantitative and cross-sectional. For instance, Freear et al. (2002) have suggested there is a need for more longitudinal research on 'angel and entrepreneurial venture behaviour'. While longitudinal research is often quantitative, variable based and snapshot oriented, our study provides an event-driven and narrative processual approach (Langley, 1999; Pentland, 1999) to the study of BAs' non-financial contributions.

Prior research on BAs has provided useful categorizations of BAs and their contributions (Sætre, 2003; Politis, 2008; Macht, 2011a). A particularly interesting aspect of BAs' non-financial contributions is the role of their skills, expertise and prior experiences. BAs with industry-relevant experience and networks that their investees can exploit are said to have 'relevant capital' (Sætre, 2003). However, not all BAs are considered to have 'relevant capital' by investees, whose interpretations shape the dynamics of the cooperation between BAs and investees. Macht (2011a) has suggested that BAs' non-financial contributions can be categorized into 'soft' people-centred and interpersonal contributions and 'hard' task-centred contributions. She pointed out that soft rather than hard contributions may be more welcome from BAs who lack industry-relevant experience, contacts and small business experience (ibid.).

With the exception of Macht's study, there is little research on how BAs who entrepreneurs do not consider possess 'relevant capital' can make non-financial contributions. This study will focus on this research gap in the literature and will provide new knowledge on how the role and non-financial contribution of a group of BAs change over time as their experience of the business and their ways of cooperating with the entrepreneurs evolve. Our case study shows how BAs without industry-specific and small business experience find a way to cooperate strategic-ally with investees and provide non-financial contributions that the entrepreneurs value.

The chapter proceeds as follows. In the second section of the chapter, we will outline previous research on BAs' non-financial contributions and introduce our theoretical approach. The third section introduces the event-driven processual research approach. In the fourth section, we will introduce the intensive case study approach, our data and the analysis method. The fifth section provides the case narrative, and in the sixth section, the findings of the research will be analysed and discussed. The final section consists of our conclusions, practical implications and suggestions for future research.

LITERATURE REVIEW

Business Angels

BAs can be defined as wealthy private individuals who invest their wealth alone or in informal or formal groups directly in unlisted companies they do not have family ties to and who tend to take an active role in the investee companies (Mason and Harrison, 2008). In contrast to other external financing available for business ventures, BA financing is not intermediated. BAs are considered 'informal investors' together with family and friend investors (Shane, 2008). BAs are a crucial source of external finance for start-ups (Morrissette, 2007). Until recently, much of the research on BAs has focused on describing BAs and on categorizing their ways of contributing non-financially. BAs are motivated by the return on their investment and by non-financial motivations, such as providing themselves with an interest, enjoyment and satisfaction (Paul et al., 2003). A significant number have experience in setting up or managing their own companies (Reitan and Sørheim, 2000; Brettel, 2003; Stedler and Peters, 2003) and often invest in companies close to home (Harrison et al., 2010). A number of empirical papers have recognized ways in which BAs contribute to their investees (see, e.g., Politis, 2008 or Fili and Grünberg, 2016 [from the risk mitigation perspective] for a review). However, these papers do not provide much detailed information on how BAs deliver their contributions. For instance, participation in the strategy work of the investee can mean a wide variety of different activities through which the contribution is actually delivered.

Although BAs by definition are individuals, they may also manage their investment in a group. Mason et al. (2013) have suggested that BAs are increasingly investing together as organized groups. In other words, instead of investing by themselves or in ad hoc groups, BAs are operating as organized groups that are often called BA networks (BANs) or syndicates. Initially, BANs were formed as an introduction service through which entrepreneurs could present their proposals to BAs, although later the services of these networks expanded (ibid.). BA syndicates are self-formed groups of BAs that invest together (ibid). Mason et al. (2013) noted that there has not been much consideration of the practical implications that the change in BA investing may have for entrepreneurs and investors or regarding policy. While Mason et al. (2013) focus on the investment process, the grouping of BAs can also be expected to impact BAs' non-financial post-investment contributions. Despite this, there has not been much discussion around the question of whether BA groups are any different from individual BAs in terms of their non-financial contributions.

Mason (2007) suggested that BA syndicates can probably contribute greater added value than individual BAs because they possess a wider range of experience. This would seem rational, but it makes assumptions about the effectiveness of the value delivery. It can be argued that a group of BAs is likely to together possess a larger variety of competencies, but one key question concerns to what degree an investee can or wants to exploit these competencies. For example, entrepreneurs and managing directors may have limited opportunities to be in contact with all their BAs. With little contact and communication, they may not take full advantage of their BAs' competencies, and some of the potential of BAs' contributions could remain unexploited. Therefore, this change toward BA investing in groups may have either positive or negative impacts on BAs' non-financial contributions. Furthermore, the impact can change over the life cycle of the business venture.

BAs' Non-financial Contributions

This section will discuss the non-financial contributions of BAs. The prior BA literature has often considered the terms 'involvement', 'value adding' and 'contribution' as equivalent (see, e.g., Macht and Robinson, 2009); very few authors have explicitly and clearly defined the differences between these concepts. We consider that BAs can get involved without delivering value, whereas the concepts of value adding or contributing explicitly or implicitly contain the notion of adding value, that is, contributing something to the business. In this chapter, we will use the term non-financial contribution, which includes the notion of adding value.

The earlier literature has recognized various roles through which BAs deliver their non-financial contributions. In her review, Politis (2008) recognized the following four roles: the sounding board/strategic role, the supervision and monitoring role, the resource acquisition role and the mentoring role. The first two roles focus on the human capital of the BAs, and the latter two focus on their social capital (ibid.). Human capital refers to intangible capital (e.g., knowledge and skills) of an individual that cannot be separated from him or her (Becker, 1993). Human capital can be accumulated, for example, through education or work experience (ibid.). Nahapiet and Ghoshal (1998, p. 243) define social capital as 'the sum of the actual and potential resources embedded within, available through, and derived from the network of relationships possessed by an individual or social unit'. It should be noted that this not only refers to network connections but also to relationships between different parties in the network and to common ground between them (Sørheim, 2005a).

According to Politis (2008), the most reported way for BAs to contribute is to take a sounding board/strategic role in which BAs act as a strategic resource for an investee company by providing business know-how and management expertise based on their experience. In the supervision and monitoring role, BAs contribute to minimize information asymmetry and to reduce agency costs (ibid). In other words, BAs do get involved to protect their investment and contribute by ensuring non-profit maximizing activities are minimized (ibid).

In the resource acquisition role, investors acquire resources for the company through their personal networks (ibid.). Finally, in the mentoring role, there is a developmental relationship between a BA and an entrepreneur (ibid). Furthermore, a BA can be an open and trusted partner in helping the entrepreneurs (ibid). Based on this, we consider that this role focuses on the psychological or emotional needs of the entrepreneurs. The mentoring role draws from BAs' entrepreneurial experience and their self-perception as a part of the entrepreneurial team (Politis, 2008).

BAs' contributions have also been studied from the perspective of entrepreneurs. According to results by Mason and Harrison (1996) some entrepreneurs perceived the lack of industry/product/market knowledge as a weakness in a BA. BAs' backgrounds in large companies were even considered a handicap (ibid). In line with these findings, Sætre (2003) stated that some entrepreneurs specifically search for BAs who can provide them with expertise and contacts in addition to funding. Based on these findings, Sætre (2003) suggested that the concept of 'relevant capital' adequately describes the capital possessed by BAs who allow their investees to take advantage of their industry experience and networks in particular.

A case study by Macht (2011b) suggested that we should also consider the influence that investees' management has when discussing BAs' contributions, as they may choose to reject BAs' contributions for various reasons. Based on the earlier discussion, it could be argued that from the perspective of the entrepreneurs, BAs who do not possess 'relevant capital' have a limited capacity to contribute, therefore, it may be that entrepreneurs or managers of the investee are more likely to reject contributions from such BAs. However, an in-depth case study by Macht (2011a) showed that BAs without industry-relevant experience or contacts or small business experience have been able to deliver contributions in the form of 'soft' people-centred and interpersonal involvement that have been appreciated by the investees. Based on this finding, Macht (2011a) suggested that BAs' involvement activities could be divided into 'soft' people-centred activities and 'hard' task-centred activities.

We will use the roles by Politis (2008), the concepts of human (Becker, 1993) and social capital (Nahapiet and Ghoshal, 1998) and the soft-hard categorization by Macht (2011a) as tools to discuss how BAs' contributions change over time. They will provide us with points of reference and allow us to observe changes in the nature of BAs' contributions. As our analysis of the prior research on BAs' and BA groups' non-financial contributions shows, much of the empirical research has focused on providing descriptive categorizations through cross-sectional research designs focusing on quantitative analysis (Avdeitchikova et al., 2008). Consequently, we know little about how BAs' and especially BA groups' non-financial contributions evolve over time. It is not surprising that some researchers have called for more longitudinal research on angel investing (Freear et al., 2002) and the BA–entrepreneur relationship (Sørheim, 2005b). A few papers on BAs' non-financial contributions based on longitudinal case data have been published (Macht, 2011a, 2011b; Macht and Weatherston, 2011), however, none of these has specifically focused on how BAs' non-financial contributions change over time. This is the area of research that we seek to contribute to with our empirical research results. Furthermore, our contribution lies in providing a conceptual framework through which this topic can be approached. We will briefly outline this framework in the following section.

EVENT-DRIVEN PROCESSUAL APPROACH

A growing number of researchers have started to emphasize processual approaches for understanding organizations (Langley and Tsoukas, 2010) and entrepreneurship (Moroz and Hindle, 2012). Process research represents one type of longitudinal research with an interest in how specific phenomena and related events, actions and activities unfold in context over time (Pettigrew, 1997; Langley, 2009). While longitudinal research tends to be quantitatively focused on variable-based variance, processual research is mostly qualitative and focused on event-driven narratives (Langley, 1999; Van de Ven and Engleman, 2004; Moroz and Hindle, 2012). The event-driven and narrative processual approach has an interest in how change unfolds in organizational and business practice and in how the substance, context and politics of change come together to shape the dynamic of the phenomena under study (Steyaert, 2007). This is why it provides a good starting point for our case study, the objective of which is to provide an event-driven story of change combined with an interest in the key actors' interpretations of the events under study. Accordingly, the objective of our research is not to aim at statistical generalizability but to provide a narrative account of the dynamics of interaction among the group of people under study.

When implementing processual research, researchers can choose between different research designs and respective data collection and analysis methods, all of which have specific strengths and weaknesses (e.g., Langley, 1999; Van de Ven and Engleman, 2004). Several researchers have pointed out that there is a close link between the event-driven processual approach and narrative research (Langley, 1999; Pentland, 1999), therefore, narrative data and a narrative analysis of the data have been emphasized (Paavilainen-Mäntymäki and Aarikka-Stenroos, 2013). For instance, while narrative interviews or conversations are more open than other types of interviews typically used in business studies, they also allow for more flexibility to follow unpredictable events in real time and sensitive or even messy events retrospectively. In addition, they allow more space for the subjective realities of the interviewees to be accounted for because interviewees' narration is different compared with answering pre-designed questions posed by the interviewer. When analysing narrative data, the narrated sequence of events forms a temporally unfolding plot that is meaningful within the context of the research and also to the research participants.

Similar to any other research approaches, the aim of the event-driven processual approach is to produce new theoretical knowledge. Related to this, Dawson (1997) has suggested that an event-driven processual approach is particularly good for unmasking cultural myths about change processes. These include linearity (the assumption that change goes through a logical sequence of stages), improvement (the assumption that change is marked by a line of continual improvement) and leadership (the assumption that there is one leader of change rather than a number of leaders with changing roles during the process of change) (ibid). This is why the event-driven processual approach is able to challenge and widen our understanding of change in this study. The approach does not aim to predict how change happens, but it helps to make hidden issues more visible and, by doing this, question the taken-for-granted assumptions around the phenomena under study.

METHODOLOGY

Our research follows the intensive case study strategy, which is well suited to studying event-driven processes that extend over longer periods of time with narrative methods of analysis (Eriksson and Kovalainen, 2008, 2010). The aim of intensive case studies is to provide an understanding of the specific aspects of the cases, most often from a longitudinal and processual perspective. Therefore, the purpose is to provide a good story worth hearing rather than new constructs, theoretical ideas or generalizable explanations (Dyer and Wilkins, 1991).

The first author's affiliation with the company under study started during the summer of 2010 when he completed an internship with the case company. Thereafter, he met several times with the entrepreneurs. The data were collected mainly during three years (July 2010 to July 2013), but one of the entrepreneurs answered some follow-up questions in 2014 and 2015 to confirm facts and refine the case description. The primary research data consist of in-depth narrative interviews with the entrepreneurs, participant observations conducted during one week in 2011 and retrospective auto-ethnographic notes (Eriksson, 2013) by the first author covering certain events during 2010–13. The secondary data include a marketing plan of the company from 2010.

The company, ContentShare (name changed to guarantee anonymity for the actors involved), was founded by three entrepreneurs (called John, Robert and Alan here). The company's home country is in Western Europe. Prior to founding the company, John and Robert were colleagues in a large professional services company. Robert and Alan had started a small business together during their university years, and this had continued while Robert was working for the professional services company. Initially, the entrepreneurs had the following titles: John was Finance and Commercial Director, Robert was Creative and Operations Director and Alan was System Architect and Technical Director. John was the de facto CEO/Managing Director, if one had to be named.

The first round of narrative interviews with Robert and John were held in 2010, including a follow-up interview with John. The first author observed the work in the company for one week in April 2011, which provided useful background information for the second round of interviews organized the next week with all three entrepreneurs. In the third round of interviews in 2012, all three entrepreneurs were included. These were the first interviews that focused specifically on the relationship with the BAs. This was the only pre-selected theme for these interviews, otherwise these interviews were open. Prior to these interviews, the interviewees had a chance to read the first author's earlier work in which he commented on their disagreement with the BAs in connection to the strategy change. This may have impacted their later comments or behaviour, although the research material does not give particular reason to believe so. The fourth round of interviews was conducted with Robert. The interview in 2012 was performed ad hoc after a casual conversation revealed that the company had received further funding and that one of the entrepreneurs was leaving the company. The next interview, in 2013, was also with Robert who had become the CEO/Managing Director of the company. The conversational interview revolved around the topics discussed in the previous interviews. The description of events since 2012 is based on Robert's interviews. The information on investors is second-hand information, as only the entrepreneurs were interviewed. These are limitations relating to the data from the case.

The data analysis followed abductive reasoning (Eriksson and Kovalainen, 2008). Before the final analysis for this chapter was performed, the authors had an interest in the entrepreneurial character of strategy work in the company. The more specific focus of this chapter was refined through an iterative analysis of the data and the literature. In this way, a data-sensitive, narrative process and a theory-guided, event-driven code structure were created. All data, except for the notes from the phone calls, were coded. The case narrative presented in the following section provides short descriptions of meaningful events presented as vignettes (Eriksson et al., 2008a, 2008b, 2011) that offer real-life descriptions of the entrepreneurs' perspectives. The vignettes are not verbatim quotes; they have been edited to be easily understandable and to ensure the anonymity of the case company and people involved.

CASE NARRATIVE

The three entrepreneurs, John, Robert and Alan, decided to found ContentShare after John had come across a software product for sharing content on the Internet. They then acquired this software and founded a company to develop it further into a tool that could be used in e-commerce. Soon after, they started to look for funding. One of their future BAs was helping them in this pursuit, and he eventually ended up investing approximately 300 000 euros in the company, together with a group of his friends in September 2009. This investment enabled a 700 000 euro subsidy. The BAs did not have family connections in the company, and all made the investment directly to the company. The BA group had more experience in large companies than in smaller ventures. Over a period of three and a half years, three people left the BA group and two new people joined it, but the 'mixture' of the backgrounds stayed almost the same. The headcount of the BA group varied from six to eight people throughout the investment period. Their investments enabled the entrepreneurs to hire a development team and to start work on a new version of the software.

Changing Strategic Focus from B2B Markets to B2C Markets

ContentShare adjusted its strategy several times during the three years (2010–13). The entrepreneurs followed the markets actively, sought input from clients or their network and tried to adapt to the changing markets. The entrepreneurs also had meetings with the whole BA group and an advisory board. The advisory board was a part of the contract with the BAs and consisted of two BAs and a third person chosen by the entrepreneurs. The meetings with the BAs and the advisory board took place approximately once every two months. They were more frequent (once every two to four weeks) if there were important decisions to be made. According to one of the entrepreneurs, these meetings were a mechanism for reviewing the strategy. The BAs also connected Content-Share with an offshore outsourcing partner. However, the outsourcing project did not prove to be particularly successful.

Initially, the entrepreneurs chose to target B2B markets to license out their software as an Internet service. This decision was influenced by the BAs who requested or even pressured the entrepreneurs to choose the B2B market focus. By the autumn of 2010, it seemed that the B2B strategy had not produced the desired financial results. The entrepreneurs then realized that they had to change the strategic focus to B2C markets. This change allowed them to take control of their marketing efforts. Earlier, the company was dependent on the marketing efforts of their B2B clients. Therefore, the company transformed from a software development company to a more commercially focused one, that is, they targeted the consumers themselves instead of providing software service for other companies.

As the B2B strategy had been something that the BAs strongly desired, the entrepreneurs had to spend time convincing the BAs that a strategic change was needed. The entrepreneurs held the majority of the shares in the company, and they could have made a decision regarding the change by themselves, but they wanted to create a consensus among the shareholders and to make the decision together.

Getting everyone on board with the change was frustrating for the entrepreneurs, as it took time to reach a decision. At this time, they had more frequent meetings with the BAs and the advisory board. These meetings had a micro-political aspect, as John later noted. Sometimes, the BAs did not have a clear opinion as a team, and instead they started arguing about the strategic direction of the company. Overall, the participation of all the BAs was confusing, as Robert retrospectively expressed.

Vignette 1: The BAs just do not have the same information as us

Alan: We are very focused on a daily basis on the work in our industry and on the start-up scene. We learn way more than our investors do and there is a certain gap. Sometimes it's very hard to get them to close that gap so that they know exactly the same things or they can reach the same conclusions that we did. So sometimes it's horrible, but mainly because at that time they don't have the current knowledge of the market mostly, I guess, and sometimes it's also their background since when you come from a consulting company it's sometimes hard to understand the life at a start-up company.

John: The IT business is very rapidly developing. As managing directors, we are much into the materials and we noticed that our investors have difficulty in keeping up with all the – how do you call it ...? With information and the changes in the industry. It's a logical thing, of course, but that makes it difficult, more difficult, to make these kinds of strategic changes. They cannot understand the change. They do not always understand the change as easily as we can because we are knowledgeable about the information in the industry.

Around the time of the strategy change, the entrepreneurs felt that they should take increasingly more responsibility for the decision-making because they had a far better understanding of the context. The entre-preneurs expressed concern that the BAs would not understand how a small start-up works; nor were they familiar with the information and communications technology (ICT) industry or the particular market in which the company operated.

The entrepreneurs visited California during the autumn of 2010 to see if it would be possible to get further funding from the capital markets in the USA or to start operations in California. During this trip, they received further encouragement regarding changing their strategy. The entrepreneurs felt that California could provide a more suitable environ-ment for a start-up like ContentShare. The entrepreneurs saw a lot of potential in the international markets in terms of both revenue and further funding, while the investors appeared to prefer a local focus at first.

Vignette 2: A visit to California shows what good investors are like

Robert: So the investors in California are a little bit more risk-taking if you compare them to the European investors or to investors in our home country … So that's one thing I found out, and another thing is also that the start-up philosophy over there is a little bit different. It's like 'Okay, I got a good idea, let's do it' and the decisions are made rather fast. If you compare it to our home country, we have more of a meeting philosophy here.

Later on, Robert expressed the following: 'If I were looking for investors in the future, and we are of course doing that right now, then we would be looking for investors that can play more of a strategic role in our company based on their background, on their network – people that could be added to our team'.

After a series of intense discussions, the entrepreneurs were able to convince the BAs about changing the strategic focus of the company. Around the time of the change, the dynamics between the entrepreneurs and the BA group were not good, as one of the entrepreneurs stated retrospectively, but a new portal for consumers was launched during the winter of 2010–11.

Vignette 3: A change for the better

> Robert: There is not really that peer pressure from the whole team of investors that we had before, where everyone was looking at each other: 'What are they (assumedly other BAs) going to decide?' and 'Should we all be involved?' During that time, a lot of miscommunication was going on.

> John: Yeah, and what I also see is that of course seven people were on the board of that entity (assumedly referring to the meetings with the BAs) and had opinions. But, of the seven people, only one or two have entrepreneurial experience. They worked for big corporations et cetera, and working for a start-up is so different.

> Robert: [...] and now we only have one investor who we communicate with, and that's a big relief because we noticed that since he had the most feeling towards IT companies and IT start-ups and he wasn't really on our backs all the time so he gave us more space to pivot with our strategy and not always needing to communicate every step we decided to take. So that was a really big improvement in our cooperation with our investors.

Relatively soon after the strategic change, there were also changes in the cooperation between the entrepreneurs and the BAs. The majority of the BAs moved into the background, and the entrepreneurs were only actively in touch with one of the BAs (referred to as Richard here). Richard became a link between the entrepreneurs and the BA group. There were still meetings once in a while with the whole group; however, these meetings were not check-ups like before, as the BAs had already been updated via Richard. John felt that this arrangement improved the relationship with the BAs and made the cooperation more transparent and peaceful. He also thought that the BAs realized that they did not necessarily know better how a start-up works.

In January 2012, the advisory board dissolved. Later on, one of the entrepreneurs commented that the advisory board had been helpful most of the time but sometimes seemed to be looking for an argument. In July 2012, there were plans to start the advisory board again with people possessing relevant experience, including John and Richard, but this did not occur.

Towards Strategic Cooperation with the BAs

Half a year after the BAs had moved into the background, there was a change in the management team of the company. John was leaving and a new CEO with prior experience as an executive at an Internet company that had succeeded in international markets was hired. This hire was enabled by a second round of funding around May 2012 that came partially from the old BAs and partially from a bank loan. The BAs' part of the funding round amounted to 350 000 euros. In the second investment round, the BAs gained the majority of shares in ContentShare. The round consisted of smaller patches of funding that were tied to user targets. Around this time, the BAs' operations had become increasingly professional; they had founded a company through which their investments were made. Furthermore, Richard had a full-time job as a fund and portfolio manager. The BAs' company also employed a consultant and an accountant. The accountant monitored the finances of the participants and gave advice when needed. All the BAs still participated in the decision-making regarding the second investment, although the negotiations were led by Richard and another BA.

By the summer of 2013, the CEO had also left the company and Robert had taken the lead. According to Robert, one reason for the CEO's departure was that both the entrepreneurs and the BAs felt that he did not have the right background for the job. Another development during the summer of 2013 was that the BA group decided to begin focusing their investment portfolio. The portfolio was reorganized so that it contained a group of companies focusing on e-commerce and online marketing. The BAs created 'core participation' by merging one of their old investee companies with a company they had recently acquired. The task of the core participation was to support other investee companies to succeed. One of the other merged companies had been ContentShare's partner prior to the merger, although they did not have enough resources to provide support.

Vignette 4: What we need

> Robert: If they (assumedly the core participation) are running out to Poland with their business, we're doing it as well, and if we say we see a lot of potential in Scandinavian markets, then they follow us by scanning the Scandinavian market to see if it's also for their business ... So that's become more and more connected to each other and more compact, and in that way also more focused. I guess a year ago we had a feeling that there was totally no focus within this company, in the investor company, and that also made it really difficult for us to tell our story and to explain our strategy. Now they are more connected to each other. So things look better for now, I guess. A lot has happened with that.
>
> [...] Because we needed a sort of partner where we could discuss our strategy because Alan and I, of course, we think we set up the strategy, but then it's always good to talk with other parties in the same market. And now we had the opportunity that we could talk with a competitor (referring to the other

companies forming the core participation) who would become our partner. So that was great.

[…] when we started this with them they asked us, me and Alan, 'Can you also provide us with feedback regarding what should be improved?' And then we said, 'Well, you need a CEO because now you've merged two companies'. One is in one city and the other part is in another one … they hired a really good guy who also had a background in publishing. And he's like, sort of, well, he's like the managing director of the whole team, and then together with him we suggested the structure in the company, so we said 'Well, we need weekly meetings with all the managers'.

The alignment in the BAs' portfolio meant that they had sharpened their strategy, which was a process that the entrepreneurs had influenced. Now there was a possibility to create strategic alignment between Content-Share and other investees. The core participation gave the BAs a chance to have control over the strategy of their investees. For the entrepreneurs, this new structure meant access to peer support within the BAs' portfolio companies. This support was provided through informal discussions, as well as more informal weekly meetings between the management of the investee companies. The CEO of the core participation chaired these events. Richard was the only person from the BA group who was attending these meetings frequently, but at least one other BA had attended when his capabilities were needed. ContentShare also had operational meetings with the other investees. Now the entrepreneurs could discuss and test strategies together with peer companies. Besides BAs' portfolio companies, ContentShare also had other strategic partnerships, for example, to reach out to international markets. This was supported by the BAs, as other investee companies were also looking for growth opportunities in international markets.

The alignment of the BAs' portfolio had already had, or was expected to have, an influence on the roles of the entrepreneurs in July 2013. Alan and a technical employee of ContentShare were helping other participants whose technological capabilities were not on the same level as theirs. It had also been discussed with the BAs that bringing in more resources for ContentShare would allow Robert to help them with new start-ups and opportunities. Thus, the cooperative relationship that was formed between the entrepreneurs and the BAs worked both ways.

Although the BAs and the entrepreneurs found a way for the BAs to contribute, a phone call in September 2014 revealed that ContentShare would eventually close. Robert remarked that, in a sense, ContentShare was a bit unlucky for their investors because it was the company that the BAs were learning with. The BAs had learned from their mistakes with

ContentShare, and they later recruited more people to the group with backgrounds in successful e-commerce companies.

ANALYSIS AND DISCUSSION

In our case, the BAs were making non-financial contributions to the company in various ways. In the beginning, the BAs acted as a sounding board and reviewed the strategic direction of the company together with the entrepreneurs. Some of them also served on the advisory board. Among the roles listed by Politis (2008), the investors adopted the sounding board/strategic role and the supervision and monitoring role. The investors also took a resource acquisition role (ibid.) by connecting the investee to an outsourcing partner. As the sounding board/strategic role and the supervision and monitoring role were dominant, their contributions relied dominantly on their human capital and thus on their experience and know-how.

Although the entrepreneurs accepted the strategic role of the BAs, they had a clear disagreement with them on the strategic direction of the company. The disagreement was based on entrepreneurs' observation that the BAs did not understand how a start-up company should be managed, nor did they understand the industry or target market of the start-up. Thus, when determining the strategic direction of the company, the entrepreneurs perceived the non-financial contributions of the BAs lacking industry-specific or small company experience negatively.

Prior research has suggested that when choosing investors, entrepreneurs may perceive the industry-relevant information as a specialized and more valuable asset than financial assets (Sætre, 2003). Due to the lack of industry-specific and small company experience and the lack of credibility this caused, the BAs in our case study were not able to take a role that investors with such experience might have been able to take. The BAs were willing to provide their human capital, but it was not considered suitable by the entrepreneurs, nor was the outsourcing project that was enabled by their social capital a success. Aside from contextually unfit advice, the way that the BAs were making their contribution was considered time consuming. It could have been assumed that a syndication of BAs would have been able to contribute greater value due to their wider range of experience (Mason, 2007). This was not the case because the entrepreneurs saw that as time passed, the input from the whole BA team slowed down decision-making and created miscommunication. Instead of creating more value added, the participation of the BA team seemed to put the contributions of the whole team in a negative light. Perhaps for the abovementioned reasons, the entrepreneurs were looking for input elsewhere instead of consulting the BAs.

The solution for better contributions was to change how the BAs provided their input. The BAs founded a company and adapted a structure in which they had a single point of contact for the company. At that point, the entrepreneurs were actively in contact with only one of the BAs, the portfolio and fund manager. This person was the most familiar with the company context and had already given the entrepreneurs some space for their decisions. By staying in contact with only one of the BAs, the entrepreneurs had more freedom to operate in a way they considered appropriate. The entrepreneurs appreciated the portfolio and fund manager's 'soft' role as a mediator between the entrepreneurs and the BA group.

The contribution by the BAs changed further as they aligned their portfolio. Through this change, the BAs were able to connect the entrepreneurs with a group of peers whose input the entrepreneurs perceived positively. The peers operated in industries that were connected to the investees' business.

As Robert mentioned, the investors also had more control over ContentShare via the core participation, but he did not consider this a negative thing. By moving to a more supportive position, the BAs were able to maintain influence over the direction of the company and to support it in a way that the entrepreneurs considered suitable. The entrepreneurs themselves had an active role in forming the cooperative setting with the core participation and weekly meetings. In this way, the entrepreneurs had direct influence over the contribution that the BAs provided. This is an aspect that the earlier literature has neglected. Very few, if any, papers have discussed the level of influence that entrepreneurs should have when determining BAs' ways to contribute. As pointed out by Macht (2011b), the investees can influence BAs' opportunities to contribute. By discussing and determining ways for the BAs to contribute together, perhaps the investees' willingness to accept the contribution could be enhanced. Perhaps this is even more important when BAs lack suitable experience. In this situation, the ways of contributing are not as self-evident as with BAs that possess relevant capital.

With the change in their role, the BAs moved towards the resource acquisition role and, in doing so, increasingly leaned on social capital in terms of their contributions. Furthermore, the role that Richard was playing appeared to be further based on social capital between him and the entrepreneurs. The BAs also maintained their sounding board/ strategic role, although this became more indirect and less intense. They could still offer their expertise when needed and could influence the strategic direction of the company through Richard and other investees. They also maintained the supervision and monitoring role, although less actively and intensively. Therefore, the BAs continued to provide task-centred and human capital-based contributions but from the softer side of their contributions, as well as contributions based on social capital, that is, the mutually formed cooperative setting seemed to become more important as time passed.

As noted by Mason et al. (2013), BAs are increasingly managing their funds as organized groups. This case has highlighted some problems that this development may withhold. Initially, all BAs in the case were contributing directly, which was perceived as an issue by the entrepreneurs. Only after the BA group became increasingly organized with a clear fund manager role were the entrepreneurs more responsive. The fund manager had a softer role as a mediator. This observation suggests that formally organized BA groups with clear roles may have better abilities to contribute in ways that are appreciated by investees. From the entrepreneurs' perspective, interacting with an organized group of BAs is easy and efficient but also provides access to their human and social capital when considered appropriate by the entrepreneurs.

Based on our findings and the discussion above, we suggest that BAs' non-financial contributions change over time as they and their investees interact and interpret each situation at hand. Furthermore, the human and social capital BAs have and might further develop within the process shape the roles and contributions that investees consider appropriate for them in specific circumstances. In our case, the roles based on human capital were available for the BAs only to a limited extent, as the entrepreneurs did not consider their contribution in this role credible enough.

Another key aspect of interaction is whether the BA and the investee are individuals or groups. As demonstrated by our case, contributions by a BA group do not necessarily mean better contributions. With an unsuitable structure, the contribution of a group can be perceived negatively and as harmful to the performance of the company. Therefore, the changing structures for delivering the BAs' contributions must satisfy both parties in order to support the delivery of the desired contribution.

CONCLUSIONS

This case study provides empirical support for the strategic role of investors (Politis, 2008) and particularly BAs whose strategic role in our study was connected to their other roles. While prior studies have, for the most part, been cross-sectional, our study shows how the strategic and other roles of BAs change over time and in interaction with the entrepreneurs.

Our findings highlight that as investees transform over time, so do BAs and their contributions as perceived by the investees. While the BAs in our case were mostly without industry-specific or small business backgrounds, over time they nevertheless found ways to contribute and were appreciated by investees. These findings suggest that BAs without experience in investee industries or small business contexts should search for other contributions to make that are not based on their human capital.

Our study has the following limitations. First, we focused on entrepreneurs' perspectives only, although we acknowledge that BAs' perspectives are equally important. Second, we have not combined these two perspectives in our study, which would have been ideal for achieving a more holistic understanding of the dynamics of change in BAs' roles and contributions.

These limitations notwithstanding, our study indicates that there is a need for further research of BA–investee cooperation. One interesting issue for further study is the cooperation of investees with BAs that the investees do not consider to possess relevant capital. In addition, more research into the cooperation between entrepreneurial and BA groups would shed light on the complexity of the relationships between them.

For practitioners, our case provides the lesson that both parties benefit from being open and explicit about their motivations and aspirations from the outset of their cooperation. By acknowledging the backgrounds of investors, the parties might be able to organize cooperation in a way that generates contributions for them both.

REFERENCES

Avdeitchikova, S., H. Landström and N. Månsson (2008), 'What do we mean when we talk about business angels? Some reflections on definitions and sampling', *Venture Capital*, **10** (4), 371–94.

Becker, G.S. (1993), *Human Capital: A Theoretical and Empirical Analysis, with Special Reference to Education*, Chicago, IL: University of Chicago Press.

Brettel, M. (2003), 'Business angels in Germany: a research note', *Venture Capital*, **5** (3), 251–68.

Dawson, P. (1997), 'In at the deep end: conducting processual research on organisational change', *Scandinavian Journal of Management*, **13** (4), 389–405.

Dyer, W.G. and A.L. Wilkins (1991), 'Better stories, not better constructs, to generate better theory: a rejoinder to Eisenhardt', *Academy of Management Review*, **16** (3), 613–19.

Eriksson, P. (2013), 'Longitudinal autoethnography', in M.E. Hassett and E. Paavilainen-Mäntymäki (eds), *Handbook of Longitudinal Research Methods in Organisation and Business Studies*, Cheltenham, UK and Northampton, MA, USA: Edward Elgar Publishing, pp. 119–37.

Eriksson, P. and A. Kovalainen (2008), *Qualitative Methods in Business Research*, London: Sage.

Eriksson, P. and A. Kovalainen (2010), 'Case study research in business and management', in A. Mills, G. Durepos and S. Wiebe (eds), *Sage Encyclopaedia of Case Research*, Thousand Oaks, CA: Sage, pp. 93–6.

Eriksson, P., E. Henttonen and S. Meriläinen (2008a), 'Managerial work and gender – ethnography of cooperative relationships in small software companies', *Scandinavian Journal of Management*, **24** (4), 354–63.

Eriksson, P., E. Henttonen and S. Meriläinen (2008b), 'Growth strategies of women-controlled SMEs: a case study of Finnish software companies', *International Journal of Business Excellence*, **1** (4), 434–47.

Eriksson, P., E. Henttonen and S. Meriläinen (2011), 'Managing client contacts of small KIBS companies: turning technology into business', *International Journal of Innovation in the Digital Economy*, **2** (3), 1–10.

Fili, A. and J. Grünberg (2016), 'Business angel post-investment activities: a multi-level review', *Journal of Management and Governance*, **20** (1), 89–114.

Freear, J., J.E. Sohl and W. Wetzel (2002), 'Angles on angels: financing technology-based ventures – a historical perspective', *Venture Capital: An International Journal of Entrepreneurial Finance*, **4** (4), 275–87.

Harrison, R., C. Mason and P. Robson (2010), 'Determinants of long-distance investing by business angels in the UK', *Entrepreneurship and Regional Development*, **22** (2), 113–37.

Langley, A. (1999), 'Strategies for theorizing from process data', *Academy of Management Review*, **24** (4), 691–710.

Langley, A. (2009), 'Studying processes in and around organizations', in D.A. Buchanan and A. Bryman (eds), *Sage Handbook of Organizational Research Methods*, London: Sage, pp. 409–29.

Langley, A. and H. Tsoukas (2010), 'Introducing perspectives on process organization studies', in T. Hernes and S. Maitlis (eds), *Process, Sensemaking, and Organizing*, Oxford: Oxford University Press, pp. 1–26.

Macht, S.A. (2011a), 'Inexpert business angels: how even investors with "nothing to add" can add value', *Strategic Change*, **20** (7–8), 269–78.

Macht, S.A. (2011b), 'The role of investee company managers in business angels' involvement: empirical insights from dyadic data', *Venture Capital*, **13** (3), 267–93.

Macht, S.A. and J. Robinson (2009), 'Do business angels benefit their investee companies?', *International Journal of Entrepreneurial Behavior and Research*, **15** (2), 187–208.

Macht, S.A. and J. Weatherston (2011), 'Towards a theory of business angels' post-investment involvement: a resource-based approach', in A. Maritz (ed.), *Regional Frontiers of Entrepreneurship Research, Proceedings of the Eighth*

AGSE International Entrepreneurship Research Exchange, Melbourne: Swinburne University of Technology, pp. 87–101.

Mason, C.M. (2007), 'Informal sources of venture finance', in S. Parker (ed.), *The Lifecycle of Entrepreneurial Ventures*, Berlin: Springer, pp. 259–99.

Mason, C.M. and R.T. Harrison (1996), 'Informal venture capital: a study of the investment process, the post-investment experience and investment performance', *Entrepreneurship and Regional Development: An International Journal*, **8** (2), 105–25.

Mason, C.M. and R.T. Harrison (2008), 'Measuring business angel investment activity in the United Kingdom: a review of potential data sources', *Venture Capital*, **10** (4), 309–30.

Mason, C.M., T. Botelho and R.T. Harrison (2013), 'The transformation of the business angel market: evidence from Scotland', Working Paper, Adam Smith Business School, University of Glasgow and University of Edinburgh Business School.

Moroz, P.W. and K. Hindle (2012), 'Entrepreneurship as a process: toward harmonizing multiple perspectives', *Entrepreneurship Theory and Practice*, **36** (4), 781–818.

Morrissette, S.G. (2007), 'A profile of angel investors', *The Journal of Private Equity*, **10** (3), 52–66.

Nahapiet, J. and S. Ghoshal (1998), 'Social capital, intellectual capital, and the organizational advantage', *Academy of Management Review*, **23** (2), 242–66.

Paavilainen-Mäntymäki, E. and L. Aarikka-Stenroos (2013), 'Narratives as longitudinal and process data', in M.E. Hassett and E. Paavilainen-Mäntymäki (eds), *Handbook of Longitudinal Research Methods in Organisation and Business Studies*, Cheltenham, UK and Northampton, MA, USA: Edward Elgar Publishing Limited, pp. 138–60.

Paul, S., G. Whittam and J.B. Johnston (2003), 'The operation of the informal venture capital market in Scotland', *Venture Capital*, **5** (4), 313–35.

Pentland, B.T. (1999), 'Building process theory with narrative: from description to explanation', *Academy of Management Review*, **24** (4), 711–24.

Pettigrew, A.M. (1997), 'What is a processual analysis?', *Scandinavian Journal of Management*, **13** (4), 337–48.

Politis, D. (2008), 'Business angels and value added: what do we know and where do we go?', *Venture Capital*, **10** (2), 127–47.

Reitan, B. and R. Sørheim (2000), 'The informal venture capital market in Norway: investor characteristics, behaviours and investment preferences', *Venture Capital*, **2** (2), 129–41.

Sætre, A.S. (2003), 'Entrepreneurial perspectives on informal venture capital', *Venture Capital: An International Journal of Entrepreneurial Finance*, **5** (1), 71–94.

Shane, S. (2008), *Fool's Gold? The Truth Behind Angel Investing in America*, Oxford: Oxford University Press.

Shane, S. (2012), 'The importance of angel investing in financing the growth of entrepreneurial ventures', *The Quarterly Journal of Finance*, **2** (02), doi:10.1142/S2010139212500097 [online].

Sørheim, R. (2005a), 'The pre-investment behaviour of business angels: a social capital approach', *Venture Capital*, **5** (4), 337–64.

Sørheim, R. (2005b), 'Business angels as facilitators for further finance: an explanatory study', *Journal of Small Business and Enterprise Development*, **12** (2), 178–92.

Stedler, H. and H.H. Peters (2003), 'Business angels in Germany: an empirical study', *Venture Capital: An International Journal of Entrepreneurial Finance*, **5** (3), 269–76.

Steyaert, C. (2007), 'Entrepreneuring as a conceptual attractor? A review of process theories in 20 years of entrepreneurship studies', *Entrepreneurship and Regional Development*, **19** (6), 453–77.

Van de Ven, A.H. and R.M. Engleman (2004), 'Event- and outcome-driven explanations of entrepreneurship', *Journal of Business Venturing*, **19** (3), 343–58.

5. Resource flexibility, early internationalization and performance

R. Isil Yavuz, Harry Sapienza and Youngeun Chu[*]

INTRODUCTION

Internationalization is an important growth strategy for new ventures. While much research in international entrepreneurship literature has examined why and with what consequences new ventures internationalize early (e.g., Zahra and George, 2002), very few studies have theorized and empirically examined new ventures' resource configuration as an antecedent of early internationalization or as an antecedent of performance in international new ventures (Gassmann and Keup, 2007). Most of these studies have pointed out the importance of resource availability (or the existence of slack resources), arguing that slack resources buffer organizations from external shocks, and provide flexibility (Verdú-Jover et al., 2006). However, these studies have largely overlooked the importance of the configurations of existing resources to the internationalization process. Given the constraints in the number of slack resources that new ventures almost always suffer from, how to configure available resources, in addition to the number of them, might have an effect on new ventures' strategies and the performance outcomes. In this chapter we focus on the flexibility of the available resources, as one possible dimension of resource configuration, controlling for the total number of resources that new ventures have. The specific research questions that we ask are: How does the flexibility of available resources affect the decisions to internationalize early? And, how does the flexibility of available resources affect performance outcomes in international new ventures?

We conceptualize resource flexibility as a resource characteristic that enables quick and low-cost reallocation of resources for alternative uses in different physical locations. We argue that resource flexibility is needed to recognize and successfully exploit international opportunities quickly before the window of opportunity disappears since opportunities for international expansion neither exist in physically close locations nor do they last long due to rapidly changing global environment. Therefore, recognition and exploitation of these opportunities needs certain resource characteristics. New ventures with more flexible resources would have the much needed capacity both to perceive international opportunities quickly and to respond to international market variations more efficiently. New ventures with less flexible resources, on the other hand, are not only less likely to give attention to international opportunities but also less able to react rapidly to resource needs in different markets that international new ventures operate in (Sapienza et al., 2006).

In order to empirically examine these ideas, we use the Kauffman Firm Survey (KFS), which is a large panel data set of new businesses that were all founded in 2004 in the USA. The hypotheses are tested on 2424 new ventures. We test the likelihood of early internationalization, and international new ventures' survival, growth and international sales intensity as a function of flexibility of new venture resources. We use a comprehensive set of control variables in all analyses to address (1) founder differences such as gender, age, education, previous start-up and industry experiences of primary founders, (2) firm characteristics such as Internet sales, intellectual property, firm size and (3) macro context such as industry.

This study advances international entrepreneurship literature. The central issue in this literature is to understand the causes and consequences of early internationalization. Although prior studies emphasize the critical role of resources in the internationalization processes of new ventures, the role of resource flexibility has not been critically examined even though there is evidence of firm heterogeneity or discretion in resource configuration by new ventures and this variation might have an impact on new ventures' international strategies and performance. For example, Gassmann and Keupp (2007, p. 352) state that:

> [...] a study of an international new venture's resources would be the first step to arrive at an understanding of its capability to internationalize. Indeed, resources that enable the generation of capabilities are especially important to international new ventures. A venture's ability to enter foreign markets can be linked to its accumulated tangible and intangible resource stocks.

To address this gap in the literature, we propose and test a set of hypotheses that examine the role of asset flexibility in the early internationalization and the performance of international new ventures. This study also has implications for practice. Does it make sense for entrepreneurs to commit available resources to long-term illiquid, location-specific assets, or keep them more mobile, or flexible? Our results show that entrepreneurs considering successful early internationalization should keep their assets more flexible.

THEORY AND HYPOTHESES

Internationalization provides new ventures with diverse learning and continuous growth opportunities. Like other growth strategies, internationalization is also an entrepreneurial strategy involving both opportunity recognition and exploitation processes (Chandra et al., 2009). In this chapter, we argue that for a new venture that usually has relatively few slack resources, the flexibility of available resources has an important influence on both recognizing and successfully exploiting opportunities in foreign markets. Flexibility is often defined as a strategic response to unanticipated opportunities and threats in the environment. It is 'a capability to generate variety so that options are available to do things differently or do something else if need arises' (Evans, 1991, p. 74).

Although we focus on resource flexibility in this chapter, prior research has also examined other types of flexibilities providing new ventures with capabilities to identify and exploit opportunities in foreign markets (Sapienza et al., 2006). For example, Sapienza et al. (2006) argued that various types of operational flexibilities, namely cognitive, structural, political and relational, help new ventures attain learning advantages of newness (LAN), which then increases the performance of new ventures in international markets (Autio et al., 2000, Sapienza et al., 2006). In line with this logic, De Clercq et al. (2014) studied 176 Chinese international new ventures and empirically showed that all these types of flexibilities help new ventures give more attention to foreign markets and increase their international learning effort. Their reasoning was that new ventures that have these types of operational flexibilities would find it easier to allocate their resources to new international initiatives.

Studies specifically examining resource flexibility, on the other hand, have traditionally focused on slack resources as a means of achieving flexibility. This literature suggests that a very low level and a very high level of slack is usually detrimental to taking new initiatives because while very little slack deprives firms of necessary funds, very high levels of slack cause management complacency and inhibit risk taking (Lin et al., 2009). A moderate level of slack, on the other hand, is necessary to undertake new initiatives, experiment with new strategies, and exploit new opportunities (George, 2005). For example, Nohira and Gulati (1996) argue that a good amount of slack increases experimentation and innovation. Similarly, Patzelt et al. (2008) found that slack resources are positively related to undertaking new initiatives such as seeking new alliances. Lin et al. (2009) also suggested that a moderate level of slack is positively related to internationalization strategy. In another study, Bradley et al. (2011) showed that slack resources are positively related to firm growth.

While this research has increased our understanding of how moderate levels of slack provide firms with flexibility and increase their risk-taking behaviour, the applicability of these arguments to new ventures is limited because new ventures often suffer from insufficient resources (Knight et al., 2004). In fact, one of the most important characteristics of new ventures that differentiates them from their established counterparts is their limited resources and the difficulty of accessing more resources even when they try (also called 'liabilities of newness') (Stinchcombe, 1965).

Therefore, we argue that for new ventures, flexibility arises not from the amount of slack, but from the ways in which new ventures configure their existing and often limited resources. New ventures might configure their resources and achieve different levels of flexibility either intentionally by the careful actions of founders and/or unintentionally in a path-dependent manner. The resulting configurations of existing resources then either facilitate or hinder new ventures' ability to respond to and exploit new opportunities such as early internationalization.

Resource Flexibility and Early Internationalization

Early internationalization refers to new ventures venturing abroad through sales of outputs or acquisition of inputs in foreign markets very early on in their life cycles, usually within the first five years of their existence (Zahra and George, 2002). Undertaking an early internationalization strategy requires early identification and exploitation of international opportunities. We argue that both international opportunity identification and exploitation is affected by the configuration of new ventures' resources. We define resources as 'tangible or intangible assets that are tied semi-permanently to the firm. Resources include capital, labor, brand names, technological know-how, machinery, and efficient procedures ... etc.' (Wernerfelt, 1984, p. 172).[1] Resource flexibility refers to the adoptability of assets for alternative uses easily and at low cost (Sapienza et al., 2006; Su et al., 2011). New ventures vary in the extent to which they keep their assets more or less flexible (Stam, 2007). While some firms tend to make specific resource investments that are tied to a certain location such as land, building and equipment, others tend to keep their assets more portable, liquid and short term, such as more cash, account receivable and inventory, which are easier to use for different purposes across locations (Zander, 2004). The configurations of available resources, then, direct entrepreneurs' attention toward particular opportunities, or entrepreneurs are attracted to opportunities that are in line with their existing resources (Sarasvathy, 2001; Dreyer and Grønhaug, 2004).

We argue that new ventures that have less flexible resources such as location-specific tangible and long-term assets would have greater difficulty in identifying opportunities in international markets. While resource commitments might create certain competencies (Ghemawat, 1991), they might also create inertia or competency traps (Levinthal and March, 1983). Location-specific resource commitments shape new ventures' search efforts and induce them to spend their energies and efforts on the domestic markets (Autio et al., 2000; Stam, 2007). This, in turn, limits entrepreneurs' propensity to think 'outside the box', reducing their attention to and identification of international opportunities. In line with this logic, for example, Bouquet (2005) finds empirical support for the hypothesis that firms' decision environments influence attention structures, and their interest in global issues.

In contrast, more flexible resources such as cash and inventory would free new ventures in their search for international opportunities because with independence comes confidence, resourcefulness and creativity. Having less location-specific resource commitments, such ventures would be less constrained to shift their attention and effort from domestic markets to international markets, and can more easily notice or identify opportunities in international markets. Thus, we posit the following hypothesis:

H1: The flexibility of available resources positively affects the likelihood of early internationalization of new ventures.

Resource Flexibility and Performance of International New Ventures

Not only the likelihood of early internationalization, but also the successful performance of new ventures after early internationalization is likely to be affected by the flexibility of new ventures' resources. Firms face several complexities and uncertainties operating in foreign markets. These include political instability, volatile exchange rates, differing legal systems, social norms and language barriers, entry barriers created by host market firms, and entry barriers created by host governments (Acs et al., 1997; Zaheer and Mosakowski, 1997).

This greater market diversity and uncertainty that international new ventures face requires a capability to react to market variations efficiently (Gupta et al., 2008). New ventures with less flexible resources may not be able to adapt their resources for alternative uses quickly and at low cost. It requires time and effort to sell a building, machinery or land, for example and use it for international operations. New ventures with more flexible resources, on the other hand, may shift their resources to international operations quickly and efficiently. This increases new ventures' ability to manage the complexities and uncertainties of foreign markets and increases new ventures' international performance.

In fact, the ability to shift resources back and forth also helps respond to the necessities of domestic markets when a need arises in domestic operations as well. For new ventures with limited resources, this flexibility has added importance to ensure both international performance and overall short-term survival and growth of international new ventures (Sapienza et al., 2006). Less flexible resource configurations, on the other hand, would limit the new ventures' ability to reallocate their resources so as to exploit growth opportunities both domestically and internationally. In fact, failure to shift resources for different uses when different market environments demand it can even endanger short-term survival and lead to lower growth (ibid.). That is, resource flexibility might have an influence both on international operations and on survival and growth of international new ventures. Thus, we posit the following hypotheses:

H2a: The flexibility of available resources increases the international sales intensity of international new ventures.

H2b: The flexibility of available resources increases the probability of short-term survival of international new ventures.

H2c: The flexibility of available resources increases the short-term growth of international new ventures.

DATA AND METHODS

Sample

Firm-level data to test the hypotheses come from a secondary data source – the Kauffman Firm Survey (KFS) –which is a large panel data set of new businesses founded in the USA in 2004. The data set consists of an initial and seven annual follow-up surveys (of the same firms) in 2005, 2006, 2007, 2008, 2009, 2010 and 2011 by the Kauffman Foundation and the data are now being used in other academic studies (e.g., Robb and Robinson, 2010). The firms included in the survey come from a randomly chosen sample of new businesses in the Dun & Bradstreet list, with high-tech firms intentionally oversampled by the Kauffman Foundation. The survey provides detailed information on firm resources, strategy and financial performance.

Early internationalization is first measured in 2007 when new ventures in our sample were three years old, and then it is measured in the following years for firms that remain in the sample. In this chapter, we present our results for year 2007 (year 3),[2] the earliest time that internationalization is measured. In order to test our first hypothesis, the effect of resource flexibility on the likelihood of early internationalization in year 3, we lag resource flexibility by one year, and measure it in year 2006. Our sample size in year 3 is 2717 and 434 (16 per cent) of them are early internationalizers. This ratio closely matches the prior national statistics reported by OECD (2001).

In order to test our second set of hypotheses (H2a, H2b and H2c), the effect of resource flexibility on the performance of international new ventures, we focus on the sample that have internationalized in year 2007 (year 3). This reduces our sample size to 434 international new ventures. Also, to test these hypotheses, we measure performance variables in 2008 (year 4), one year after internationalization, to give enough time to observe the effect of resource flexibility on short-term performance.

Dependent Variables

The dependent variable in H1 is early internationalization. Early internationalization is measured as a dummy variable. A new venture is considered to be an early internationalizer if it has made any sales to individuals, businesses, or governments outside the USA at year 3. This operationalization is also consistent with the prior literature, which defines early internationalization as any sales of outputs or acquisition of inputs across borders within the first five years of a new venture's existence (Zahra and George, 2002).

The first dependent variable in H2a is international sales intensity. This variable is measured as the percentage of international sales to total sales in year 3. The specific question is: 'In 2007 what percentages of your company's total sales were to individuals, businesses, or governments outside the USA?' This is a five-category variable where the categories are 1 = less than 5 per cent, 2 = 5–25 per cent, 3 = 26–50 per cent, 4 = 51–75 per cent and 5 = 76–100 per cent. This measure shows a new venture's success in internationalization based on sales. This operationalization of early international intensity (as foreign sales as a percentage of total sales) is also used in prior studies (Carpenter et al., 2003; Fernhaber et al., 2009).

The second dependent variable in H2b is firm survival. Firm survival is measured as a dummy variable to the following questions in the year following early internationalization: 'Did your company permanently close operations?' Yes = 1, No = 0 (reverse coded to indicate firm survival). The data included firm exits due to mergers or acquisitions. However, we have not considered them as firm failure because although mergers measure the discontinuity of the firm, only closing permanently captures permanent exit, which is more likely to be due to underperformance. This conceptualization and measurement is in line with extant research on firm failure (Thornhill and Amit, 2003).

The last dependent variable in H2c is firm growth. We measure firm growth as the growth of sales in the year following early internationalization. This variable is computed as follows:

$$Total\ Sales\ Growth_{2008} = (Total\ Sales\ Volume_{2008} - Total\ Sales\ Volume_{2007})/Sales\ Volume_{2007}$$

This operationalization is also consistent with the current literature (e.g., Fernhaber and Li, 2010). We chose sales growth as a performance indicator in our study because sales growth is necessary for new ventures to fund future operations and to ensure their long-term survival (Robinson, 1999).

Independent Variable

The independent variable is the flexibility of firm resources, measured as a continuous variable. It is computed as the dollar value of liquid assets (cash, account receivable and inventory) over the dollar value of total assets ($ Liquid Assets/$ Total Assets), the year prior to year 3, when early internationalization is measured to test H1. The same variable is measured in year 3 to test hypotheses H2a, H2b and H2c.

Prior studies have utilized a wide range of measures to assess resource flexibility such as firm size, debt ratio, current ratio, profitability, cash flow sensitivity, retained earnings, dividend payments and so on (e.g., Bellone et al., 2010; Denis and McKeon, 2012; Hoberg et al., 2014).

However, most of this research has focused on big established companies where these measures are more relevant to assess flexibility. On the other hand, new ventures suffer from limited access to external debt and equity, and often do not have even profitability for the first few years. Therefore, we conceptualized flexibility as the ratio of liquid assets to total assets that are available to the venture. This conceptualization of asset flexibility is also consistent with literature on corporate finance asserting that liquid assets are more readily allocated for alternative investments than fixed assets, and therefore make the companies more flexible (Fazzari et al., 1988). Moreover, in their recent paper, Kim and Bettis (2014) also used the same operationalization in examining the value of cash as a strategic asset to facilitate adaptive advantages.

Control Variables

We incorporated a comprehensive set of control variables that have been found to affect early internationalization and performance in the prior literature. Prior studies indicate that the founders' demographic characteristics matter. They have suggested that male entrepreneurs are more likely to internationalize early and attain better performance than female entrepreneurs (Orser et al., 2004; Reavley et al., 2005). Founders' education and immigrant status is also known to affect new venture internationalization and performance (Yavuz et al., 2012). We also control for the founders' previous industry experience. Studies show that previous industry experience positively influences firm strategies (Dencker et al., 2009).

We also include in our study main industrial activity (i.e., whether the firm is providing a product or a service) (Westhead et al., 2001), Internet sales (Madsen and Servais, 1997), the existence of intellectual property (Andersson et al., 2004), firm size, or the amount of total assets, known to be positively related to early internationalization and performance (Westhead et al., 2001; Andersson et al., 2004). We also control for whether a new venture is operating in a high-technology industry that tends to internationalize earlier relative to new ventures in other industries (Shrader et al., 2000). Table 5.1 summarizes the definitions of the variables.

Table 5.1   Variable definitions

Variable	Abbreviation of Variables	Definition
Likelihood of Early Internationalization$_{(2007)}$	Early International	Dummy = 1 if firm has international sales, 0 otherwise
International Sales Intensity$_{(2007)}$	International Intensity	1 = less than 5%, 2 = 5–25%, 3 = 26–50%, 4 = 51–75% and 5 = 76–100%
Firm Survival$_{(2008)}$	Survival	Dummy = 0 if firm is out of business, 0 otherwise
Firm Growth$_{(2007 \text{ to } 2008)}$	Growth	(Sales Volume$_{2008}$ – Sales Volume$_{2007}$)/ Sales Volume$_{2007}$
The Flexibility of Firm Resources$_{(2006)}$	Liquid to Total Assets	(\$ Cash + \$ Account Receivable + \$ Inventory)/\$ Total Assets
Firm Size$_{(2006)}$	Total Assets	Ln (Total Assets)
Gender of the Primary Founder$_{(2007)}$	Male	Dummy = 1 if founder is male, 0 otherwise
Education of the Primary Founder$_{(2007)}$	Education	1 = High school or less, 2 = Technical/ trade/vocational degree, 3 = Some college, no degree, 4 = Associate's degree, 5 = Bachelor's degree, 6 = Some graduate school, no degree, 7 = Master's degree, 8 = Professional school, doctorate
Immigrant Status of the Primary Founder	Immigrant Status	Dummy = 1 if non-US born, 0 otherwise
Previous Industry Experience of the Primary Founder$_{(2007)}$	Industry Exp.	Years of experience that the founder has had in the industry in which the firm competes
Product or Service Company$_{(2007)}$	Providing Product	Dummy 1 = if firm provides product, 0 otherwise
Internet Sales$_{(2007)}$	Internet Sales	Dummy 1 = if firm has Internet sales, 0 otherwise
Intellectual Property$_{(2007)}$	Intellectual Property	Dummy = 1 if firm has either patents, copyrights or trademarks, 0 otherwise
High Technology Industry$_{(2007)}$	High-tech Industry	Dummy = 1 if firm is operating in a technology generating industry, 0 otherwise

RESULTS

Table 5.2 reports descriptive statistics and pairwise correlations for all variables used to test H1. Pairwise correlations among the variables are generally as expected. The values in Table 5.2 indicate that resource flexibility is positively and significantly (as expected) related to early internationalization. Although bivariate correlations between variables are not too high (> 0.80) to suggest multicollinearity, we still employed a variance inflation factor test (VIF) where scores greater than 10 imply multicollinearity. Our results show that there are no variables with a VIF score greater than 10; we conclude that multicollinearity is not a problem for our analyses.

We use logistic regression to test our first hypothesis because our dependent variable, early internationalization, is a binary variable measuring whether a new venture has any international sales in year 3. As can be seen in the first column of Table 5.3, resource flexibility has a positive and significant effect on the likelihood of early internationalization with $z = 4.69$, $p < 0.001$, proving strong support for the H1. We calculated the odds ratio, which shows the odds that a firm will early internationalize given greater degree of resource flexibility, compared to the odds that a firm will early internationalize with lower degree of resource flexibility. The odds ratio is 2.54 in our logistic regression. This means that one unit increase in the flexibility of resources increases the likelihood of early internationalization by 2.5 times.

Table 5.3 also shows the effect of our control variables on early internationalization. Consistent with prior literature (e.g., Andersson et al., 2004; Federico et al., 2009) results show that new ventures with highly educated entrepreneurs, immigrant entrepreneurs, entrepreneurs with greater previous industry experience are significantly more likely to be early internationalizers than new ventures with less educated, native or less industry experienced entrepreneurs. Moreover, new ventures that provide product (instead of service), that have Internet sales (instead of physical sales only) and that have intellectual property (instead of having no intellectual property) are significantly more likely to be early internationalizers.

Table 5.2 Descriptive statistics and pairwise correlations for the full sample (H1)

	Variables	Mean	s.d.	1	2	3	4	5	6	7	8	9	10	11
1	Early International	0.16	0.37											
2	Resource Flexibility	0.58	0.36	0.13*										
3	Total Assets (ln)	10.75	2.06	0.13*	−0.11*									
4	Male	0.75	0.43	0.04*	−0.02	0.15*								
5	Education	6.43	2.09	0.12*	0.22*	0.01	−0.01							
6	Immigrant	0.10	0.30	0.08*	0.06*	0.03	0.05*	0.12*						
7	Industry Exp.	13.57	10.73	0.04*	0.08*	0.08*	0.20*	0.04*	−0.07*					
8	Providing Product	0.48	0.49	0.20*	0.05*	0.15*	−0.02	−0.08	0.00	−0.08*				
9	Internet Sales	0.26	0.44	0.28*	0.04	0.02	−0.00	0.03	0.01	−0.10*	0.22*			
10	Intellectual Property	0.22	0.42	0.21*	0.08*	0.08*	0.01	0.18*	0.02	0.01	0.18*	0.20*		
11	High-tech Industry	0.12	0.33	0.08*	0.12*	0.04	0.11*	0.16*	0.09*	0.10*	0.03	0.02	0.14*	

Note: $* p < 0.05$.

Table 5.3   *Logistic estimate of the likelihood of early internationalization as a function of resource flexibility*

Estimators → Variables ↓	Odds Ratio	Standard Error	z	$p > |z|$
Resource Flexibility	2.54	0.51	4.69	0.000
Total Assets (ln)	1.16	0.04	4.62	0.000
Male	1.20	0.19	1.14	0.255
Education	1.13	0.04	3.69	0.000
Immigrant	1.61	0.30	2.50	0.012
Industry Exp.	1.01	0.01	2.31	0.021
Providing Product	2.34	0.32	6.31	0.000
Internet Sales	3.56	0.45	10.01	0.000
Intellectual Property	1.72	0.24	3.93	0.000
High-tech Industry	1.17	0.21	0.90	0.366
Constant (α)	0.00	0.00	−13.68	0.000
Log Likelihood	−859.513			
Pseudo R^2	0.164			
N	2308			

Table 5.4 reports descriptive statistics and pairwise correlations for the sample of international new ventures to test H2a, H2b and H2c. The values in Table 5.4 indicate that resource flexibility is positively and significantly (as expected) related to early international intensity and short-term growth, but it does not relate to short-term survival.

Table 5.4 Descriptive statistics and pairwise correlations for the international sample (H2a, H2b, H2c)

	Variables	Mean	s.d.	1	2	3	4	5	6	7	8	9	10	11	12	13
1	International Intensity	1.88	1.17													
2	Firm Survival	0.96	0.20	-0.04												
3	Firm Growth	12.44	2.16	0.07	0.03											
4	Resource Flexibility	0.69	0.32	0.08	0.03	0.11										
5	Total Assets	11.52	2.06	0.04	0.11*	0.75*	-0.02									
6	Male	0.79	0.41	0.09	0.05	0.14*	-0.00	0.14*								
7	Education	6.96	1.94	0.12*	0.05	0.05	0.08	0.01	-0.01							
8	Immigrant Status	0.15	0.36	0.09	0.01	-0.01	0.11*	0.01	0.02	0.22*						
9	Industry Exp.	14.53	11.33	0.13*	0.03*	0.18*	-0.03	0.19*	0.18*	0.04	-0.05					
10	Providing Product	0.71	0.46	-0.05	0.00	0.07*	0.18*	0.15*	0.04	-0.16*	-0.04	-0.08*				
11	Internet Sales	0.53	0.50	-0.20*	-0.08*	-0.20*	-0.06	-0.18*	-0.03	-0.10*	-0.12*	-0.19*	0.28*			
12	Intellectual Property	0.42	0.49	-0.02	0.03	0.03	0.09	0.07	0.00	0.19*	-0.04	0.05	0.16*	0.18*		
13	High-tech Industry	0.18	0.39	0.05	-0.03	0.09*	-0.01	0.11*	0.11*	0.25*	0.10*	0.16*	0.09	0.06	0.19*	

Note: * $p < 0.05$.

83

The first column in Table 5.5 presents results from the estimates of ordered probit regression testing H2a, whether resource flexibility affects international sales intensity. The coefficient for international intensity is significant with $z = 2.06$, $p < 0.05$, providing support for H2a. This result implies that firms with more flexible resources tend to achieve higher levels of international sales as a percentage of total sales.

The second column in Table 5.5 presents results from the estimates of probit regression testing H2b, whether resource flexibility affects the short-term survival of international new ventures. The odds ratio for resource flexibility is insignificant, meaning resource flexibility has no significant effect on the short-term survival of international new ventures.

The third column in Table 5.5 provides results for our last hypothesis, H2c where the dependent variable is overall sales growth. The results of an OLS estimation shows that the coefficient of resource flexibility is positive and significant with $z = 1.40$, $p < 0.001$, meaning that resource flexibility has a positive and significant effect on the growth of international new ventures such that one unit increase in resource flexibility increases total sales by 1.40 units for international new ventures.

It is also important to note that consistent with low bivariate correlations between variables presented in Table 5.4, none of our control variables, except total assets, has a significant effect on either the survival or the growth of international new ventures (see Table 5.5). These results suggest that the number of available resources is the most significant control variable explaining new venture survival and growth. As for international intensity, on the other hand, being male and having international sales also have marginally significant positive effects on international sales intensity at $p < 0.10$ level.

In order to check the robustness of our results, we also employed different operationalization of resource flexibility. We have used cash to total assets (\$ Cash/\$ Total Assets) instead of liquid to total assets and re-run our analyses with this measure. Moreover, we have used different time periods to measure our dependent and independent variables. Our results are largely robust to these alternative specifications.

To sum up, results show that resource flexibility, measured as liquid assets over total assets, has a positive and significant effect on the early internationalization of new ventures. Moreover, resource flexibility has a positive and a significant effect on the both the intensity of international sales and overall short-term sales growth of international new ventures. However, there is no relationship between resource flexibility and international new ventures' short-term survival.

Table 5.5 *Logistic estimate of the international sales intensity, short-term survival, and short-term sales growth as a function of resource flexibility*

Estimators → Variables ↓	International Sales Intensity (Ordered Probit)				Short-term Survival (Probit)				Short-term Sales Growth (OLS)			
	Coef.	s.d.	z	$p > |z|$	Coef.	s.d.	z	$p > |z|$	Coef.	s.d.	t	$p > |t|$
Resource Flexibility	0.42	0.20	2.06	0.039	-0.01	0.33	-0.02	0.988	1.40	0.28	5.06	0.000
Total Assets	-0.00	0.03	-0.02	0.987	0.11	0.05	2.27	0.023	0.78	0.05	14.69	0.000
Male	0.28	0.16	1.78	0.075	0.25	0.25	1.02	0.310	0.23	0.24	0.97	0.331
Education	0.01	0.04	0.35	0.724	0.09	0.06	1.51	0.131	-0.00	0.05	-0.07	0.946
Immigrant Status	0.13	0.19	0.71	0.476	0.06	0.38	0.15	0.882	-0.18	0.24	-0.74	0.462
Industry Exp.	0.07	0.01	1.26	0.208	0.00	0.01	0.20	0.844	0.01	0.01	1.51	0.131
Providing Product	0.01	0.15	0.07	0.947	0.03	0.21	0.13	0.898	-0.17	0.20	-0.88	0.382
Internet Sales	-0.24	0.13	-1.81	0.071	-0.36	0.26	-1.36	0.173	-0.22	0.18	-1.24	0.217
Intellectual Property	-0.13	0.13	-1.03	0.303	0.07	0.24	0.29	0.774	-0.01	0.17	-0.08	0.936
High-tech Industry	0.03	0.16	0.18	0.858	-0.46	0.306	-1.49	0.136	-0.05	0.22	-0.22	0.823
Constant					-0.01	0.68	-0.01	0.991	2.43	0.76	3.19	0.002
Wald Chi² χ^2/F	20.28				20.06				33.25			
Log likelihood	-456.600				-60.681				N/A			
Pseudo R^2/R^2	0.02				0.08				0.61			
N	376				366				290			

DISCUSSION

We investigate the heterogeneity in the decision and performance of early internationalization. We hypothesize that a greater degree of resource flexibility in new ventures facilitates their identification of international opportunities earlier in their life cycles and also enhances their performance following initial entry into foreign markets. We find evidence consistent with these claims. We find that new ventures with a greater ratio of liquid assets make sales outside the USA not long after their inception. We also find that after initial sales made outside the USA, new ventures increase performance both in terms of international sales intensity and in terms of overall sales growth if they have a greater ratio of liquid assets. This is consistent with our argument that flexibility in resource configuration provides new ventures with capabilities to respond to opportunities in foreign markets.

However, we do not find a significant effect of liquid assets over total assets on international new ventures' short-term survival. This finding is interesting because prior literature has shown that liquid assets tend to prevent companies from financial distress and increase their probability of survival (Holtz-Eakin et al., 1994). One potential explanation for our finding would be that new ventures need some level of resource flexibility to be able to internationalize. Once this level of flexibility is achieved and new ventures internationalize, even though there is variation among international new ventures in terms of the flexibility of their resources, it may not be of a sufficiently high magnitude that it significantly affects the survival rates of international new ventures.

Another explanation might be that the resource flexibility only influences how new ventures respond to opportunities, but not to threats. It could be that because the opportunity to internationalize will only be available for a very short period of time, resource flexibility might be useful to capture these opportunities, positively affecting international sales intensity and short-term growth. On the other hand, what really matters for survival might be the number of available resources regardless of their configurations. As long as new ventures have sufficient resources, they might be able to find the time and the ways to utilize these resources to avoid failure. Our results do not rule out this explanation because the number of available resources has a significant positive effect on new venture survival while resource flexibility has no such significant effect. Future research should delve into this issue in more detail.

Our theoretical arguments and empirical findings provide novel insights into what affects early internationalization. We do not focus on potential factors that would affect internationalization by any firm. Rather, we highlight how resource flexibility can facilitate and enhance start-ups' internationalization. Although studying early internationalizing firms is becoming an important part of the growing international entrepreneurship literature, many studies still stick to the traditional internationalization theories and try to apply them to this emerging new phenomenon. While we agree that there is overlap between the two, we also strongly believe that this new phenomenon requires us to illuminate another dimension that has not been considered as a factor related to internationalization – for example, resource flexibility. We believe that consideration of resource flexibility distinguishes internationalization by ventures from that by established firms (i.e., traditional internationalization perspectives) that tend to have a lot of slack resources. The empirical findings that we demonstrate provide further theoretical development to explain this emerging phenomenon of internationalization by new ventures. Guided by our theoretical predictions, we were able to identify the effect of firm's resource flexibility on the early internationalization and performance of international new ventures. We believe that the study of international entrepreneurship or international business, in general, could benefit from our findings.

Limitations and Future Research

Both the limitations and the findings of the study present avenues for future research. First, the data for this study come from new ventures that are started in the USA. It is important to note that the USA provides a more stringent context to test the hypotheses of this study because it is a country where access to resources is relatively easy. Therefore, we expect that the findings hold more strongly in other countries where firms suffer from limited resources much more, and the distinction between firms with more and less flexible resources would be more salient in determining their strategic actions.

Second, future studies should build on this research and measure resource flexibility in different ways. While we used objective data, the ratio of liquid assets to total assets, future studies could also design survey questions and ask entrepreneurs directly about the ease with which they are able to use their resources for alternative options. Moreover, although we have focused specifically on resource flexibility in this chapter, future research could examine other types of flexibilities such as cognitive, structural, political and relational, emphasized by prior studies (Autio et al., 2000; Sapienza et al., 2006; De Clercq et al., 2014). In addition, we also think that human resource flexibility (i.e., the extent to which new ventures hire full-time employees versus outsourcing, for example) could be a potentially fruitful direction as well. We suggest that future studies combine these different types of flexibilities and examine the conditions under which these flexibilities might be more or less important in affecting early internationalization and new venture performance.

Third, we have undertaken two-step analyses where we first measured the effect of resource flexibility on the propensity to internationalize early in the full sample. And then we examined the influence of resource flexibility on performance of international new ventures excluding the ones that have stayed domestic. While this was our strategy given our focus on international new ventures, future research might examine both domestic and international new ventures to understand the mechanisms by which resource flexibility influences new venture performance. These studies could examine how early internationalization and maybe other types of strategies could mediate or moderate the relationship between resource flexibility and new venture survival and growth.

Finally, there might be other factors that might affect the need for resource flexibility such as the industry in which new ventures operate. Although in this study we controlled for industry (i.e., whether the new ventures operate in high-tech industries or not), future research should examine the effect of industry in more depth and also look into possible interaction effects of resource flexibility and industry on the early internationalization decisions and performance of international new ventures. Analysing these factors might also shed better light on our insignificant result regarding the effect of resource flexibility on the survival of international new ventures. It could be that survival effects of resource flexibility might be different in different industries. Hence, future research should address these possibilities and increase our understanding of the relationship between resource flexibility and new venture performance.

CONCLUSIONS AND CONTRIBUTIONS

This study is one of the first empirical attempts to examine the effect of resource flexibility on early internationalization and performance. In doing so, this chapter provides theoretical insights into the flexibility of firm resources as an important resource characteristic affecting new ventures' internationalization and performance outcomes. Research in this field has not paid much attention to differing characteristics of early internationalization by start-ups – originating from their resource-constrained nature. Such constraints that new ventures face lead them from focusing on internationalization from the number of available resources to focusing on effective configuration of their existing resources. This study addresses this research gap in the literature, and theorizes and empirically tests how resource flexibility influences early internationalization.

Furthermore, although there are plenty of conceptual articles on the importance of resources for new venture performance, there are very few recent empirical studies that explain the resource determinants of performance in international new ventures (Gassmann and Keupp, 2007). One such study is by Chang et al. (2012) that showed how slack resources increased sales growth in the sample of 335 international new ventures. Given the resource-limited nature of new ventures, in this chapter, we have analysed the effect of resource flexibility on the survival and growth of international new ventures after controlling for the total number of available resources.

Empirically, this study utilizes a large longitudinal database of a cohort of firms so that we are able to lag our dependent variables and examine performance outcomes in later years, and use different time specifications to ensure the reliability of our results. We have also used a comprehensive set of control variables that prior studies have shown to have an effect on early internationalization and performance. Last, we have used a variety of performance measures (namely, international sales intensity, short-term survival and short-term growth) in the same study. All these are attempts to address some of the empirical gaps in the prior studies of international new ventures.

Practically, our study has the potential to provide guidelines to entrepreneurs considering early internationalization. Given that resource allocation decisions are critical decisions that entrepreneurs have to make, we suggest that flexible resource configuration helps successful early internationalization. Moreover, this study has important implications for financial resource providers. Many funding agencies require new ventures to make specific investments with the money they provide to them. However, our results indicate that this practice may in fact limit the flexibility of new ventures to exploit many fruitful opportunities and limit their growth. Therefore, we suggest that financial resource providers be more lenient in the specific uses of these funds and let new ventures keep cash reserves to pursue growth opportunities such as early internationalization. Finally, our study has implications for policy-makers seeking to encourage the formation of international new ventures. Policy-makers can benefit from our results in devising entrepreneurial policies and educational programmes.

NOTES

* We gratefully acknowledge the support of the Ewing Marion Kauffman Foundation through access to the KFS data in the NORC Data Enclave. All errors remain ours.
1. We use the term 'resources' and 'assets' interchangeably in this chapter.
2. We conducted our analyses for each alternative year and results are robust to different time specifications and estimation techniques.

REFERENCES

Acs, Z.J., M. Shaver and B. Yeung (1997), 'The internationalization of small and medium sized enterprises: a policy perspective', *Small Business Economics*, **9** (1), 7–20.

Andersson, S., J. Gabrielsson and I. Wictor (2004), 'International activities in small firms: examining factors influencing the internationalization and export growth of small firms', *Canadian Journal of Administrative Sciences*, **21** (1), 22–34.

Autio, E., H. Sapienza and J. Almeida (2000), 'Effects of age at entry, knowledge intensity, and imitability on international growth', *Academy of Management Journal*, **43** (5), 909–24.

Bellone, F., P. Musso, L. Nesta and S. Schiavo (2010), 'Financial constraints and firm export behavior', *The World Economy*, **33** (3), 347–73.

Bouquet, C.A. (2005), *Building Global Mindsets: An Attention-Based Perspective*, New York: Palgrave Macmillan.

Bradley, S.W., J. Wiklund and D. Shepherd (2011), 'Swinging a double-edged sword: the effect slack on entrepreneurial management and growth', *Journal of Business Venturing*, **26** (5), 537–54.

Carpenter, M.A., T.G. Pollock and M.M. Leary (2003), 'Testing a model of reasoned risk-taking: governance, the experience of principals and agents, and global strategy in high technology IPO firms', *Strategic Management Journal*, **24** (9), 803–20.

Chandra, Y., C. Styles and I. Wilkinson (2009), 'The recognition of first time international entrepreneurial opportunities: evidence from firms in knowledge-based industries', *International Marketing Review*, **26** (1), 30–61.

Chang, S.H., Y.L. Jaw and H.J. Chiu (2012), 'A behavioral perspective of international new ventures: slack, early internationalization, and performance', *Journal of Global Business Management*, **8** (2), 200–211.

De Clercq, D., H. Sapienza and L. Zhou (2014), 'Entrepreneurial strategic posture and learning effort in international ventures: the moderating roles of operational flexibilities', *International Business Review*, **23** (5), 981–92.

Dencker, J., M. Gruber and S. Shah (2009), 'Pre-entry knowledge, learning, and the survival of new firms', *Organization Science*, **20** (3), 516–37.

Denis, D.J. and S.B. McKeon (2012), 'Debt financing and financial flexibility: evidence from proactive leverage increases', *Review of Financial Studies*, **25** (6), 1897–929.

Dreyer, B. and K. Grønhaug (2004), 'Uncertainty, flexibility, and sustained competitive advantage', *Journal of Business Research*, **57** (5), 484–94.

Evans, J.S. (1991), 'Strategic flexibility for high technology maneuvers: a conceptual framework', *Journal of Management Studies*, **28** (1), 69–89.

Fazzari, S., G. Hubbard and B.C. Petersen (1988), 'Financial constraints and corporate investment', *Brooking Papers on Economic Activity*, **19** (1), 141–95.

Federico, J.S., H.D. Kantis, A. Rialp and J. Rialp (2009), 'Does entrepreneurs' human and relational capital affect early internationalization? A cross-regional comparison', *European Journal of International Management*, **3** (2), 199–215.

Fernhaber, S.A. and D. Li (2010), 'The impact of inter-organizational limitation on new venture international entry and performance', *Entrepreneurship Theory and Practice*, **34** (1), 1–30.

Fernhaber, S.A., P.P. Macdougall-Covin and D.A. Shepherd (2009), 'International entrepreneurship: leveraging internal and external knowledge sources', *Strategic Entrepreneurship Journal*, **3** (4), 297–320.

Gassmann, O. and M.M. Keupp (2007), 'The competitive advantage of early and rapidly internationalising SMEs in the biotechnology industry: a knowledge based view', *Journal of World Business*, **42** (3), 350–66.

George, G. (2005), 'Slack resources and the performance of privately-held firms', *Academy of Management Journal*, **48** (4), 661–76.

Ghemawat, P. (1991), *Commitment*, New York: Free Press.

Gupta, A.K., V. Govindarajan and H. Wang (2008), *The Quest for Global Dominance*, Hoboken, NJ: Wiley.

Hoberg, G., G. Phillips and N. Prabhala (2014), 'Product market threats, payouts, and financial flexibility', *Journal of Finance*, **69** (1), 293–324.

Holtz-Eakin, D., D. Joulfaian and H. Rosen (1994), 'Entrepreneurial decisions and liquidity constraints', *The RAND Journal of Economics*, **25** (2), 334–47.

Kim, C. and R.A. Bettis (2014), 'Cash is surprisingly valuable as a strategic asset', *Strategic Management Journal*, **35** (13), 2053–63.

Knight, G., T. Madsen and P. Servais (2004), 'An inquiry into born-global firms in Europe and the USA', *International Marketing Review*, **21** (6), 645–65.

Levinthal, D. and J. March (1983), 'The learning myopia', *Strategic Management Journal*, **14** (S2), 95–112.

Lin, W.T., K. Cheng and Y. Liu (2009), 'Organizational slack and firms' internationalization: a longitudinal study of high-technology firms', *Journal of World Business*, **44** (4), 397–406.

Madsen, T.K. and P. Servais (1997), 'The internationalization of born-globals: an evolutionary process?', *International Business Review*, **6** (6), 561–83.

Nohira, N. and R. Gulati (1996), 'Is slack good or bad for innovation?', *Academy of Management Journal*, **39** (4), 1245–64.

Organisation for Economic Co-operation and Development (OECD) (2001), *Development Co-operation Report*, Paris: OECD.

Orser, B., A. Riding and J. Townsend (2004), 'Exporting as a means of growth for women-owned Canadian SMEs', *Journal of Small Business and Entrepreneurship*, **17** (3), 153–74.

Patzelt, H., D.A. Shepherd, D. Deeds and S.W. Bradley (2008), 'Financial slack and venture managers' decisions to seek a new alliance', *Journal of Business Venturing*, **23** (4), 465–81.

Reavley, M., T. Litchy and E. McClelland (2005), 'Exporting success: a two country comparison of women entrepreneurs in international trade', *International Journal of Entrepreneurial and Small Business*, **2** (1), 57–78.

Robb, A. and D. Robinson (2010), 'The capital decisions of new firms', *NBER Working Paper No. 16272*.

Robinson, K.C. (1999), 'An examination of the influence of industry structure on eight alternative measures of new venture performance for high potential independent new ventures', *Journal of Business Venturing*, **14** (2), 165–87.

Sapienza, H., E. Autio, G. George and S.A. Zahra (2006), 'A capabilities perspective on the effects of early internationalization on firm survival and growth', *Academy of Management Review*, **31** (4), 914–33.

Sarasvathy, S.D. (2001), 'Causation and effectuation: toward a theoretical shift from economic inevitability to entrepreneurial contingency', *Academy of Management Review*, **26** (2), 243–64.

Shrader, R., B. Oviatt and P. McDougall (2000), 'How ventures exploit tradeoffs among international risk factors: lessons for accelerated internationalization of the 21st century', *Academy of Management Journal*, **43** (6), 1227–47.

Stam, E. (2007), 'Why butterflies don't leave: locational behavior of entrepreneurial firms', *Economic Geography*, **83** (1), 27–50.

Stinchcombe, A.L. (1965), 'Social structure and organizations', in J. March (eds), *Handbook of Organizations*, Chicago, IL: Rand McNally.

Su, Z., E. Xie and D. Wang (2011), 'Entrepreneurial strategy making, resources, and firm performance: evidence from China', *Small Business Economics*, **36** (2), 235–47.

Thornhill, S. and R. Amit (2003), 'Learning about failure: bankruptcy, firm age and the resource based view', *Organization Science*, **14** (5), 497–509.

Verdú-Jover, A., F.J. Lloréns and V.J. García-Morales (2006), 'Environment–flexibility coalignment and performance: an analysis in large versus small firms', *Journal of Small Business Management*, **44** (3), 334–49.

Wernerfelt, B. (1984), 'A resource-based view of the firm', *Strategic Management Journal*, **5** (2), 171–80.

Westhead, P., M. Wright and D. Ucbasaran (2001), 'The internationalization of new and small firms: a resource-based view', *Journal of Business Venturing*, **16** (4), 333–58.

Yavuz, R.I., H. Sapienza and S. Zaheer (2012), 'Founders' immigrant status, early internationalization and performance in high technology industries', *Frontiers of Entrepreneurship Research*, **36** (16), Article 2.

Zaheer, S. and E. Mosakowski (1997), 'The dynamics of the liabilities of foreignness', *Strategic Management Journal*, **18** (6), 439–64.

Zahra, S. and G. George (2002), 'International entrepreneurship: the current status of the field and future research agenda', in M. Hitt, D. Ireland, M.

Camp and D. Sexton (eds), *Strategic Entrepreneurship: Creating a New Mindset*, Oxford: Blackwell Publishing, pp. 255–88.

Zander, I. (2004), 'The micro foundations of cluster stickiness – walking in the shoes of the entrepreneur', *Journal of International Management*, **10** (2), 151–75.

6. Overcoming the 'smallness challenge' in asymmetrical alliances

Krister Salamonsen

INTRODUCTION

Research has shown that firms that participate in strategic alliances reap greater benefits than firms that compete independently due to, for example, the pooling of resources and knowledge (Hamel, 1991; Das and Teng, 2000). In fact, strategic alliances have become a central component of many companies' growth strategies (Kale and Singh, 2009). However, in the wake of increasing numbers of strategic alliances, the failure[1] rate of alliances ranges between 50 and 70 per cent (Hughes and Weiss, 2007; Chao, 2011).

A recent study notes that most of the existing literature on alliances focuses on partnerships between two or more large firms and that too few studies examine alliances between small firms and large firms (Yang et al., 2014). From the perspective of a small firm, an asymmetrically sized strategic alliance can potentially result in a situation in which the large firm controls the alliance's activities by engaging in opportunistic behaviour, which inhibits collaboration and even jeopardizes the survival of the alliance (Vandaie and Zaheer, 2014).

The proximity perspective has earned a central position in several research streams, including streams relating to different forms of inter-firm collaboration (Balland, 2012; Fitjar and Rodríguez-Pose, 2013). Several dimensions of proximity have emerged, including geographical, organizational, cognitive, cultural, institutional, social and technological. This variety has led to conceptual ambiguity in the field, which may have limited the development of comparable research (Knoben and Oerlemans, 2006). This chapter focuses on small firms' geographical, organizational and technological proximity towards large alliance partners for the following reasons. First, geographical proximity facilitates interaction and the exchange of knowledge and information between actors (Torre and Gilly, 2000; Letaifa and Rabeau, 2013). Thus, geographical proximity is expected to be an important factor for small firms in asymmetrically sized alliances. Organizational proximity concerns the partners' ability to share and complement each other's information, knowledge and resources (Meister and Werker, 2004; Torre and Rallet, 2005). The concept of organizational proximity also encompasses the characteristics of functional (or dysfunctional) organizations, including cognitive, social, institutional and/or cultural dynamics (Knoben and Oerlemans, 2006). Consequently, without further specification, organizational proximity functions as a measure of several different organizational aspects. Finally, technological proximity refers to the sharing of technological experience and knowledge bases between collaborating firms (Lane and Lubatkin, 1998; Knoben and Oerlemans, 2006) and to the degree of heterogeneity in the firms' respective competencies and capabilities (Boschma, 2005). Technological proximity thus affects the ability of collaborators to benefit from the exchange of, for example, experience, technology, resources and knowledge.

The chapter asks the following research question: How can geographical, organizational, and technological proximity influence small firms' relationships with large partners? To address this issue I use empirical data from small firms in five asymmetrically sized alliances in the Norwegian oil and gas industry, and theoretical insights from the alliance and proximity literature.

CONCEPTUAL FRAME OF REFERENCE

Interfirm relationships receive increasing attention from scholars, and a number of approaches are being used to investigate these phenomena. A strategic alliance – that is, a collaborative arrangement between two or more firms (Hitt et al., 2000) – has been described in the literature as a valuable mode of collaboration. The strategic alliance concept has been adopted in different research streams and has earned considerable attention in entrepreneurship and management literature in particular. For example, studies have demonstrated that strategic alliances can facilitate resource complementarities among partners (Harrison et al., 2001), increase firm performance through innovation (Lahiri and Narayanan, 2013), and generate growth by enabling entry into new markets (Salamonsen and Henriksen, 2015).

Alliances can be characterized broadly as horizontal, vertical, or diagonal. A horizontal alliance is a relationship between firms operating at the same level in the value chain (Perry et al., 2004). A vertical alliance is usually based on a buyer–supplier relationship between the partners and involves the combination of the partners' respective assets and capabilities to achieve collective ends (Belderbos et al., 2012). Diagonal alliances are partnerships where firms from different industries collaborate to gain from each other's resources and market positions (Doole and Lowe, 1997). Several studies have illustrated that horizontal and vertical alliances differ in terms of competitive tension, opportunistic behaviour, resource dependency, and stability (Park and Russo, 1996; Rindfleisch, 2000). For example, the partners in vertical alliances share resources and inputs more often than partners in horizontal alliances (Rindfleisch, 2000). In addition, vertical and horizontal alliances often differ with respect to objectives and performance outcomes. For example, studies have shown that horizontal alliances are more effective at generating radical innovations, whereas vertical alliances often strive for (and achieve) productivity growth and incremental innovations (Belderbos et al., 2004).

Resources and knowledge critical to a firm's development and prosperity are often beyond the reach of small firms; thus, small firms in particular may extract value from alliances (Doz and Hamel, 1998; Van-Gils and Swart, 2009). Despite numerous valuable contributions to the growing body of alliance literature, rather few studies have investigated alliances between large firms and small firms (Yang et al., 2014). The current knowledge is thus based primarily on the results of studies that focus on alliances between two or more large firms. An alliance between a large firm and a small firm is characterized by size asymmetry, and this asymmetry has been shown to potentially facilitate unfavourable outcomes for the small firm. For example, in many asymmetrically sized alliances, a small firm's only option is to abide by the rules and regulations established by the large partner (Stuart, 1998; Ahuja et al., 2009; Yang et al., 2014).

However, recent studies have illustrated that there is more to asymmetrical alliances than the preconceived notion of David versus Goliath. For example, some studies have shown that contrary to the distribution of value (Dyer et al., 2008), each partner in an asymmetrical alliance may procure the full value generated by the collaboration when value is defined and measured differently by each partner (Pérez et al., 2012). This concept indicates that the incentives for entering into an alliance may differ among the firms involved. Another study found that small firms in possession of valuable technological knowledge are more likely to have their interests met when negotiating governance issues with their large partners (Bosse and Alvarez, 2010). This finding shows that partner interdependence may yield increased benefits for small firms in asymmetrical alliances (Gulati and Sytch, 2007; Villanueva et al., 2012). Furthermore, small firms frequently possess assets that large firms are incapable of developing internally, such as local knowledge and access to local markets (Prashantham and Birkinshaw, 2008). As such, small firms can provide value to large-partner alliances. Conversely, small firms may gain legitimacy and increased access to resources through their large partners (Hoang and Rothmaermel, 2005; Ahuja et al., 2009; Salamonsen and Henriksen, 2015).

One way to consider the strategic alliance relationship is to employ the proximity framework. The proximity concept has received much attention from scholars in recent years and has been used in innovation studies (Boschma, 2005), cluster studies (Silvestre and Dalcol, 2009), and studies of interfirm collaboration (Balland, 2012). The benefit of the proximity perspective is that it provides a framework for better understanding the factors that influence interfirm collaboration (Knoben and Oerlemans, 2006).

Several proximity dimensions have emerged in the literature, including geographical, organizational, cultural, technological, cognitive, institutional and social (see Knoben and Oerlemans, 2006, for a review). As stated in the introduction, this study focuses on geographical, organizational and technological proximity. Table 6.1 provides the definitions and characteristics of these proximity dimensions in interorganizational collaboration.

The degree of organizational and technological proximity between alliance partners depends on the firms' previous experiences with industrial practices and with interfirm relationships (D'Este et al., 2012). If a firm can draw on earlier experiences, it will be better able to adapt to a partner's routines (Li et al., 2008) and to learn from the partner's skills and knowledge bases (Kumar and Nti, 1998). Technological proximity coincides with organizational proximity because both dimensions relate to the sharing of knowledge across organizational borders. For example, the degree of complexity will affect the ability to transfer and process technology (Sorenson et al., 2006).

The above discussion regarding geographical, organizational and technological proximity illustrates the potential importance of these dimensions in interfirm relationships. By employing these theoretical approaches in the context of small firms' role in asymmetrically sized alliances, this chapter may provide novel insights into an underdeveloped theme in the alliance literature.

Table 6.1   Geographical, organizational and technological proximity

Proximity Dimension	Definition	Characteristics	Developments in the Literature
Geographical	The ability and extent to which collaborating actors can have face-to-face relations (Capello, 1999)	Fosters knowledge transfer and innovation among collaborating partners (Lane and Lubatkin, 1998; Knoben and Oerlemans, 2006)	Temporary geographical proximity (Gallaud and Torre, 2005) Co-location might harm entrepreneurship and innovation (Broekel and Boschma, 2012; Letaifa and Rabeau, 2013)
Organizational	The set of routines – explicit or implicit – that allows for coordination between individuals of organizations without having to define beforehand how to do so (Rallet and Torre, 1999)	Relational dimension that encompasses social and cognitive proximity (Knoben and Oerlemans, 2006) Fosters the ability of collaborating firms to achieve learning and innovation based on a shared understanding and language (Kirat and Lung, 1999; Meister and Werker, 2004)	Organizationally proximate partners are less likely to suffer from opportunism and uncertainty (Cassi and Plunket, 2014)
Technological	The level of overlap of the knowledge bases of two collaborating actors (Lane and Lubatkin, 1998)	May facilitate effective communication, learning processes, and knowledge sharing (Cantner and Meder, 2007; Cassi and Plunket, 2014)	When firms are too technologically proximate learning may be limited, and when firms lack this proximity learning may be limited because partners have difficulty in accessing each other's knowledge (Menzel, 2008; Cecere and Ozman, 2014)

METHODOLOGY

Research Design and Data Collection

A case study approach (Yin, 2009) was employed to explore how geographical, organizational and technological proximity influence small firms' position in five asymmetrically sized alliances in the Norwegian oil and gas industry. Qualitative techniques were selected because the objective of the research was to understand interfirm dynamics and processes, which are facets that are difficult to capture using quantitative techniques (Oinas, 1999). Moreover, the case study approach makes it possible to acquire rich, real-world accounts of these phenomena (Eisenhardt and Graebner, 2007). The studied cases are referred to as strategic alliance A (SAA) through to strategic alliance E (SAE) to preserve anonymity. Data collection included 11 interviews with small firm representatives, all of which followed a semi-structured interview guide. The interviews were complemented by a number of secondary data sources, including websites, press releases and other relevant documentation provided by the interviewees. Due to the small size of the subject firms, interviews were conducted with top and middle managers (e.g., founders, CEOs and project managers).

The small firm in SAA was interviewed twice annually in 2010 and 2011 and once annually in 2012, 2013 and 2014 (for a total of seven interviews), whereas data were collected from the small firms in SAB–SAE in 2013 and 2014. The interviews were conducted at the firms' locations (SAA and SAB) or by telephone (SAC–SAE) and lasted for 45 minutes on average. All interviews were recorded and transcribed verbatim, resulting in 52 pages of transcripts.

Data Analysis

Overall, the analysis followed the three-step framework suggested by Miles and Huberman (1984). First, the contents of the interview transcripts were reduced using NVivo software to code each case into four cross-case categories that could address the research question. The four categories – alliance asymmetries, geographical proximity, organizational proximity and technological proximity – were predetermined and theoretically derived based on the approach of the chapter. The cases were compared to each other to identify similarities and differences between them, as suggested by previous studies (Yin, 1981; Eisenhardt, 1989). As a result of the reduction process and the identification of similarities and differences between the cases, a cross-case analysis of the five cases was then performed according to the four data categories. This analysis represents the final step in the Miles and Huberman framework, namely, the conclusion-drawing and verification process. A holistic view of how the cases developed was obtained by exploring the features of and contrasts between the cases. After the coding process and cross-case analysis were completed, brief discussions were held with the interviewees to ensure that the interpretations and presentation of the empirical data accurately reflected the small firms' experiences.

A different aspect refers to analysing and categorizing the degrees of proximity (see Tables 6.2 and 6.4). Regarding the geographical dimension, I characterize the degree as 'low' or 'high' based on the geographical distance (kilometres) that separates the small firm from its large partner. In this study, the small firms in SAA–SAC are located more than 500 km from their large partner, while in SAD and SAE, the small and large firms are nearly co-located. A more complex task is to categorize the degrees of organizational and technological proximity. A review of the literature shows that no uniform model exists for the empirical measurement of organizational and technological, and other non-spatial proximity dimensions. Consequently, to categorize the degrees of organizational and technological proximity I relied on theoretically driven criteria as identified in the literature. Organizational proximity was labelled low, medium, or high based on the small firms' accounts of coordination and frequency in their communication with the large partner (Rallet and Torre, 1999). Technological proximity was labelled low, medium, or high based on the small firms' degree of independence from the large partner, that is, comparable general knowledge bases but different specialized knowledge bases (Colombo, 2003; Fung, 2003).

Case Presentation

Five cases are investigated in this chapter: SAA to SAE. The large firms are globally integrated service providers, each of which has an annual turnover in excess of one billion euros and several thousand employees. The large firms' core competencies relate primarily to engineering, project management, construction and maintenance and modification in global energy sectors.

The oil and gas industry comprises a number of sub-sectors wherein firms supply different products and services at different stages of the industry's life cycle. In essence, the industry comprises three actors (Cumbers and Martin, 2001): (1) oil companies that engage in oil exploration and production (E&P); (2) integrated service providers that are responsible for the majority of E&P-related services to oil companies;

and (3) a network of suppliers that deliver goods and/or services either directly to oil companies or through alliances with integrated service providers (Hatakenaka et al., 2006). The five small firms in this study are characterized as suppliers, whereas their large partners are characterized as integrated service providers. Table 6.2 presents the similarities and differences across the small firms in this study.

Table 6.2   Small firm characteristics

	SAA[a]	SAB	SAC	SAD[a]	SAE
Firm establishment	1998	1969	1988	1982	1981
Number of employees (2013)	98	17	23	88	69
Turnover (million euros, 2013)	21	7	2.3	27	15.3
Core activities	Fabrication, maintenance and modification	Welding and fabrication	Staff provision and fabrication	Fabrication	Fabrication, maintenance and modification
Alliance experience	Low	Medium/ high	Medium	Low	Low
Industry experience	Low	High	Medium/ high	Medium/ high	Medium
Alliance establishment	2009	1975	2005	2008	2005
Collaboration in the alliance	Maintenance and modification	Welding and fabrication	Staff provision and fabrication	Fabrication	Fabrication
Geographic distance to the large partner	High	High	High	Low	Low

Note: a. The small firms in SAA and SAD represent divisions of larger parent companies.

In Table 6.2, 'alliance experience' refers to the small firms' experiences from previous alliances or other types of interfirm collaboration. 'Alliance establishment' refers to the year when the small firms established an alliance relationship with their large partner. Finally, 'collaboration in the alliance' refers to the particular activities where the small firms collaborate with the partner.

CROSS-CASE ANALYSIS

Size Asymmetry

The empirical findings identified several differences relating to the effects of size asymmetry across the cases (Table 6.3). For example, the small firms in SAA and SAE suffered from the large firms' opportunistic behaviour more than the small firms in SAB–SAD. Regarding SAA, the small firm experienced a depreciation in its initial contract obligations soon after the alliance was established. The interviewee referred to this event as the firm's first experience with 'the cynical side of the industry', and he described himself and his colleagues as having acted naively. With respect to SAE, the small firm has endured short-term assignments that last only for months at a time, which has caused uncertainty about future revenue generation and thus impeded the small firm's ability to develop long-term strategies.

The interviewee at SAE stated that the unpredictable schedule of alliance activities had been ongoing for years and was likely to continue. In contrast, the CEO and other key individuals at the small firm in SAA spent vast resources in 2010 to clarify its role in the alliance. This included several meetings with the large partner and required extensive legal advice. The interviewee stated: 'We really had to speak up for ourselves to get our part of the contract. It's not easy to deal with a major corporation like [them]. There are many people with different ideas about how things should be done'. The actions taken by the small firm in SAA improved the relationship because it enhanced the large firm's understanding and acceptance of the small firm's capabilities.

The small firms in SAB and SAC did not suffer appreciably as a result of size asymmetry. However, the interviewee at each of these small firms acknowledged that they depended upon their contract with the large partner due to the substantial impact of the alliance on revenue generation and capacity utilization. In addition, each interviewee stated that the large partner had determined the contractual terms. Although the duration of the contracts did not present any issues for the small firms in SAB and SAC, the rates and volume requirements were enforced by the large partners. The small firm in SAD reported no apparent signs of smallness liabilities.

Table 6.3   Quotes illustrating asymmetry dynamics

	SAA	SAB	SAC	SAD	SAE
Effects of size asymmetry	'We struggle to get our part of the contractual value. We have literally been run over since day one'	'We simply have to accept that they set the ground rules of the collaboration. They represent a major share of our revenue generation and capacity'	'We are definitely dependent upon their willingness to use our services'	No effects of size asymmetry were observed	'We never have any long-term outlook about our role in the alliance. For example, we don't know if we will have work to do three months from now'
Factors mitigating size asymmetry	'Our company has grown a lot in recent years in terms of internal skills and resources and external network relationships, so our position is improving' 'We are one of very few actors in this part of the country that actually has the capacity to take on such extensive contract obligations'	'We have been around since the 1970s, so our reputation is established in the industry, even internationally' 'Only a few others in all of Europe can do what we are capable of'	'We report to only a few individuals in their organization, so I don't get the feeling of them being "up there" and us being "down here"' 'We definitely gain from our closeness to the offshore supply base'	'We deliver our products to customers all over the world, so we don't depend exclusively on [them]'	'Because we are nearly co-located, we are able to respond quickly if they face urgent circumstances'

Each of the small firms reported factors that mitigated the effects of size asymmetry. The small firms in SAB and SAD each reported that they contributed unique skills and technologies to their alliance, which increased the degree of partner complementarity and interdependence and thereby increased the small firms' role and power in the partnership. In the other cases (SAA, SAC and SAE), locational factors mitigated the effects of size asymmetry. For example, the small firms in SAA and SAC were located close to the offshore installations where they operated with the large partner, which gave these small firms the ability to respond quickly to sudden demands. The small firm in SAB was also located close to the offshore installation but reported no advantage due to this proximity. The small firm in SAE reported that it gained a significant advantage from its co-location with the large partner. Specifically, the interviewee stated that the large partner played a major role in developing the small firm into a supplier to the oil and gas industry because the large firm wanted to have a supplier nearby. The small firm in SAD was also located close to the large partner, but this was considered more of a convenience than a necessity.

The Influence of Proximity

All five cases were characterized by different degrees of geographical proximity between the small and large firms, and the empirical findings revealed several other variations across the cases (Table 6.4). For example, the small firms in SAA, SAB and SAC were located far from their large partners but close to the offshore installations. Interviewees at the small firms in SAB and SAC stated that the lack of geographical proximity presented no barrier to alliance activities, whereas the interviewees at the small firm in SAA found that the lack of proximity was a major hindrance to effective management of the relationship. The small firms in SAD and SAE were located close to their large partners. In SAD, the co-location enabled effective communication but was not necessary for the small firm to fulfil its obligations. The small firm in SAE argued that co-location was the principal reason for the establishment of the alliance.

As stated in the theoretical discussion, organizational proximity incorporates the different characteristics of functional (or dysfunctional) organizational relationships (e.g., social and cognitive proximity) that affect the ability of collaborators to share and complement each other's information, knowledge and resources. At the social level, the small firms in SAB–SAE reported that they had long-term relationships with their large partners, which facilitated effective communication and interaction in these alliances. In particular, the small firms in SAB–SAD endured high degrees of organizational proximity to their partners due to mutual understanding, similar degrees of knowledge about the structure of the industry, and similar degrees of embeddedness in national networks. SAA was characterized by relatively low organizational proximity in several respects. For example, the lack of social relationships complicated the establishment of the alliance function, and the small firm's lack of engineering experience in the oil and gas industry led to misunderstandings about the collaboration.

As was the case with organizational proximity, the small firms in SAB–SAD yield a high technological interrelatedness to their large partner. In contrast, the empirical findings for SAA and SAE clearly illustrated low technological proximity between the partners. An interviewee at the small firm in SAA highlighted this issue by stating that 'our main objective [with the alliance] is to build competence and to learn about this industry. They represent our entry ticket'. In addition, the small firms in SAA and SAE were both subject to audit revisions before the alliances were established, and the audits exposed fundamental shortcomings related to compliance with the strict standards of the oil and gas industry. This issue illustrates how the industry experience and maturity of the small firms in SAA and SAE differed from those of the small firms in SAB–SAD. Also indicative of the low technological proximity between the partners in SAA and SAE was the large firms' frequent monitoring of the small firms' operations. Whereas the small firms in SAB–SAD fulfilled their respective obligations independently of their large partners, the small firms in SAA and SAE depended heavily on direct oversight by and assistance from their large partners.

Several aspects may explain these divergent empirical findings. First, the small firms differed with respect to their levels of experience in the oil and gas industry. Specifically, the small firms in SAB–SAD each had years of industry experience and strong capabilities, skills and resource development, which enhanced their respective abilities to manage large-partner relationships. In contrast, the small firms in SAA and SAE each suffered from a lack of knowledge about key components of the industry. This in turn may have increased the propensities of their large partners to engage in opportunistic behaviour.

A second possible explanation relates to the small firms' respective contributions to the dyads. The small firms in SAB–SAD provided products and services that were of a higher complexity than those of the small firms in SAA and SAE. Furthermore, the products and services of the small firms in SAB–SAD were less available in the market than the more standardized maintenance and modification services provided in SAA and SAE.

Table 6.4   Quotes illustrating the level of proximity

	Geographical Proximity	Organizational Proximity	Technological Proximity
SAA	*Low* 'Unfortunately they have become more of a customer than a partner; thus, the geographical distance doesn't really matter. I don't think we have met with them more frequently than we meet with any other customer'	*Low–medium* 'Since we established the alliance, our main contact [at the large firm] has changed four times. As a result, they don't know the initial intentions or history of the alliance. They simply treat us like any other customer' 'We soon understood that we were way behind in terms of internal routines and formal systems. In order to comply with their demands, we had to establish and comply with extremely detailed HSE&Q [Health, Safety, Environment & Quality] systems. It's really nothing like what we were used to in traditional onshore industries'	*Low* 'Before we entered into the alliance, they conducted major audits during which they assessed all aspects of our organization. Since the alliance was established, their inspectors have made additional follow-up visits' 'When they visit, they monitor everything we do, and a number of tests must be passed. Our employees refer to it as taking an exam' 'It's simple. We depend on their skills and competencies, particularly related to engineering'
SAB	*Low* 'It [distance to partner] really does not matter a whole lot. If we need to meet with them, we always have the airport. Actually, we depend more on local suppliers and the infrastructure that surrounds us'	*High* 'Through the years, we have continually developed our HSE and quality assurance systems. This represents a common language and it improves our relations with them' 'Over the years, we have established strong, trust-based relationships with several key individuals in their organization. This way, we always have someone to discuss things with'	*High* 'Sometimes they take part in, for example, materials testing, but really, the objective of their visits is more to safeguard the overall progress of our work' 'Our technology and skills are matched by maybe two or three competitors throughout Europe'

	Geographical Proximity	Organizational Proximity	Technological Proximity
SAC	*Low* 'I can't say that the distance matters a whole lot. Only a few times have I missed the opportunity to have them visit us to oversee complex procedures. I can imagine, however, that geographic distance could be more of a general problem for those trying to enter the industry'	*Medium–high* 'As a board member in [a national petroleum society], I have established relationships with the key individuals in the industry, including those we collaborate with today. This really was a door opener' 'We have established trust-based relationships with several individuals in their organization. Some of them we have worked with for more than a decade' 'In the 1990s, we were part of an inter-regional alliance that delivered a number of services to [the partner], so we have known them for years'	*Medium–high* 'What we learn from them does not concern technology or how to do our job better. Rather, we learn about the philosophy under which such large corporations operate, and we gain information about the future prospects of the industry' 'A central part of our job is to make sure offshore personnel are up to date in terms of certifications, and standards and regulations. Actually, we frequently hold courses for their [large firm's] workers too'
SAD	*High* 'They are very satisfied with the partnership agreement, particularly because we are more or less co located. It makes it much easier for them to follow up on our commitments' 'It's nice to have the option to simply call and ask if they can pay us a visit. Particularly in projects with short deadlines that depend on quick feedback'	*Medium–high* 'Our sales and project departments consist almost exclusively of engineers with varying degrees of [oil and gas] industry experience. This increases the effectiveness of communication' 'Our partner always has kick-off seminars before projects are initiated. During these seminars, we get to meet with the end customers [oil companies] and discuss potential design modifications' 'For a period, we had follow-up meetings at least once a week' 'Our people often have discussions with their project managers, and together they come up with more practical solutions'	*High* 'Many of our employees have worked here for more than 20 years. You develop a lot of competence when you do similar or related tasks for such a long time' 'When we receive an inquiry [from the partner] we build, ourselves, complete structures based on the specifications of that inquiry' 'We don't necessarily learn new or better ways of designing hydraulic systems. However, in each and every project we learn new things about how the overall process works'

Table 6.4 (continued)

	Geographical Proximity	Organizational Proximity	Technological Proximity
SAE	*High* 'Our facilities are located only 40 km from them, and this eases the logistics' 'If they need something to be done in a hurry, we have a clear advantage compared to our competitors located elsewhere'	*Medium* 'They have really helped us to develop our routines and standards to enable us to take part in the oil and gas industry and to become a local supplier. Our interests were congruent' 'We have known them for years [geographical proximity], so we had no problems getting in touch with them'	*Medium–low* 'One of their inspectors frequently visits us and monitors our operators. In some periods, even twice a week. He speaks with our engineers and managers and tells people to fix things that are not up to the required standards' 'They [large partner] conducted a thorough examination of our firm, and they had a number of inspections ... In order to comply with their demands we had to upgrade most of our assets and infrastructure, and we had to qualify for a number of certifications'

DISCUSSION

Earlier studies have demonstrated that size asymmetries often have the potential to damage interfirm relationships due to opportunistic behaviour by large partners (Holmlund and Kock, 1996; Yang et al., 2014). The empirical evidence in this study indicated that the 'smallness challenge' was present in all five cases, albeit to different degrees. Furthermore, the empirical findings showed that the small firms' proximity to their large partner mitigated issues related to size asymmetry.

Current knowledge about the role of geographical proximity is characterized by contradictory claims. Some have found that geographical proximity has a positive effect on interfirm relationships due to the embeddedness of information and knowledge within geographically defined areas (Asheim and Isaksen, 2002). Conversely, other scholars have found that geographical proximity may hinder entrepreneurship and innovation (Letaifa and Rabeau, 2013). The current study finds evidence to support both sides of this scholarly debate but, more importantly, suggests that for small firms the role played by geographical proximity varies according to their firm characteristics. More specifically, the findings suggest that geographical proximity is not an essential component as long as small firms possess or develop other, non-spatial forms of proximity. This relates to recent studies that propose that proximity dimensions may overlap with and substitute for one another (Mattes, 2012; Hansen, 2015).

An additional finding regarding geographical proximity is that despite the lack of geographical proximity to the large partner, the small firms in SAA and SAC benefited from their closeness to the locations where collaboration activities occurred. Furthermore, empirical data indicated that the large partners perceived the lack of geographical proximity as a means of accessing distant markets. This relates to a recent study that found that due to the variety in firms' motives and objectives, a proximate partner may be preferred in some cases whereas a remote partner might be preferred in other cases (Pérez et al., 2012; Hansen, 2014). This finding also illustrates how otherwise weak firms may represent valuable strategic partners for large firms.

A final observation regarding geographic proximity relates to the notion of temporary geographical proximity. The findings of this study illustrated that, as found in previous studies (Torre and Rallet, 2005), a single personal visit or meeting can be sufficient for effective alliance management. However, the findings also indicated that in cases in which the partners were unfamiliar with each other and/or differed significantly in terms of relevant technological or industrial knowledge, temporary geographical proximity was insufficient for the small firm to benefit from the dyad.

Organizational proximity emerged as a crucial determinant in the establishment and operational phases of the alliances across all five cases, thus supporting previous publications (Letaifa and Rabeau, 2013). First, the empirical findings highlight the differences in how the small firms were able to communicate with their large partners. The partners in SAB–SAE were either co-located, had long-term relationships with each other, or possessed strong extra-regional network positions. These social dimensions facilitated effective communication in dyads SAB–SAE, as illustrated in Table 6.4. A second note on organizational proximity relates to the knowledge bases of the small firms' management teams and other key personnel. The data clearly indicated that the small firms in SAB–SAD were able to generate innovative solutions through joint problem solving, whereas the small firms in SAA and SAE lacked individuals who possessed sufficient knowledge to engage in such creative behaviour. This cognitive dimension thus also favoured the small firms in SAB–SAD. Finally, the findings illustrated the importance of adhering to formal routines and norms, such as health, safety, environmental and quality assurance programmes. Initially, the small firms in SAA and SAE had no such programmes in place; thus, a fundamental component was missing in these cases.

With regard to technological proximity, the data support two major findings. First, the small firms in SAA and SAE depended on frequent visits by their large partners to perform certain contractual obligations. Conversely, the small firms in SAB–SAD stated that visits from the large partner were merely of a follow-up nature. This clearly illustrates the different degrees of technological proximity across the five cases. Second, the findings illustrate that the small firms with a high degree of technological proximity were the least prone to opportunistic behaviour by the large partner. More specifically, the small firms in SAB–SAD possessed technologies and assets that were more complex and valuable than those possessed by the small firms in SAA and SAE, which facilitated mutual interdependence between the alliance partners of SAB–SAD. This finding is in line with several recent publications (Gulati and Sytch, 2007; Bosse and Alvarez, 2010; Villanueva et al., 2012).

A final observation is that the small firms that experienced opportunistic behaviour by their partners (SAA and SAE) were immature in terms of industry experience. Despite this fact, both firms managed to enter into and survive in large-partner alliances for five and nine years, respectively. This suggests that once a small firm has survived the critical early stages of the relationship, it can focus on strengthening its position in the dyad by developing proximity to its partner.

CONCLUSIONS AND IMPLICATIONS

This chapter posed the following research question: How can geographical, organizational and technological proximity influence small firms' relationships with large partners? By focusing on five small firms' geographical, organizational and technological proximity to their large partners, this chapter provides valuable insights in a unique context. Existing knowledge relating to alliances between large firms and small firms has illustrated that size asymmetry can potentially severely undermine the role of the small firm (Holmlund and Kock, 1996; Stuart, 1998; Ahuja et al., 2009; Yang et al., 2014). The findings indicate that the non-spatial dimensions of proximity can mitigate the 'smallness challenge' in large-partner alliances. For example, personal relationships, common industry experience, a shared understanding of technology, and mutual dependence emerged as central components of the small firms that succeeded in their large-partner collaboration. This particular finding suggests that non-spatial proximity may in fact compensate for a lack of geographical proximity in asymmetrical alliances. This provides new insight into the recent debates over the role of geographical proximity in interfirm relationships.

The analysis and discussion identified several variations across the cases. In particular, the small firms in SAA and SAE suffered from liabilities of smallness due to low degrees of proximity in non-spatial dimensions, whereas in SAB–SAD the small firms reported high degrees of proximity in non-spatial dimensions. In the cases of SAA and SAE, the lack of organizational and technological proximity led the alliances in the direction of transaction-based customer–supplier relationships. Furthermore, it could be argued that when small firms possess non-spatial dimensions of proximity, they contribute their entrepreneurial behaviour to the large partners; this type of behaviour is difficult to pursue in large organizations due to their institutionalized and fixed organizational structures. This example illustrates the value that small firms may contribute to large-partner alliances.

The results of this study contribute to recent developments in the proximity literature by providing empirical accounts in the context of asymmetrical alliances. Specifically, the results yield novel insights into the impact of small firms' different motives and objectives on interfirm relationships (Hansen, 2014) and demonstrate that the dimensions of proximity may overlap with and substitute for one another (Mattes, 2012; Hansen, 2015). Furthermore, this study provides insight into the means by which firms can overcome the 'smallness challenge' in large-partner alliances and thereby reduce the risk of alliance failure.

Finally, this chapter has implications for small-firm managers. First, non-spatial proximity is critical for a small firm's ability to overcome opportunistic behaviour by its large partner. For managers, this suggests that a lack of geographical proximity to central markets does not necessarily imply that permanent co-location is the only means to access potential partners. Rather, managers should emphasize the formation of strategic ties to establish social relationships and legitimacy in the industry before entering into alliances. In addition, small-firm managers should position and develop their firms' internal resources and technologies in a manner that promotes partner interdependence.

Limitations and Future Research

This study has several limitations related to its methodological approach. First, the data collection was based on the accounts provided by a single individual at four of the five small firms. However, these individuals were chosen specifically because they possessed comprehensive knowledge about their respective firms' historical and current activities. Furthermore, the data were collected at a single moment in time (except for SAA), and longitudinal processes were thus not thoroughly captured. A different limitation relates to the variety of the selected cases. In retrospect, the case selection might have benefited from the inclusion of small firms who had experienced failure in large-partner alliances. This might have yielded more variety in the findings and thus further strengthened the value of the results.

As the global rate of alliance formation increases, further research should focus on the reasons why some alliances fail. One interesting approach would be to conduct longitudinal designs that explain in more detail how the value of non-spatial proximity evolves over time. A novel approach would be to also include large partners in the data collection process, thereby exposing eventual contradictory perceptions about the partners that compose asymmetrical alliances. Finally, this study provides insights that could benefit from large-scale longitudinal surveys with explorative purposes. A quantitative approach might provide further evidence about how the 'smallness challenge' can be mitigated in asymmetrically sized alliances and perhaps further reduce the conceptual ambiguity of the proximity framework.

NOTE

1. Failure refers to termination or the failure of the alliance to deliver value to the partners (Chao, 2011).

REFERENCES

Ahuja, G., F.J. Polidoro and W. Mitchell (2009), 'Structural homophily or social asymmetry? The formation of alliances by poorly embedded firms', *Strategic Management Journal*, **30** (9), 941–58.

Asheim, B.T. and A. Isaksen (2002), 'Regional innovation systems: the integration of local "sticky" and global "ubiquitous" knowledge', *Journal of Technology Transfer*, **27** (1), 77–86.

Balland, P.-A. (2012), 'Proximity and the evolution of collaboration networks: evidence from research and development projects within the global navigation satellite system (GNSS) industry', *Regional Studies*, **46** (6), 741–56.

Belderbos, R., V. Gilsing and B. Lokshin (2012), 'Persistence of, and interrelation between, horizontal and vertical technology alliances', *Journal of Management*, **38** (6), 1812–34.

Belderbos, R., M. Carree and B. Diederen et al. (2004), 'Heterogeneity in R&D cooperation strategies', *International Journal of Industrial Organization*, **22** (8–9), 1237–64.

Boschma, R.A. (2005), 'Proximity and innovation: a critical assessment', *Regional Studies*, **39** (1), 61–74.

Bosse, D.A. and S.A. Alvarez (2010), 'Bargaining power in alliance governance negotiations: evidence from the biotechnology industry', *Technovation*, **30** (5–6), 367–75.

Broekel, T. and R. Boschma (2012), 'Knowledge networks in the Dutch aviation industry: the proximity paradox', *Journal of Economic Geography*, **12** (2), 409–33.

Cantner, U. and A. Meder (2007), 'Technological proximity and the choice of cooperation partner', *Journal of Economic Interaction and Coordination*, **2** (1), 45–65.

Capello, R. (1999), 'Spatial transfer of knowledge in high technology milieux: learning versus collective learning processes', *Regional Studies*, **33** (4), 353–65.

Cassi, L. and A. Plunket (2014), 'Proximity, network formation and inventive performance: in search of the proximity paradox', *The Annals of Regional Science*, **53** (2), 395–422.

Cecere, G. and M. Ozman (2014), 'Innovation, recombination and technological proximity', *Journal of the Knowledge Economy*, **5** (3), 646–67.

Chao, Y.-C. (2011), 'Decision-making biases in the alliance life cycle', *Management Decision*, **49** (3), 350–64.

Colombo, M.G. (2003), 'Alliance form: a test of the contractual and competence perspectives', *Strategic Management Journal*, **24** (12), 1209–29.

Cumbers, A. and S. Martin (2001), 'Changing relationships between multinational companies and their host regions? A case study of Aberdeen and the international oil industry', *Scottish Geographical Journal*, **117** (1), 31–48.

Das, T.K. and B.-S. Teng (2000), 'A resource-based theory of strategic alliances', *Journal of Management*, **26** (1), 31–61.

D'Este, P., F. Guy and S. Iammarino (2012), 'Shaping the formation of university–industry research collaborations: what type of proximity does really matter?', *Journal of Economic Geography*, **13** (4), 537–58.

Doole, I. and R. Lowe (1997), *International Marketing Strategy: Contemporary Readings*, London: International Thomson Business Press.

Doz, Y.L. and G. Hamel (1998), *Alliance Advantage: The Art of Creating Value through Partnering*, 1st edition, Boston, MA: Harvard Business Press.

Dyer, J.H., H. Singh and P. Kale (2008), 'Splitting the pie: rent distribution in alliances and networks', *Managerial and Decision Economics*, **29** (2–3), 137–48.

Eisenhardt, K.M. (1989), 'Building theories from case study research', *The Academy of Management Review*, **14** (4), 532–50.

Eisenhardt, K.M. and M.E. Graebner (2007), 'Theory building from case studies: opportunities and challenges', *Academy of Management Journal*, **50** (1), 25–32.

Fitjar, R.D. and A. Rodríguez-Pose (2013), 'Firm collaboration and modes of innovation in Norway', *Research Policy*, **42** (1), 128–38.

Fung, M.K. (2003), 'Technological proximity and co-movements of stock returns', *Economic Letters*, **79** (1), 131–6.

Gallaud, D. and A. Torre (2005), 'Geographical proximity and circulation of knowledge through interfirm relationships', *Scienze Regionali*, **2005/2** (2), 21–35.

Gulati, R. and M. Sytch (2007), 'Dependence asymmetry and joint dependence in interorganizational relationships: effects of embeddedness on a manufacturer's performance in procurement relationships', *Administrative Science Quarterly*, **52** (1), 32–69.

Hamel, G. (1991), 'Competition for competence and interpartner learning within international strategic alliances', *Strategic Management Journal*, **12** (S1), 83–103.

Hansen, T. (2014), 'Juggling with proximity and distance: collaborative innovation projects in the Danish cleantech industry', *Economic Geography*, **90** (4), 375–402.

Hansen, T. (2015), 'Substitution or overlap? The relations between geographical and non-spatial proximity dimensions in collaborative innovation projects', *Regional Studies*, **49** (10), 1672–84.

Harrison, J.S., M.A. Hitt, R.E. Hoskisson and R.D. Ireland (2001), 'Resource complementarity in business combinations: extending the logic to organizational alliances', *Journal of Management*, **27** (6), 679–90.

Hatakenaka, S., P. Westnes, M. Gjelsvik and R.K. Lester (2006), 'The regional dynamics of innovation: a comparative case study of oil and gas industry development in Stavanger and Aberdeen', *International Journal of Innovation and Regional Development*, **3** (3–4), 305–23.

Hitt, M.A., M.T. Dacin and E. Levitas et al. (2000), 'Partner selection in emerging and developed market contexts: resource-based and organizational learning perspectives', *The Academy of Management Journal*, **43** (3), 449–67.

Hoang, H. and F.T. Rothmaermel (2005), 'The effect of general and partner-specific alliance experience on joint R&D project performance', *The Academy of Management Journal*, **48** (2), 332–445.

Holmlund, M. and S. Kock (1996), 'Buyer dominated relationships in a supply chain – a case study of four small-sized suppliers', *International Small Business Journal*, **15** (1), 26–40.

Hughes, J. and J. Weiss (2007), 'Simple rules for making alliances work', *Harvard Business Review*, **85** (11), 122–31.

Kale, P. and H. Singh (2009), 'Managing strategic alliances: what do we know now, and where do we go from here?', *Academy of Management Perspectives*, **23** (3), 45–62.

Kirat, T. and Y. Lung (1999), 'Innovation and proximity – territories as a loci of collective learning processes', *European Urban and Regional Studies*, **6** (1), 27–38.

Knoben, J. and L.A.G. Oerlemans (2006), 'Proximity and inter-organizational collaboration: a literature review', *International Journal of Management Reviews*, **8** (2), 71–89.

Kumar, R. and K.O. Nti (1998), 'Differential learning and interaction in alliance dynamics: a process and outcome discrepancy model', *Organization Science*, **9** (3), 356–67.

Lahiri, N. and S. Narayanan (2013), 'Vertical integration, innovation, and alliance portfolio size: implications for firm performance', *Strategic Management Journal*, **34** (9), 1042–64.

Lane, P.J. and M. Lubatkin (1998), 'Relative absorptive capacity and inter-organizational learning', *Strategic Management Journal*, **19** (5), 461–77.

Letaifa, S.B. and Y. Rabeau (2013), 'Too close to collaborate? How geographic proximity could impede entrepreneurship and innovation', *Journal of Business Research*, **66** (10), 2071–8.

Li, D., L. Eden, M.A. Hitt and R.D. Ireland (2008), 'Friends, acquaintances, or strangers? Partner selection in R&D alliances', *Academy of Management Journal*, **51** (2), 315–34.

Mattes, J. (2012), 'Dimensions of proximity and knowledge bases: innovation between spatial and non-spatial factors', *Regional Studies*, **46** (8), 1085–99.

Meister, C. and C. Werker (2004), 'Physical and organizational proximity in territorial innovation systems', *Journal of Economic Geography*, **4** (1), 1–2.

Menzel, M.-P. (2008), 'Dynamic proximities – changing relations by creating and bridging distances', *Papers in Evolutionary Economic Geography*, No. 08.16, 1–26.

Miles, M.B. and A.M. Huberman (1984), 'Drawing valid meaning from qualitative data: toward a shared craft', *Educational Researcher*, **13** (5), 20–30.

Oinas, P. (1999), 'Voices and silences: the problem of access to embeddedness', *Geoforum*, **30** (4), 351–61.

Park, S.H. and M.V. Russo (1996), 'When competition eclipses cooperation: an event history analysis of joint venture failure', *Management Science*, **42** (6), 875–90.

Pérez, L., J. Florin and J. Whitelock (2012), 'Dancing with elephants: the challenges of managing asymmetric technology alliances', *The Journal of High Technology Management Research*, **23** (2), 142–54.

Perry, M.L., S. Sengupta and R. Krapfel (2004), 'Effectiveness of horizontal strategic alliances in technologically uncertain environments: are trust and commitment enough?', *Journal of Business Research*, **57** (9), 951–6.

Prashantham, S. and J. Birkinshaw (2008), 'Dancing with gorillas: how small companies can partner effectively with MNCs', *California Management Review*, **5** (1), 23–41.

Rallet, A. and A. Torre (1999), 'Is geographical proximity necessary in the innovation networks in the era of global economy?', *GeoJournal*, **49** (4), 373–80.

Rindfleisch, A. (2000), 'Organizational trust and interfirm cooperation: an examination of horizontal versus vertical alliances', *Marketing Letters*, **11** (1), 81–95.

Salamonsen, K. and J.T. Henriksen (2015), 'Small businesses need strong mediators: mitigating the disadvantages of peripheral localization through alliance formation', *European Planning Studies*, **23** (3), 529–49.

Silvestre, B.D.S. and P.R.T. Dalcol (2009), 'Geographical proximity and innovation: evidences from the Campos Basin oil and gas industrial agglomeration – Brazil', *Technovation*, **29** (8), 546–61.

Sorenson, O., J.W. Rivkin and L. Fleming (2006), 'Complexity, networks and knowledge flow', *Research Policy*, **35** (7), 994–1017.

Stuart, T.E. (1998), 'Network positions and propensities to collaborate: an investigation of strategic alliance formation in a high-technology industry', *Administrative Science Quarterly*, **43** (3), 668–98.

Torre, A. and J.-P. Gilly (2000), 'On the analytical dimension of proximity dynamics', *Regional Studies*, **34** (2), 169–80.

Torre, A. and A. Rallet (2005), 'Proximity and localization', *Regional Studies*, **39** (1), 47–59.

Vandaie, R. and A. Zaheer (2014), 'Surviving bear hugs: firm capability, large partner alliances, and growth', *Strategic Management Journal*, **35** (4), 566–77.

Van-Gils, A. and P.S. Swart (2009), 'Alliance formation motives in SMEs: an explorative conjoint analysis study', *International Small Business Journal*, **27** (1), 5–37.

Villanueva, J., A.H. Van de Ven and H.J. Sapienza (2012), 'Resource mobilization in entrepreneurial firms', *Journal of Business Venturing*, **27** (1), 19–30.

Yang, H., Y. Zheng and X. Zhao (2014), 'Exploration or exploitation? Small firms' alliance strategies with large firms', *Strategic Management Journal*, **35** (1), 146–57.

Yin, R.K. (1981), 'The case study crisis: some answers', *Administrative Science Quarterly*, **26** (1), 58–65.

Yin, R.K. (2009), *Case Study Research: Design and Methods*, 4th edition, Thousand Oaks, CA: Sage Publication.

7. Evolution of the scientrepreneur? Role identity construction of science-based entrepreneurs in Finland and in Russia

**Päivi Karhunen and Irina Olimpieva*

INTRODUCTION

In the contemporary world scientists are expected to contribute to economic development by commercializing their research findings (Hakala, 2009), and eventually by becoming entrepreneurs in science-based ventures. As the underlying values of academic science and commerce are traditionally considered to conflict (e.g., Jain et al., 2009), it is worth asking whether and how the role identities of a scientist and an entrepreneur can be accommodated in the same person.

Some scholars view a scientist's involvement in commercial activities as a threat to their academic identity (Hakala, 2009; Jain et al., 2009). Others, in contrast, argue that contemporary academic identities should, by definition, accommodate entrepreneurial ideals, as research work is becoming increasingly entrepreneurial in nature (Etzkowitz, 1995), with scientists competing for external funding and being subject to accountability. At the same time, entrepreneurship research has begun to view entrepreneurial knowledge, or expertise (e.g., Sarasvathy, 2008), as an integral part of entrepreneurial behaviour. Similarly to academic research, where scientific discoveries are based on scientists applying their domain-specific expertise, entrepreneurial expertise is a means for discovering and exploiting entrepreneurial opportunities (Shane and Venkataraman, 2000; Politis, 2005). This further supports the argument for narrowing the normative gap between science and entrepreneurship.

Nevertheless, we argue that the normative gap between science and entrepreneurship varies between countries due to institutional differences. In this study we analyse the role identities of science-based entrepreneurs in two very different institutional contexts, Finland and Russia. By science-based entrepreneurs, we refer to individuals who are currently engaged in entrepreneurial activities and have been involved in academic research at some stage of their professional careers. This includes individuals pursuing entrepreneurship and academic duties in parallel, as well as those who have at least temporarily left their academic position for entrepreneurial purposes.

In doing so, we contribute to existing research on science-based entrepreneurship, which has largely taken the context as given (Jain et al., 2009). Furthermore, we extend the scope of prior research, which has been limited to individuals currently holding an academic position (ibid.). Our biographical interview data include 12 Finnish and 11 Russian science-based entrepreneurs representing different career paths and combinations of science and entrepreneurship.

Our results suggest, first, that the increasing entrepreneurial orientation of the academic world has resulted in the emergence of a new identity, that of the 'scientrepreneur'. The strategies employed to manage this new role identity aim to bridge its scientific and entrepreneurial dimensions rather than to reconcile the discrepancies between two separate identities. Second, we propose that the speed and character of this evolution might be influenced by the institutional context. In Russia, the transition from socialism to a market economy and the subsequent institutional crises in Russian science forced scientists to become entrepreneurs, which created a temporary tension between the scientific and entrepreneurial aspects of the hybrid role identity.

THEORETICAL FRAMING

Our theoretical framing is based on the role identity construct, which captures the notion that individuals inhabit roles associated with a set of behavioural expectations held by society, but internalized in different ways by the role occupants (McCall and Simmons, 1978; Jain et al., 2009; Hoang and Gimeno, 2010). Much of the research on role identities pertains to careers and professions. Its focus has varied from the formation of professional role identities (e.g., Ibarra, 1999) to career transitions, including the transition to entrepreneurship (Hoang and Gimeno, 2010). This research argues that the process of founding a start-up enterprise typically requires individuals to transition to the new work role of founder, and the transition may be difficult if the founder role conflicts with the individual's previous professional role (ibid).

In the case of science-based entrepreneurship, making the transition from the role of scientist to that of founder can involve a role conflict, as these two role identities are often viewed as being in opposition to one another (Jain et al., 2009). The traditional understanding of academic identity is associated with concepts such as the search for truth and autonomy, an academic calling and a passion for knowledge (Hakala, 2009). Thus, commercial entrepreneurship, which is primarily motivated by utilitarian principles and profit-seeking, challenges this identity. Jain et al. (2009) indeed found in their empirical study that scientists involved in commercial activity often adopt a hybrid role identity consisting of two separate parts: a focal academic self and a secondary commercial persona. Due to a tension between the demands of these two roles, the scientists under study used various tactics to protect the integrity of their academic identity from commercial influences.

In contrast to the findings by Jain et al. (2009), we argue that academic and entrepreneurial role identities may no longer exist in such sharp contrast. This argument is supported by a number of recent studies on the extent to which academic work is increasingly accommodating entrepreneurial ideals (Behrens and Gray, 2001; Stuart and Ding, 2006; Mendoza, 2007; Libaers and Wang, 2012). At the same time, entrepreneurship research has started to recognize entrepreneurial knowledge, or entrepreneurial expertise (e.g., Sarasvathy, 2008), as an integral part of entrepreneurial behaviour. Similarly to academic research, where scientific discoveries are based on scientists using domain-specific expertise, entrepreneurial expertise is a means for discovering and exploiting entrepreneurial opportunities (Shane and Venkataraman, 2000; Politis, 2005).

Furthermore, as science and academic institutions are increasingly dependent on the resources and expectations of their institutional environment (Hackett, 1990), we agree with the claim by Chreim et al. (2007) that a study of role identities must bridge multiple levels of analysis. This is necessary for understanding how an individual's role identity construction is enabled and constrained by institutional forces, both directly and through organizational arrangements. Providing the 'rules of the game' (North, 1990), formal institutions may directly affect individuals by imposing limitations and/or incentives for individuals to engage in particular behaviour. In our research setup, they can work as factors for migrating between science and entrepreneurship. Additionally, informal institutions may indirectly influence individuals' role identities by providing beliefs, values and preferences, which shape individuals' attitudes and perceptions during the course of their professional socialization. The differences in institutional contexts can be traced through country-specific organizational structures, which serve as the main agents of institutional change (ibid.). Hence, in our study we assess institutional forces by focusing on a particular country's approach to science and the respective organization of the research sector. In sum, our empirical analysis is guided by the question of whether the identities of a scientist and an entrepreneur are compatible in two different institutional environments.

DATA AND RESEARCH METHOD

Our empirical data consist of 23 biographical interviews, 12 of which were conducted in Finland and 11 in the Russian city of Tomsk. The data were collected as part of a four-country research project on high-tech entrepreneurs, defined as founders of enterprises engaged in manufacturing high-tech products. The informants were identified from public sources, including enterprise directories, and company information available on their websites and other electronic sources. In the Russian case, a snowballing method was also used due to the limited availability of public data. For the purposes of this study, we retrieved from the data interviews with entrepreneurs who have been engaged in academic science at some stage of their professional career. This was defined as having a PhD degree and/or being employed as a research scientist.

Thus, the profiles of our informants (see Table 7A.1 in the Appendix to this chapter for more details) are heterogeneous in terms of their combination of academic and entrepreneurial activities, including individuals who have left science to become entrepreneurs and those who have pursued entrepreneurship in parallel to a career in science. Approximately a third of the informants fall into the latter group. In the empirical analysis, we will refer to quotes from the interviewees via the name of the informant, location (FI for Finland and RU for Russia) and year of birth.

A native speaker conducted the interviews in the informants' mother tongue. The average duration of the interviews was two hours. The biographical interview method was used, meaning that the informant selected the course of the interview and the interviewer's role was just to direct the interview to cover certain themes relevant to the study questions. In addition to the basic biographical data, the interviews covered factors related to the informants' identity by discussing the motivation and reasoning for their particular choices in life.

The empirical part of this chapter is based on a two-stage analysis. First, we organized the interview data according to the following predefined categories relevant to role identity construction:

- understanding of one's scientific versus entrepreneurial self;
- contrast versus compatibility between the identities as a scientist and entrepreneur;
- influence of the institutional environment on the two identities.

Examples of the codes that we applied for organizing the data as well as the interview quotes, which the codes were based on, are presented in Table 7A.2 in the Appendix to this chapter.

Second, we constructed profiles of Finland and Russia as contexts for science-based entrepreneurship in order to identify those institutional and organizational features that interact with individual-level determinants in role identity construction.

FINLAND AND RUSSIA AS CONTEXTS FOR SCIENCE-BASED ENTREPRENEURSHIP

We begin our empirical analysis by briefly describing Finland and Russia as institutional contexts for science-based entrepreneurship. Since our point of departure is the identity of the informant as scientist, we consider the following country-specific features as important for our analysis:

- general institutional development of science in recent decades, including the role of fundamental science as the main source for the values and normative system of science;
- the organizational structure of science, including the links between science and industry;
- the role of and attitudes towards science-based entrepreneurship;
- features of R&D funding and institutional support for science-based entrepreneurship.

In Finland, the priorities determining science and university policies have traditionally been derived from the needs of society and the national economy, such as the construction of the welfare state in the 1970s, and technology-based economic development in the 1980s (Kaukonen and Nieminen, 1999). Therefore, it can be argued that Finnish academic science, with universities at its core, has been less of an 'ivory tower' than in countries with a long tradition of fundamental science. Furthermore, the introduction of a national science and technology policy in the 1970s has resulted in university research gradually being integrated with the national innovation system (Lemola, 2002), thus blurring the boundary between academic and applied science.

The research sector in Finland includes universities as the main bases for academic research; the universities collaborate closely with state research institutes and industry laboratories. The close links between industry and academia are also fostered by the dominant public funding mechanisms, which emphasize such cooperation, and by significant R&D investments by the private sector. In addition, academic research funding in Finland is increasingly shifting from budgetary funding to competitive funding.

Nevertheless, science-based entrepreneurship is a relatively recent phenomenon in Finland, where self-employment was not the norm for university graduates until the 1980s (Kaukonen and Nieminen, 1999). It emerged in the 1990s due in part to the economic recession at the start of the decade and consequent high unemployment among highly educated workers and also in part to the information technology boom later in the decade, which provided opportunities for knowledge-based entrepreneurship. Nowadays entrepreneurship is increasingly integrated with university curricula and university students have a positive attitude towards self-employment. As part of the state policy promoting academic entrepreneurship, university-based structures supporting technology transfer and start-ups were first developed in the 1990s (Kaukonen and Nieminen, 1999; Lemola, 2002).

In Russia, science has largely retained the generic features it inherited from the Soviet model of science, most distinctively its structural division into fundamental and applied sectors. With the Soviet model, fundamental research was conducted at the institutes of a prestigious and independent Academy of Science and was viewed more as a basis for ideological competition with capitalist countries (Graham, 1993) than a source of industrial development. Industrial research and development (R&D) was conducted at the research institutes subordinated to industrial ministries, parts of which were hosted by state enterprises, whereas universities mainly focused on educational functions. As a distinctive social and cultural system (Kara-Murza, 2014), Soviet science was never seen as a means for generating ideas to be sold in the market place, but rather as a unique environment for the self-realization of extraordinary personalities. Unlike in Western countries, where science gradually accepted entrepreneurial values under the pressure of economic necessity (e.g., Etzkowitz, 2003), the culture of Soviet science was 'frozen' within the framework of a planned economy and remained almost intact until the beginning of the 1990s.

The Soviet linear innovation model (Meske, 1998) assumed strong organizational links between industry-level institutions and enterprises. However, the centrally planned system did not have efficient mechanisms supporting the inter-industry diffusion of innovations (Radosevic, 2003). The institutional links between science and industry were weak in terms of a low demand for advanced technologies on the part of enterprises (Yegorov, 2009).

Another important feature of the Soviet institutional system of science was the discrepancy between military and civilian research reflected in the so-called technological gap between military hi-tech and civilian low-tech research (Kaukonen, 1994). The continuous technological lag of the Soviet Union along a broad technological frontier, especially since the mid-1970s (Radosevic, 2003), was the main reason that scientists who left for scientific institutes to pursue business opportunities at the beginning of the 1990s could not convert advanced scientific ideas into a commercial product and had to merely fulfil orders for maintaining obsolete equipment and technologies. At the same time, scientists from the advanced academic and military-oriented institutes successfully traded scientific ideas and technologies abroad even during the worst of economic times (Yurevich and Tsapenko, 1996).

The origins of science-based entrepreneurship in Russia lie in the Soviet economic reforms of the late 1980s, which introduced the possibility to establish private cooperatives and delegated more financial autonomy to state enterprises and other institutions. At the same time, the subsequent economic crises forced Soviet scientists to undertake a number of various commercial activities in order to survive after the funding of science institutions collapsed in the early 1990s (Olimpieva, 2005). Such 'necessity entrepreneurship' (Reynolds et al., 2001) was a common phenomenon among academically educated people in Russia in the 1990s. Academic entrepreneurship as it is understood in the West was not promoted until the 2000s, when entrepreneurial ideas started to impact the state's policies regarding science, innovation and higher education.

The institutional path dependency in contemporary Russian science is evident in the preservation of the 'sectoral' structure of science (Dezhina and Kiseleva, 2008), in the persistent 'gap' between military and civil research (Roffey, 2013) and in the low demand for advanced technologies from the civil industries (Dezhina and Ponomarev, 2014). Despite multiple initiatives to strengthen university research, the positive changes witnessed in the university sector have not yet become a stable trend and have a rather contradictory character (Dezhina, 2014). Similarly, the initial state mega-projects aimed at providing institutional support for hi-tech entre-preneurship in Russia, such as the Skolkovo innovation city project, also have an enclave-like character to them (Radosevic and Wage, 2014).

The overall amount of research funding, which was drastically reduced in the late 1980s and early 1990s, is still relatively low by international comparison (National Research University, 2013). Most funding for academic research continues to be state budgetary funding despite attempts to engineer the system in a more competitive direction (Dezhina and Kiseleva, 2008).

In sum, Finland and Russia represent very different contexts for science-based entrepreneurship, as summarized in Table 7.1.

Table 7.1   Finland and Russia as institutional contexts for science-based entrepreneurship

	Finland	Russia
Institutional evolution of science	The development of science is integrated with economic modernization and the building of an innovation economy; the boundary between fundamental and applied science is blurred	Soviet institutional model of science with emphasis on fundamental research and military technologies; institutional crisis in the early 1990s, path dependency of Russian science
Organization of science	Universities are the main sites of academic research; close links to state (applied) research institutes and industry laboratories	'Sectoral' structure of science; low effectiveness of state policy regarding the organizational restructuring of science, low demand from industry
Science-based entrepreneurship	Academic entrepreneurship actively promoted since the 1990s in state policies and university education	Forced entrepreneurship at the beginning of the 90s; low efficiency and enclave-like character of institutional support for scientific entrepreneurship since 2000
Funding of R&D	Public funding increasingly competitive and implied industry–academia cooperation since the 1980s; substantial share of private R&D funding	Overall amount of research funding low by international comparison; R&D financing dominated by the state, insignificant private R&D funding

The table shows that Finland has enjoyed a consistent institutional and organizational evolution of science in correspondence with economic development and industrial demand, where university research is an integral part of the innovation system and the ideas of an entrepreneurial university are widely applied. Russia, in contrast, is burdened by the legacy of Soviet science with its distinct boundaries between fundamental and applied science, an emphasis on military research and poor cooperation between industry and academia. While entrepreneurial ideas have also started to penetrate the Russian university and science sector, they have done so later than in many other countries.

ROLE IDENTITIES OF SCIENCE-BASED ENTREPRENEURS

We begin our analysis of role identities in Finland and in Russia by analysing the values and properties that the respondents associate with the role of a scientist and how they give meaning to this role. Then we continue by assessing their perceptions of the entrepreneurial role identity.

What Does it Mean to be a Scientist in Finland and in Russia?

In this section, we explore the extent to which our informants associated traditional 'ivory tower' scientists with an academic calling and passion for knowledge (Hakala, 2009) or with entrepreneurial scientists (Etzkowitz, 1995) who have integrated commercial values into their academic identity. We argue that our Russian informants are closer to the former category than their Finnish counterparts, who have internalized the values of entrepreneurial science.

Informants in both countries emphasized the practical value of science, which may indeed distinguish them from those scientists who are not engaged in any commercial activities. This emphasis means that research has value only when its results can be applied in practice:

> Although we do fundamental research, I always wonder whether it will be useful for certain applications. Of course, you can do fundamental research on just about anything, and publish in top-tier journals, but then it does not necessarily benefit anyone. (Eetu, 1957, FI)

However, the Finnish and Russian informants differed in their conceptualization of 'practical application'. The Russian informants felt that their results have been applied in practice already when they have been incorporated into a concrete device or technology, irrespective of the market demand for it:

> No, this [device] is not an object for sale. It is rather ... the result of serious scientific and technological work. (Vitaly, 1952, RU)

The Finnish informants, in contrast, view the application in terms of its usage to solve technological problems relevant to the industry or to respond to global societal challenges.

The Finnish informants also emphasized the practical angle of research when discussing their motivations to enter the field of science:

> The [research] project was fun because you did not need to isolate yourself; instead, you saw that there was a real need in the company. It was highly motivational. (Toni, 1967, FI)

In contrast, most Russian informants, especially among the older generation, viewed their career as a scientist as desirable and much anticipated from a professional standpoint after graduation. For them, the career choice was based on a prior, internal motivation rather than on the actual experience of doing research work:

> I always had a strong desire for a real scientific work, something experimental. (Valentina, 1953, RU)

What Does it Mean for a Scientist to be an Entrepreneur?

We continue our analysis by analysing what it means for our informants to be entrepreneurs, including the potential difficulties and role conflict associated with entry into the founder role (Hoang and Gimeno, 2010). We found that the Finnish informants did not view entrepreneurship as something 'alien' for a scientist, but rather as part of a natural continuum for research work. The Russian informants, in contrast, avoided defining themselves as entrepreneurs, whom they perceive as individuals seeking to maximize profits and with other less noble motivations.

All of the Finnish informants claimed that entry into the founder role was relatively easy. Some of the Finnish informants explicitly defined themselves as entrepreneurial individuals, for whom scientific discovery had stimulated their entrepreneurial intentions and endeavours:

> There was no necessity. Instead, the driving force was probably my great interest in entrepreneurship. (Pauli, 1962, FI)

Moreover, the strong practical emphasis of the Finnish informants is evident in the ways in which they perceive their entrepreneurial roles. They view commercializing their research results through a start-up company as a natural part of the research process, and sometimes even one of a scientist's obligations:

> I wanted to start my own business because I had invented many things, and [I wanted to] try to continue inventing. At the research institute, I saw that part of the inventions stay at the institute, while those that are given to large firms are not necessarily adopted in practice. (Eetu, 1957, FI)

Nevertheless, some Finnish informants acknowledged feeling competing pressures from their previous role as scientist and current role as entrepreneur:

> Recently my role has probably been 80 per cent entrepreneur. A few years ago it was 50–50. It is a difficult equation. There are still some things at the university where I should provide advice and assistance, although I am not employed by the university. (Justus, 1983, FI)

Similarly, those informants who were not able to finish their PhD studies due to being absorbed by entrepreneurial activities perceived it as kind of a failure. They, however, pragmatically noted that the firm is now top priority, with their own studies being last in line.

The Russian data reveal considerable generational differences in the process of making the transition from scientist to entrepreneur. For the first generation of scientists-entrepreneurs, those who were motivated by economic necessity, shifting from one role to another was especially traumatic. They stressed the fact that engaging in purely commercial activities in the early 1990s was not a voluntary choice:

> [We had] to feed ourselves somehow. As soon as the possibility emerged to earn money in the scientific-technological field, we immediately quit pure commerce and focused on science-based activities. (Vadim, 1956, RU)

This can be explained by their having been socialized in the normative system of the Soviet academy, where the image of the unworldly 'real scientist' was predominant. The largest discrepancies between their identities as scientist and entrepreneur were typical of informants with a background in academic or military-oriented institutions, a stronghold of the Soviet scientific culture.

At the same time, some of the informants spoke of a major change in their own attitudes towards entrepreneurship:

> During the first years, it was disgusting to do all that [commercial activity] because of a lack of money, the necessity to feed your kids, etc. But then we got interested in it and began to enjoy both the process and the money. (Sergey, 1950, RU)

However, even for the younger Russian generation, transitioning from science to business is not always as natural as for their Finnish counterparts:

> I had my first breakaway when I realized that I would not be able to survive there [in the academic environment]. Although, by that time I had already betrayed my fundamental education once by getting involved in contractual research. (Andrey, 1979, RU)

Furthermore, when speaking of their entrepreneurial identity most Russian informants tried to distance themselves from being perceived as a purely commercial entrepreneur. First, they emphasized either the sophisticated nature of technological products or the high scientific qualifications necessary to produce them:

> [...]if you are a high-tech [entrepreneur] you should possess some fundamental knowledge, have a deep understanding of what you are doing. (Olga, 1980, RU)

The second distinction has to do with financial gain as the driving force for business activity:

> Simple business people only want to earn money, while entrepreneurs in high-tech want to earn money by developing something new. The principle difference is that it is important for them to obtain money for their creativity. (Artem, 1984, RU)

Compatibility Between Identities as Scientist and Entrepreneur

In this section, we present our findings regarding the compatibility between identities as scientist and entrepreneur; whether they are contrasting and separate, as Jain et al. (2009) suggest, or whether they have a similar underlying logic, as suggested by the Sarasvathian approach (2008). We found that they are compatible in the Finnish case, associated with similar characteristics. In the Russian case, however, the identity as scientist clearly predominates and decisively affects an individual's identity as entrepreneur.

As to the direct question of whether or not the informants considered themselves to be scientists or entrepreneurs, nearly all of the Finnish respondents pragmatically elaborated on this question in terms of dividing their working time between different obligations. Most acknowledged that their role as an entrepreneur tends to be predominant:

> Two years ago I would have said that I am 50–50 researcher and entrepreneur, but currently I am 95 per cent entrepreneur and 5 per cent researcher. It is surprising how fast you slip completely out of the research world. (Joni, 1983, FI)

At the same time, the Finnish informants viewed both science and entrepreneurship as a source of new knowledge and a means of satisfying one's curiosity:

> Your appetite for knowledge is [constantly] growing and you aim to feed it with things related to entrepreneurship. (Pekka, 1950, FI)

In contrast, the Russian informants discussed their identity as scientist or entrepreneur mainly through the content of their work. They often referred to creativity, which is at the core of their definition of science, and found it even in their everyday business routines:

> [...] of course, I had to quit with all the formulas and symbols and maths. What I am actually doing here is marketing. However, my fundamental education allows me to find interesting perspectives in these tasks, some creative elements, because I would feel sick to live without it. (Andrey, 1979, RU)

Moreover, the Russian informants talked about their self-identification as a scientist or entrepreneur in terms of professionalism in different fields. From this perspective, none of them directly considered themselves to be an entrepreneur, which by definition is strongly associated with the marketplace and commerce:

> Q: Do you consider yourself professionally to be more of a scientist or an entrepreneur?

> A: No-no-no, entrepreneur to the least extent [possible]. (Vitaly, 1952, RU)

The respondents instead described themselves as being practically oriented researchers or experts, such as a 'developer' of technology or a technological product:

> No, I do not consider myself a professional entrepreneur; I am a professional in the area of developing [technological] devices and technologies. (Mikhail, 1956, RU)

This illustrates again how the informants wanted to distance themselves from 'ordinary' entrepreneurs.

Discussing the Role of Institutional Context in Shaping Role Identities

We conclude our empirical analysis by discussing the potential institutional influences on role identity construction to demonstrate the importance of multiple-level analysis in identity research (Chreim et al., 2007).

The influence of the institutional context shows, first, in the career paths of the informants. In both countries entrepreneurship was not always a planned or even anticipated turn in their professional careers. The difference, however, was that for Finnish informants it was a voluntary choice, that is, they represent opportunity-based entrepreneurs (Reynolds et al., 2001), as the following quote illustrates:

> Entrepreneurship became just timely and I started to become interested in it. (Justus, 1983, FI)

In the Russian case, in contrast, the question was about the necessity of entrepreneurship (ibid.). The decision to engage in entrepreneurship was motivated by economic realities, as there was not enough funding for everyone involved in science at the time. This was particularly evident for the older generation of informants.

Curiously, in both countries, the economic conditions of the early 1990s appeared to be a turning point for some in terms of their professional careers, though in opposite respects. During the deep economic recession in Finland in the early 1990s, work in the academic world provided a safety net since public research funding was not drastically cut:

> It happened that in the faculty there was a large research project, and the professor asked if I would do my Master's thesis on that project. I said that I probably would, as there did not seem to be any opportunities in the industry. That was the beginning, and I realized that doing research is actually fun and interesting. (Saku, 1966, FI)

In Russia, in contrast, the sharp decline in the state financing of science in the late 1980s and the severe economic crises at the beginning of the 1990s forced scientists to resort to entrepreneurship for economic survival. Quite often, establishing a private enterprise during that period served as a survival strategy so that they could continue engaging in 'real' scientific activities:

> After we were told that looking for money was our own business, we made the decision that we should do something to support [our] scientific research ... So, that's how the first firm was established. (Vitaly, 1952, RU)

Another primary difference between the institutional contexts had to do with the normative position of entrepreneurship in the Finnish and Russian academic contexts. This was evident in the ways in which the informants discussed the legitimacy of entrepreneurship in the different academic settings. In Finland, the narratives illustrate how entrepreneurship has become increasingly accepted in recent decades. Those informants who had studied between the 1960s and the early 1980s talked about how initially pioneering entrepreneurial individuals were treated nearly as traitors to science:

> N.N. was a top-level student who submitted a top-level doctoral thesis and then started an enterprise. Everybody was horrified because (a) he was wasting a promising research career and (b) he didn't know anything about entrepreneurship, so he would certainly fail. But he made his business [into] a great success. (Mikko, 1959, FI)

Informants representing the younger generation, in contrast, painted a different picture:

> Already before we established our firm, the research at our department was very commercially oriented ... So the tradition of moving from research to business was already there, and probably this was also a field that attracted commercially oriented people. (Lasse, 1975, FI)

The informants' biographies also illustrate the importance of organizational arrangements that supported the transition to entrepreneurship:

> Our institute was supportive of entrepreneurship, so you could work part-time at the institute and part-time in your company. You could do that for half a year, and then take a leave of absence. In practice, there was a safety net for 1.5 years, meaning that you could have returned to the institute if your business did not take off. (Pertti, 1971, FI)

Furthermore, the Finnish context for entrepreneurial science is reflected in the ways in which the informants treated their scientific work and entrepreneurship as parallel endeavours:

> Our research activity has always been kind of small entrepreneurship. We have worked largely on project funding, which is kind of [like] doing something for yourself. You sell a good project idea to the industry and to Tekes [the national funding agency], and then implement it with a small team. And then you sell the next one. (Saku, 1966, FI)

The legitimization of entrepreneurship in the Russian academic environment seems to lag about one decade behind that of Finland. Normative resistance was particularly strong in the early 1990s when the first private firms were organized at scientific institutes. The older generation of informants provided many examples of how they were censured by their colleagues for their entrepreneurial activities:

> When I was leaving the institute, the head of the laboratory said to me: 'You know, the Academy of Sciences is 250 years old and it would stay for another 250 years and nothing would happen to it. As for your so-called business – today it is here and tomorrow it is not'. (Anton, 1963, RU)

On the other hand, the comments regarding the current situation reflect changes in this respect:

> There are no longer pure scientists sitting inside the 'ivory tower' developing scientific ideas, as in earlier times ... With the 'era of sales', the brains started working in a different way, to create not just something [interesting], but something that you can sell in the market. (Mikhail, 1956, RU)

Interestingly, for Russian informants the formal institutional affiliation does not serve as the primary criterion for their self-identification as a scientist. There seems to be an institutional symbiosis, one where the private enterprise establishes the core and the academic institution the shell for externally funded research activities:

> [The firm] grew out of the [Russian Academy of Sciences, RAS] institute ... The people who still work over there ... come to work for us in collaborative projects. The [RAS] institute in a sense is no longer a driver of scientific progress, but it is a potentially good receiver of grants. We are the real producers of scientific ideas in these collaborative enterprises. (Anton, 1963, RU)

On the other hand, especially for the younger Russian informants, maintaining an affiliation with the university is a formality, one that grants them access to an innovative support infrastructure. In Finland, in contrast, the institutional boundary between the research-based spin-offs and their home institutions is clear. Although some Finnish informants referred to the relationship between their start-up and the university or institute as 'symbiotic', they at the same time stressed that the relations are governed by formal contracts.

CONCLUSION AND IMPLICATIONS

This study focused on the role identity construction of science-based entrepreneurs in two very different institutional contexts, Finland and Russia. We conclude the chapter by discussing the research implications of our study as well as its limitations and making suggestions for future research.

Research Implications

Our analysis of biographical interviews in part supports existing empirical research on the identities of scientists involved in commercial activities (Jain et al., 2009; Libaers and Wang, 2012), but they also highlight the contextual determinants that influence role identity construction.

In spite of differences at the contextual level, at the micro level the data support the notion of a hybrid role identity similar to what was described by Jain et al. (2009). However, there are important differences, which we argue are a result of the marketization of the science sector. Jain et al. (2009) assessed the hybrid role identity by placing the role of scientist at the core. This perspective needs to be modified to accommodate the demands of the entrepreneurial role – or even to be protected from such demands. This reflects our findings from the Russian data. In contrast, with our Finnish data the two identities seem to be mutually supportive rather than conflicting. First, some individuals did not perceive of any such hierarchy between the two identities, even to the extent that they consider themselves to be '100% scientists-entrepreneurs' (Pekka, 1950, FI). In other words, the roles of a scientist and an entrepreneur cannot be separated, as the commercialization of research results through entrepreneurship is viewed as an integral part of one's work as a scientist. Second, the informants repeatedly drew parallels between science and entrepreneurship, highlighting the entrepreneurial nature of scientific work. This points to the Sarasvathian (2008) idea of entrepreneurial expertise as being comparable to scientific expertise.

This leads us to propose that instead of speaking of the identities of scientist and entrepreneur as two contrasting identities, the extent to which entrepreneurial ideals have penetrated the academy is creating a new hybrid identity that we call scientrepreneur. In Finland, its evolution has been 'linear', starting from scientists gradually transforming themselves into entrepreneurial scientists and then scientific entrepreneurs. Such linearity was enabled by simultaneous macro-level developments in the institutional context, including the gradual integration of science and universities into the national innovation system.

In Russia, in contrast, the evolutionary process created an additional identity. Such an identity was characteristic of the early years of systemic transition from central planning to market economy in the early 1990s. This identity refers to forced, or reluctant, entrepreneurs, with a considerable amount of tension between the scientific and entrepreneurial parts of the hybrid role identity. It had the characteristics of an entrepreneurial scientist and necessity-based entrepreneurship typical of the early transition period. We base our argument on the generation gap between those informants whose professional socialization was influenced by the norms and values of the Soviet academy and those who studied and started their professional trajectories in the post-Soviet era.

Moreover, the mutual compatibility of the roles as scientist and entrepreneur is demonstrated by the ways in which our informants reportedly manage their hybrid role identities. In both cases, this is done by ascribing similar attributes to both roles. For the Finnish informants, the notion of practical applicability emerged as the leitmotif during the interviews, referring to scientific research having value only through its practical application to solve the problems of firms or meet societal challenges. The Russian informants in contrast emphasized that intellectual challenges and creativity are the core determinants of both roles. We assume that these differences reflect country-specific features with respect to the values and normative systems of science impacting scientific entrepreneurship.

Finally, the compatibility of the roles as scientist and entrepreneur is demonstrated by the ways in which our informants move between their academic and commercial activities. Our data illustrate that our Finnish informants' scientific and private business activities are governed by formal institutions, which support such movement and yet also help establish clear boundaries between them. In Russia, in contrast, the legacy of the transition period is still visible. In the early 1990s, many scientists managed to survive using informal and semi-formal mechanisms and by blurring the institutional boundaries between their employer organization and their own private activities. Still today, the relationship between scientific organizations and the entrepreneurial activities of scientists is often not transparent, with the former providing the shell and the latter the core for science-based entrepreneurship.

Limitations and Future Research

As with any scientific research project, our study has its limitations that at the same time open up new avenues for research. The first limitation is empirical; it is related to the comparison of two countries that can be considered as two extremes of national innovation ecosystems. Future research could examine the generalizability of our findings by, for example, examining whether the Russian case reflects the situation in other transitional and emerging economies. Similarly, the pattern that we discovered in Finland may be characteristic of Nordic welfare economies and countries with state-led innovation systems, but may not be applicable to such countries as the USA, where the economy and its innovation system are more market driven.

The other limitations of our study are methodological. First, the biographical interview as a research method may lead to retrospective bias when the informants elaborate on past events from their current perspective. Hence, future studies might apply other methods, such as longitudinal case studies with real-time data collection. In addition to interviews, additional studies could apply ethnographic methods, such as participant observation, and conduct an analysis of artefacts, such as firm slogans and mission statements. Finally, the purposive sampling of our study led to a sample where all of the informants were scientists involved in commercial activities. Hence, the starting point was that all informants have at least one shared feature: an interest in commercializing their research. The question as to the degree to which our results reflect the similarities and differences between Finnish and Russian scientific communities as a whole remained beyond the scope of our study. Hence, future research could extend the analysis to include scientists who are not engaged in entrepreneurial activities.

NOTE

* The authors acknowledge financial support from the Academy of Finland (Grants No. 264948 and No. 275592), and from the Rusnano Corporation (Grant No. 89763). The study is also included in the research programme of the Finnish Centre of Excellence in Russian Studies, funded by the Academy of Finland.

REFERENCES

Behrens, T.R. and D.O. Gray (2001), 'Unintended consequences of cooperative research: impact of industry sponsorship on climate for academic freedom and other graduate student outcome', *Research Policy*, **30** (2), 179–99.

Chreim, S., B.E. Williams and C.R. Hinings (2007), 'Interlevel influences on the reconstruction of professional role identity', *Academy of Management Journal*, **50** (6), 1515–39.

Dezhina, I. (2014), 'New science policy measures in Russia: controversial observations', *Russian Analytical Digest, Newsletter*, No. 155, October.

Dezhina, I.G. and V.V. Kiseleva (2008), *Gosudarstvo, nauka i biznes v innovatsionnoy sisteme Rossii* [State, Science and Business in the Innovation System of Russia], Moscow: IEPP.

Dezhina, I. and A. Ponomarev (2014), 'Advanced manufacturing: new emphasis in industrial development', *Foresight-Russia*, **8** (2), 16–29.

Etzkowitz, H. (1995), 'The norms of entrepreneurial science: cognitive effects of new university–industry linkages', *Research Policy*, **27** (8), 823–33.

Etzkowitz, H. (2003), 'Research groups as "quasi-firms": the invention of the entrepreneurial university', *Research Policy*, **32** (1) 109–21.

Graham, L.R. (1993), *Science in Russia and the Soviet Union: A Short History*, Cambridge, UK: Cambridge University Press.

Hackett, E.J. (1990), 'Science as a vocation in the 1990s: the changing organizational culture of academic science', *Journal of Higher Education*, **61** (3), 241–79.

Hakala, J. (2009), 'The future of the academic calling? Junior researchers in the entrepreneurial university', *Higher Education*, **57** (2), 173–90.

Hoang, H. and J. Gimeno (2010), 'Becoming a founder: how founder role identity affects entrepreneurial transitions and persistence in founding', *Journal of Business Venturing*, **25** (1), 41–53.

Ibarra, H. (1999), 'Provisional selves: experimenting with image and identity in professional adaptation', *Administrative Science Quarterly*, **44** (4), 764–91.

Jain, S., G. George and M. Maltarich (2009), 'Academics or entrepreneurs? Investigating role identity modification of university scientists involved in commercialization activity', *Research Policy*, **38** (6), 922–35.

Kara-Murza, S. (2014), 'Sovetskaya nauka kak sistema' [Soviet science as a system], *Digest*, 3 March, accessed 26 June 2014 at http://centero.ru/digest/sovetskaya-nauka-kak-sistema [in Russian].

Kaukonen, E. (1994), 'Science and technology in Russia: collapse or new dynamics?', *Science Studies*, **7** (2), 23–36.

Kaukonen, E. and M. Nieminen (1999), 'Modeling the triple helix from a small country perspective: the case of Finland', *Journal of Technology Transfer*, **24** (2–3), 173–83.

Lemola, T. (2002), 'Convergence of national science and technology policies: the case of Finland', *Research Policy*, **31** (8–9), 1481–90.

Libaers, D. and T. Wang (2012), 'Foreign-born academic scientists: entrepreneurial academics or academic entrepreneurs?', *R&D Management*, **42** (3), 254–72.

McCall, G.J. and J.L. Simmons (1978), *Identities and Interactions*, New York: Free Press.

Mendoza, P. (2007), 'Academic capitalism and doctoral student socialization: a case study', *Journal of Higher Education*, **78** (1), 71–96.

Meske, W. (1998), 'Toward new S&T networks: the transformation of actors and activities', in W. Meske, J. Mosoni-Fried, H. Etzkowitz and G. Nesvetailov (eds), *Transforming Science and Technology Systems: The Endless Transition?*, Amsterdam: IOS Press, pp. 3–26.

National Research University (2013), *Science and Technology Indicators in the Russian Federation: Data Book*, Moscow: National Research University Higher School of Economics (HSE).

North, D. (1990), *Institutions, Institutional Change and Economic Performance*, Cambridge, UK: Cambridge University Press.

Olimpieva, I. (2005), 'Informal character of organizational changes in post-socialist firms', in R. Lang (ed.), *The End of Transformation?* Muenchen/Mering: Rainer Hampp Verlag, pp. 255–67.

Politis, D. (2005), 'The process of entrepreneurial learning: a conceptual framework', *Entrepreneurship Theory & Practice*, **29** (4), 399–424.

Radosevic, S. (2003), 'Patterns of preservation, restructuring and survival: science and technology policy in Russia in the post-Soviet era', *Research Policy*, **32** (6), 1105–24.

Radosevic, S. and I. Wade (2014), 'Modernization through large S&T projects: assessing Russia's drive for innovation-led development via Skolkovo Innovation Centre', *Economics and Business Working Paper No. 131*, November 2014, London: Centre for Comparative Economics UCL School of Slavonic and East European Studies.

Reynolds, P.D., S.M. Camp and W.D. Bygrave et al. (2001), *The Global Entrepreneurship Monitor, 2001 Executive Report*, London and Wellesley, MA: London Business School and Babson College.

Roffey, R. (2013), 'Russian science and technology is still having problems – implications for defense research', *Journal of Slavic Military Studies*, **26** (2), 162–88.

Sarasvathy, S. (2008), *Effectuation: Elements of Entrepreneurial Expertise*, Cheltenham, UK and Northampton, MA, USA: Edward Elgar Publishing.

Shane, S. and S. Venkataraman (2000), 'The promise of entrepreneurship as a field of research', *Academy of Management Review*, **25** (1), 217–26.

Stuart, T.E. and W.W. Ding (2006), 'When do scientists become entrepreneurs? The social structural antecedents of commercial activity in the academic life sciences', *American Journal of Sociology*, **112** (1), 97–144.

Yegorov, I. (2009), 'Post-Soviet science: difficulties in the transformation of the R&D systems in Russia and Ukraine', *Research Policy*, **38** (4), 600–609.

Yurevich, A. and I. Tsapenko (1996), 'Mify o nauke' [Myths about science], *Voprosy Filosofii*, **5**, 37–45.

APPENDIX

Table 7A.1   Profiles of science-based entrepreneurs in Finland and in Tomsk Province, Russia

Name	Year of Birth	Profile as Scientist and Entrepreneur
Harri	1945	Went into industrial science after receiving MSc, where he did his PhD. First owned his own firm, established as a spin-out of his employer's. Now co-owner and board member of two university start-ups
Pekka	1950	Academic career ranging from university scientist to professor; established two spin-offs in parallel to his academic career; now co-owner of and board member in one of them
Eetu	1957	Academic career ranging from research institute scientist to professor; established two spin-offs in parallel to his academic career; now co-owner of and board member in them
Mikko	1959	Went into industrial science after receiving MSc; later the head of a university laboratory. Has established several university research spin-offs; currently an IP manager in the most recent of them
Pauli	1962	Project researcher at the university after receiving MSc; did not finish his PhD studies. Co-founder of university spin-off; currently works full-time as its CEO
Kari	1963	Went into industrial engineering after receiving MSc; then began PhD studies but changed to industrial science. Co-founder of an industrial research spin-off; currently works full-time as its CEO
Saku	1966	Academic career ranging from university researcher to professor; established spin-off in parallel to his academic career, but divested his share. Currently no active entrepreneurial activity
Toni	1967	Master's and PhD theses as part of a university research group; went into industrial science after receiving PhD. Co-founder of a spin-out from the employer's firm; now its chief technology officer
Pertti	1971	Research institute scientist after receiving PhD. Co-founder of a spin-off, now its full-time CEO

Name	Year of Birth	Profile as Scientist and Entrepreneur
Lasse	1975	University researcher after receiving MSc; did not finish PhD studies. Co-founder of a spin-off, now member of its board and employed full-time as financial manager in a large firm
Joni	1983	Institute project researcher after receiving MSc; did not finish PhD studies. Co-founder of a university spin-off, now its full-time CEO
Justus	1983	Project researcher at university after receiving MSc; did not finish PhD studies. Co-founder of a spin-off, now its full-time technology director
Sergey	1950	After receiving MSc, worked in the RAS institute, where he got his PhD; established a firm in 1990 to survive the economic crisis; now a chief designer of the institute and CEO of the firm
Vitaly	1952	Received MSc, PhD and Doctor of Science from the university; in 1994 established a firm to obtain funding for academic activity; now CEO in two firms and university professor
Valentina	1953	After receiving MSc, worked in the university, where she got her PhD and Doctor of Science degrees; co-founder of the two firms where she works now
Mikhail	1956	Doctor of Science, academic career ranging from researcher to the head of a laboratory and university professor; in 1994–95 co-founder of several commercial firms for economic survival; now CEO in four firms in parallel with academic activity
Vadim	1956	PhD from the university, planning to get Doctor of Science degree; in late 1980s worked in scientific cooperative; now works as a senior researcher in the RAS institute and as a deputy director of a firm affiliated with the institute
Anton	1963	After receiving PhD, worked as a researcher at the RAS institute; established first commercial firm in 1989 to survive the economic crisis; now is the co-owner of several innovative companies
Alexey	1970	No place to work after graduation because of economic crisis; serial entrepreneurship in different fields; now works as the CEO of a large technological company

Table 7A.1 (continued)

Name	Year of Birth	Profile as Scientist and Entrepreneur
Andrey	1979	After receiving PhD, left the university because of a lack of professional perspectives; worked as a technical expert and CEO in a large company, then organized an innovative firm at the university (incubator)
Olga	1980	After receiving MSc and PhD from the state university, worked in a technology transfer centre, then established a firm with the university; currently working on Doctor of Science thesis
Vladimir	1981	After receiving PhD, worked in a large company; then started a firm in the university's business incubator. Now combines work at the university with work in his own company
Artem	1984	After receiving MSc, worked in a large techno-company; did not realize his desire to complete a PhD; returned to the university and organized his own firm in the university's business incubator

Table 7A.2   Examples of interview codes

Name	Role of Scientist	Code	Scientist as Entrepreneurs	Code
Harri	A career as industrial scientist [a nine-to-five job] suited me very well because of family reasons	Just a job	The leap from industrial laboratory to entrepreneurship was not that big, as I was already immersed to business as well	Smooth transition
Pekka	As a scientist, my findings can potentially influence the lives of millions of people	Societal challenges	My obligation as scientist is to make sure that our findings are applied and brought into practice	Part of job

Name	Role of Scientist	Code	Scientist as Entrepreneurs	Code
Eetu	Although we do fundamental research, I always wonder whether it will be useful for the certain applications	Practical application	It is interesting to see the business world through one's own enterprise. You can develop and test your own ideas to see if they work in practice	Part of job
Mikko	I went into the industrial research after graduation to gain an industrial perspective into my field of study	Practical application	The foundation of our firm was partly motivated by a very supportive environment for entrepreneurship at the department	Institutional support
Pauli	I worked as project researcher at the university, and pursued some doctoral studies . . . Now it seems that I'll never finish them, but you never know	Just a job	[. . .] the driving force was probably my great interest in entrepreneurship . . . Perhaps it is related to my personality, I have more entrepreneurial spirit than an average scientist	Entrepreneurial spirit
Kari	I went to an industrial R&D lab, because a job there combined my interest in research with a link to business	Practical application	We have a kind of 'save the world' mentality in our business, to solve environmental problems with our technology	Environmental challenges
Saku	[. . .] doing research is fun and interesting . . . there is always something new	Interest in science	Our research activity has always been kind of small entrepreneurship	Parallels
Toni	The [research] project was fun because you did not need to isolate yourself; instead, you saw that there was a real need in the company	Practical application	I approached to my work in the industrial R&D group as entrepreneurship, it was very independent	Entrepreneurial spirit

Table 7A.2 continued

Name	Role of Scientist	Code	Scientist as Entrepreneurs	Code
Pertti	Earlier I saw myself as an inventor, but after establishing the firm I had to leave the inventing to others	Pragmatism	I was interested in entrepreneurship, and our research institute started at that time to support the establishment of spin-offs	Motivation, institutional support
Lasse	I had been working in the research group for half a year, when I realized that this area is a huge commercial opportunity	Practical application	I have always been a relatively commercially oriented person, so it was very easy for me to take the role of the commercial primus motor	Entrepreneurial spirit
Joni	[. . .] currently I am 95% entrepreneur and 5% researcher. It is surprising how fast you slip completely out of the research world	Just a job	We come from atmospheric science, so we understand a lot of climate change. We want to bring these values to the business	Global challenges
Justus	I gradually drifted to science, starting from a summer job at the faculty	Unplanned career	Entrepreneurship became just timely and I started to become interested in it	Opportunity
Sergey	We were ready to work in the laboratory without limitations and without salaries. It was professional interest	Motivation, interest in science	During the first years it was disgusting to do all that [commercial activity] because of a lack of money, the necessity to feed your kids etc.	'Forced' entrepreneur

Name	Role of Scientist	Code	Scientist as Entrepreneurs	Code
Vitaly	My education was motivated by the interest in science and especially in some basic studies. I always admired scientific research and daring engineering solutions	Motivation, interest in science	After we were told that looking for money was our own business, we made a decision that we should do something to support scientific research	'Forced' entrepreneur
Valentina	It was first of all interesting to work in science	Motivation, interest in science	We are not just business people . . . we have not left the [academic] environment at all, we keep teaching, and doing science as well	Distancing from 'pure' entrepreneurs
Mikhail	There are no longer pure scientists, sitting inside the 'ivory tower' developing scientific ideas	Applied vs academic science	I do not consider myself as a professional entrepreneur, I am a professional in the field of developing [technological] devices and technologies	Content of work
Vadim	Our main customer is the Ministry of Defence	R&D funding	As soon as the market for science and technology in Russia developed, we immediately quit 'pure' commerce and focused on science-based activities	'Forced' entrepreneurs

Table 7A.2 continued

Name	Role of Scientist	Code	Scientist as Entrepreneurs	Code
Anton	[The firm] is the real scientific institute. We are real producers of scientific ideas in collaborative enterprises with RAS institutes	Informal institutional ties	When I was leaving the institute the head of the laboratory said to me: 'You know, the Academy of Sciences is 250 years old and it would stay for another 250 years . . . As for your so-called business – today it is here and tomorrow it is not'.	Rigid transition
Alexey	I was doing 'pure' science only when I was working on my thesis, where I managed to make a tiny-small contribution	Applied vs academic science	We ceased to be in demand by the economy even before we graduated from the institute	'Forced' entrepreneurs
Andrey	The resources that I use for my project [the firm] are not easy to get … So, although I did not initially belong to the university, it is better for me now to get an affiliation	Informal ties with the university	What I am actually doing here is marketing. However, my fundamental education allows me to find interesting perspectives in these tasks, some creative elements, because I would feel sick to live without it	Creativity
Olga	I am very interested in many scientific problems and questions but at the same time, I am already more in entrepreneurship	Practical application	If you are a high-tech [entrepreneur] you should possess some fundamental knowledge, have a deep understanding of what you are doing	Distancing from 'pure' entrepreneurs

Name	Role of Scientist	Code	Scientist as Entrepreneurs	Code
Vladimir	I have always worked 'in tandem' with the university. In fact, I have never left the university	Informal ties with the university	I opened my first own firm, a computer game saloon, at the age of 17	Entrepreneurial spirit
Artem	The most valuable quality is not the acquired academic knowledge, but the ability to think outside the box	Role of creativity	Simple business people only want to earn money, while entrepreneurs in high-tech want to earn money by developing something new	Distancing from 'pure' entrepreneurs

8. The intention–behaviour link of higher education graduates

Elina Varamäki, Sanna Joensuu-Salo and Anmari Viljamaa*

INTRODUCTION

Previous research on entrepreneurial intentions has focused on testing entrepreneurial intention and personal-level variables (see Liñán and Fayolle, 2015). The tendency has been to go beyond the original theory of planned behaviour model (Ajzen, 1991) and provide new insights into the mental processes leading to the formation of entrepreneurial intentions. It has been also suggested that new scales be proposed for entrepreneurial intention models (Fayolle and Liñán, 2013). There is still a research gap in longitudinal settings (e.g., Matlay and Carey, 2007; Fayolle and Liñán, 2013). Also the link between intentions and actual start-up remains relatively unexplored (Sequeira et al., 2007; Carsrud and Brännback, 2011).

In this study entrepreneurial intentions refer to the commitment to start a new business (Krueger and Carsrud, 1993) by a graduate, either directly after graduation or later. Some studies suggest that higher education reduces the likelihood of entrepreneurship (Kangasharju and Pekkala, 2002; Henley, 2005; Pihkala, 2008; Nabi et al., 2010; Joensuu et al., 2013) while others suggest the opposite (Blanchflower and Meyer, 1994; Ertuna and Gurel, 2011; Lanero et al., 2011; Zhang et al., 2014). Reasonable arguments exist in favour of both views. On one hand, participating in higher education gives a person a resource advantage that may enable a successful career in entrepreneurship; on the other hand, with a higher education diploma a person is a more desirable employee and may well find salaried employment a more attractive alternative than entrepreneurship. Also, it is a fact that most higher education programmes do not aim to promote entrepreneurial behaviour in the first place (e.g., Aronsson, 2004).

Fayolle and Liñán (2013) reviewed recent literature on entrepreneurial intentions and classified 220 papers published in 2006–12 into five categories. The first category consists of studies on core model, methodological and theoretical issues. The second and largest category includes studies on the influence of personal-level variables on entrepreneurial intentions. Impact of gender has received a lot of attention, as has the impact of role models. The third group consists of papers on entrepreneurship education and intentions, with a main focus on impacts of entrepreneurship education on entrepreneurial intentions on various levels, ranging from comprehensive to higher education. The fourth group includes papers focusing on context and institutions; the papers relate formation of entrepreneurial intentions to specific environments, for example, national cultures. The fifth group consists of papers focusing on the entrepreneurial process and intention–behaviour link. This group remains the smallest as longitudinal analyses are inherently challenging; it is in this group that new studies are most needed (Sequeira et al., 2007; Carsrud and Brännback, 2011; Fayolle and Liñán, 2013), and to which this chapter aims to contribute.

Liñán and Fayolle (2015) have continued with the systematization and categorization of studies on entrepreneurial intentions. In addition to previous categories, they identified in entrepreneurial intention studies new research areas related to sustainable entrepreneurship and social entrepreneurship.

The chapter examines the realization of students' entrepreneurial intentions in entrepreneurial behaviour after graduation. We apply Ajzen's (1991) theory of planned behaviour (TPB) to entrepreneurial intentions of higher education students and test their relevance as antecedents of actual behaviours after graduation. The students' intentions and their antecedents have been measured during their studies and then a follow-up study has been conducted a few years after graduation. Hence, this study offers a longitudinal follow-up for entrepreneurial intention–behaviour link of higher education students. The focus is on the formation of behaviour rather than intentions. The specific objectives are: (1) to analyse the link between entrepreneurial intentions, their antecedents and entrepreneurial behaviour (i.e., start-up behaviour) after graduation and (2) to analyse the role of gender and entrepreneurial role models in entrepreneurial behaviour.

LITERATURE REVIEW AND DEVELOPMENT OF HYPOTHESES

Entrepreneurial Intentions

In studying intentions we adopt an existing intention model, namely Ajzen's (1991) TPB, which has become the dominating model in empirical literature on entrepreneurial intentions (Schlaegel and Koenig, 2014). The TPB suggests that intention is the immediate antecedent of behaviour and, thus, the stronger the intention to engage in a specific behaviour, the more likely its actual performance should be (Ajzen, 1991). However, it has been shown that mere goal intention accounts for no more than 28 per cent of variance in goal-directed behaviour (Sheeran, 2002), and psychological mechanisms (commitment, implementation intention) have a major role in the process (Adam and Fayolle, 2015). The core of the TPB is the idea that intentions have three conceptually independent determinants, namely attitude towards the behaviour, subjective norm and perceived behavioural control (Ajzen, 1991):

- *Attitude towards the behaviour* refers to the degree to which a person has a favourable or unfavourable evaluation or appraisal of the behaviour in question. The more positive an individual's perception regarding the outcome of starting a business is (see, e.g., Shapero and Sokol, 1982; Autio et al., 1997; Krueger et al., 2000; Segal et al., 2005; Van Gelderen and Jansen, 2006; Pruett et al., 2009) the more favourable their attitude towards that behaviour and, consequently, the stronger the individual's intention to go ahead and start a business.
- *Subjective norm* refers to the perceived social pressure to perform or not to perform a behaviour, that is, starting a business. Subjective norm is based on beliefs concerning whether important referent individuals or groups approve or disapprove of an individual establishing a business, and to what extent this approval or disapproval matters to the individual (Ajzen, 1991, p. 195). Generally speaking, the more the opinion of a particular referent group or individual matters to the individual, and the more encouraging of enterprising activity the individual believes them to be, the stronger the individual's intention to start a business. Cialdini and Trost (1998) suggested that social norms have the greatest impact when conditions are uncertain. Pruett et al. (2009) operationalized social

norms as family experience and support in addition to knowledge of others who had started businesses.

- *Perceived behavioural control* (PBC) refers to the perceived ease or difficulty of performing the behaviour. It is based on beliefs regarding the presence or absence of requisite resources and opportunities for performing a given behaviour (see Bandura et al., 1980; Swan et al., 2007). In general, the greater this perceived behavioural control, the stronger the individual's intention to start up in business. According to Ajzen (1991) this is most compatible with Bandura et al.'s (1980) concept of perceived self-efficacy. In entrepreneurial intention literature, perceived behavioural control and entrepreneurial self-efficacy have been used almost interchangeably (Schlaegel and Koenig, 2014).

According to Ajzen and Fishbein (2004), the three theoretical antecedents should be sufficient to predict intentions, but only one or two may be necessary in any given application. In other words, the theory of planned behaviour posits that the relative importance of the three factors can vary from one context to another. In most of the studies the best predictor of intentions has been perceived behavioural control (Shapero and Sokol, 1982; Boyd and Vozikis, 1994; Krueger et al., 2000; Autio et al., 2001; Melin, 2001; Kristiansen and Indarti, 2004; Liñán, 2004; Henley, 2005; Segal et al., 2005; Urban, 2006; Sequeira et al., 2007; Wilson et al., 2007; Prodan and Drnovsek, 2010; Chen and He, 2011; Drost and McGuire, 2011; Finisterra do Paco et al., 2011; Lee et al., 2011; Pihie and Bagheri, 2011). The second most common predictor has been attitudes (Zampetakis et al., 2009; Moi et al., 2011) followed by subjective norm (Aizzat et al., 2009; Pihie et al., 2009; Engle et al., 2010; Siu and Lo, 2013). Kautonen et al. (2013) found that attitude, subjective norm and perceived behavioural control jointly explain 59 per cent of the variation in intention. In a recent meta-analysis, perceived behavioural control had a significantly larger effect than either attitude or subjective norm (Schlaegel and Koenig, 2014).

The Intention–Behaviour Relationship

TPB suggests that intention is the immediate antecedent of behaviour (Ajzen, 1991), and even a 0.9–0.96 intention–behaviour correlation has been reported (Ajzen et al., 2009). However, antecedents of intentions can also have a direct effect on actual behaviours. Ingram et al. (2000) found that perceived behavioural control has a direct effect on start-up behaviours (see also Jung et al., 2001; Sequeira et al., 2007; Townsend et al., 2010). Kautonen et al. (2013) also found that perceived behavioural control contributes to the prediction of behaviour over and above its mediated influence via intention. In fact, Ajzen (1991) suggests PBC has a double role in the TPB: to the extent that perceived behavioural control is realistic, that is, the person's perceptions are accurate, and that perceived behavioural control also predicts the actual behaviour instead of full mediation via intentions. In Ajzen's model, PBC may have a direct effect on behaviour, but attitudes and subjective norms affect behaviour via intention. Kolvereid and Isaksen (2006) did not, however, find a correlation between perceived behavioural control and start-up.

Kautonen et al. (2015) also argue that the intention to start a business is not necessarily the starting point of the entrepreneurial process. Thus, an explicitly stated intention is not required as an antecedent of behaviour in all cases. Furthermore, as the antecedents of intentions are in themselves conceptually independent of intentions, there is no reason to assume that the antecedents cease to exist for individuals who have proceeded beyond intentions to actual behaviours.

Based on previous research, we suggest following hypotheses:

H1: Entrepreneurial intention measured during studies has a direct and positive link on entrepreneurial behaviour after graduation.

H2: Perceived behavioural control measured during studies has a direct and positive effect on entrepreneurial behaviour after graduation.

H3: Attitudes towards entrepreneurship and subjective norm have no direct effect on behaviour.

The Role of Gender and Entrepreneurial Role Models in Entrepreneurial Intentions

In previous entrepreneurial intention studies, gender has received the greatest attention followed by role models (Fayolle and Liñán, 2013). Both existing enterprise statistics and research on intentions (e.g., Crant, 1996; Wilson et al., 2004; Wang and Wong, 2004; Shay and Terjesen, 2005; Sequeira et al., 2007; Liñán and Chen, 2009; cf. Pruett et al., 2009; Yordanova and Tarrazon, 2010; Lee et al., 2011; Zhang et al., 2014) have shown that women have less desire to start new businesses than men. A recent European Commission (2012) study on alumni of entrepreneurship programmes found that female alumni score lower on entrepreneurial self-efficacy than their male counterparts, but higher than the control group (cf. Wilson et al., 2007; Kickul et al., 2008). In Zhao et al.'s (2005) study, gender was not related to entrepreneurial self-efficacy but was directly related to entrepreneurial intentions. In their study women also had lower entrepreneurial intentions than men. Yordanova and Tarrazon (2010) found that gender effect on entrepreneurial intentions is fully mediated by perceived behavioural control and partially mediated by perceived subjective norms and attitudes. Finally, Joensuu et al. (2013) demonstrated in a longitudinal study of higher education students that not only do women have lower intentions to begin with but also that their intentions decrease more during their studies. Hence, gender is included in our theoretical model as a factor influencing entrepreneurial intentions and actual start-up behaviours.

Role models have been found to be a significant factor in entrepreneurial intentions (Kolvereid, 1996; Van Auken et al., 2006; Bosma et al., 2012). In Uygun and Kasimoglu's (2013) study, entrepreneurs who started their enterprises in sectors where their role models were already active, role models first affected self-efficacy, and then self-efficacy caused a positive effect on perceived feasibility. In cases where entrepreneurs chose different sectors from their role models, Uygun and Kasimoglu argued that role model had a direct influence on perceived desirability and self-efficacy. Engle et al. (2011) examined the relative social influence of family, friends and role models on entrepreneurial intent in 14 countries. They found that each of the individual social groups is a significant predictor of entrepreneurial intent.

Despite the fact that gender and entrepreneurial role models have been extensively studied in previous research, we wanted to test their effect in a longitudinal setting and suggest the following hypotheses:

H4: Gender (male) has a positive effect on entrepreneurial behaviour after graduation.

H5: Entrepreneurial role models have a positive effect on entrepreneurial behaviour after graduation.

RESEARCH METHODOLOGY

Data Collection Process

The instrument used in the study has been developed and piloted in Finland (see Joensuu et al., 2014). The scales are largely based on Kolvereid (1996). However, in some parts of the instrument (e.g., attitudes), new scales were proposed and the validity tested using national data during 2008–09.

The data was collected in two waves: the first wave during studies and the second wave after graduation. Longitudinal data gathering is demanding and much data is lost in the process. During their studies the students answered the questionnaire each year from the first until the fourth study year. However, we could not find a measurement from all years for the same individuals who answered the questionnaire after graduation. Therefore, the latest available intention measurement for each student from study time was accepted in the analysis. Data in the first wave was gathered during the years 2008–12. The average age of the respondents varied from 21 to 23. The percentage of female students varied from 56 per cent to 60 per cent. The number of respondents varied from 616 respondents (year 2008) to 5036 (year 2011) respondents.

The second wave for this study was collected by sending a self-administered questionnaire in autumn 2013 for the alumni of Seinäjoki University of Applied Sciences who had graduated 1.5–3.5 years ago at Bachelor level. Altogether, 1045 responses were received (response rate 46 per cent). For these respondents, a measurement result for entrepreneurial intentions during studies could be identified for 282 students: 100 students had a measurement from the fourth year, 106 students from the third year, nine students from the second year and 67 students from the first year.

Ten of the students were already starting a business during their studies (five men and five women). Three of them were still entrepreneurs after graduation, and two were part-time entrepreneurs. All students who were starting their own business during their studies were left out of the analysis, leaving a sample of 272 graduated students in the final analysis.

There were considerably more women (201) than men (71) in the data. Eighteen per cent had a mother with a professional background as an entrepreneur and 36 per cent had a father with a professional background as an entrepreneur. The majority of respondents were working as an employee in some organization (79.8 per cent); 2.2 per cent were working as an entrepreneur or freelancer; 7.4 per cent were unemployed; 5.5 per cent were studying full-time; and 4.4 per cent were on their maternity or parental leave.

Most of the responses were from students who had graduated from Social Services, Health and Sports (40 per cent) and Social Sciences, Business and Administration (17 per cent). Other study fields were Technology, Communications and Transport (13 per cent), Culture (13 per cent), Natural Sciences (4 per cent), Natural Sources and the Environment (6 per cent) and Tourism, Catering and Domestic Services (6 per cent).

Altogether six respondents had become entrepreneurs after graduation. In addition, 11 respondents were part-time entrepreneurs, that is, had a business in addition to their main occupation.

Variables

The dependent variable is actual start-up behaviour after graduation. Because of the small number of entrepreneurs, two groups were combined: in the analysis there were altogether 17 graduates who were either full-time or part-time entrepreneurs (12 men and five females). Behaviour was a dichotomous variable, no coded as 0 and yes coded as 1.

Independent variables are entrepreneurial intention, subjective norm, perceived behavioural control, attitudes, gender and entrepreneurial role models. An index of entrepreneurial intention was created by averaging six items. The variable demonstrates good reliability (Cronbach's alpha = 0.85, min 1.0, max 6.7, mean 3.4, s.d. 1.1).

Subjective norm was measured with a procedure suggested by Ajzen (1991). Originally the support from people close to the individual (belief items) was measured with three items (seven-point scale from 1 to 7) and importance of support was measured by three items (seven-point scale from 1 to 7) referring to each of the aforementioned belief questions (three items). For statistical analysis the motivation to comply items were transformed to a -3 to $+3$ scale. The belief-based items (coded as ranging from 1 to 7) and the corresponding motivation to comply items (coded as ranging from -3 to $+3$) were multiplied, and then added to create an index of subjective norm (ranging from -63 to $+63$). The variable demonstrates acceptable reliability (Cronbach's alpha = 0.71, min -45.0, max 51.0, mean -1.5, s.d. 16.0).

An index of perceived behavioural control was created by averaging five item scores. The variable demonstrates acceptable reliability (Cronbach's alpha = 0.74, min 1.0, max 6.4, mean 4.0, s.d. 1.0).

An index of entrepreneurial attitude was created by averaging nine item scores. The variable demonstrates acceptable reliability (Cronbach's alpha = 0.76, min 2.4, max 7.0, mean 4.9, s.d. 0.8).

Gender was coded 0 for female students and 1 for male students. Entrepreneurial role models were measured with the entrepreneurship of mother or father of the respondent. Mother's and father's professional background is coded 0 for 'not an entrepreneur' and 1 for 'entrepreneur'.

All the variables and their items (Table 8A.1) and correlations among studied variables (Table 8A.2) are presented in the Appendix at the end of the chapter.

Testing Procedures

As a first step, we compared respondents with high and low intentions scores. We classified an individual as having a high level of intention when he or she scored over 4 and a low level of intention when the score was 4 or below (scale 1–7).

In the second step the data were analysed using logistic regression analysis with SPSS 21. Logistic regression analysis was used to test a model in which intentions measured during studies explain actual start-up behaviour after graduation. Logistic regression is suited for situations where the dependent variable is dichotomous. In logistic regression, regression coefficients can be used to estimate odds ratios for each of the independent variables in the model. In our model, independent variables were entrepreneurial intentions, attitudes, subjective norm, perceived behavioural control, gender and entrepreneurial role models. Gender, father's professional background as an entrepreneur and mother's professional background as an entrepreneur were used as categorical variables. Categorical variables were used as indicators: contrasts indicate the presence or absence of category membership. The reference category was represented in the contrast matrix as a row of zeros.

RESULTS

There were 200 students with a low intention score (score 4 or below) and 72 with a high intention score (score over 4). Of the graduates who had a high intention score during studies, 13 per cent had become entrepreneurs after graduation. Only 4 per cent of the graduates with a low intention score during studies had become entrepreneurs. The difference between groups is statistically significant (chi^2 6.528, ** $p <$ 0.01). Table 8.1 presents the cross-tabulation of these groups.

In the first regression model we included only intentions measured during studies. Intentions explain start-up behaviour statistically significantly (Exp (B) 2.261, *** $p < 0.001$). H1 is thus supported. The model fits the data well (Hosmer-Lemeshow non-significant chi^2 (10.708), omnibus test chi^2 13.429, *** $p < 0.001$, Nagelkerke R^2 0.13). However, the model is not able to classify the students who became entrepreneurs correctly. This problem is common in situations where the outcome event is rare, as in this case. The model classifies the respondents who did not become entrepreneurs 100 per cent correctly.

In a second model (Table 8.2) we included intentions and also subjective norm, attitudes, perceived behavioural control measured during studies and gender and entrepreneurial role models as independent

Table 8.1   Level of intention during studies and entrepreneurial behaviour after graduation

Level of Intention During Studies	Not an Entrepreneur after Graduation	Entrepreneur after Graduation	Together
Low	192 (96.0%)	8 (4.0%)	200 (100%)
High	63 (87.5%)	9 (12.5%)	72 (100%)
Together	255 (93.8%)	17 (6.3%)	272 (100%)

Note: Chi^2 6.528, $p = 0.01$**.

variables. In this model only perceived behavioural control and gender had statistical value in predicting the start-up behaviour. Perceived behavioural control significantly explains the start-up behaviour (Exp (B) 2.405, $*$ $p <$ 0.05), and so does gender (Exp (B) 6.605, $**$ $p < 0.01$). H2 is supported. Also H4 is supported: gender (male) has a positive effect on entrepreneurial behaviour. On the other hand, H5 is rejected, that is, effect of role models is non-existent. It is interesting that the role of intentions in explaining the behaviour decreases when PBC is included in the model. This suggests that the belief in one's own capabilities as an entrepreneur is far more important than the mere intention to become an entrepreneur. Attitude toward entrepreneurship is not significant in explaining the entrepreneurial behaviour, nor is subjective norm. Thus, H3 is supported. The fit measures of the model are good (omnibus test chi^2 30.708, $***$ $p <$ 0.001, Nagelkerke R^2 0.29, Hosmer-Lemeshow test chi^2 2.893, sig. 0.941). The model classifies 94.3 per cent of cases correctly.

Table 8.2   Logistic regression, variables in equation

	B	S.E.	Wald	df	Sig.	Exp(B)
Entrepreneurial intentions	0.345	0.348	0.984	1	0.321	1.412
Perceived behavioural control	0.877	0.409	4.594	1	0.032*	2.405
Attitudes	–0.272	0.516	0.277	1	0.598	0.762
Subjective norm	–0.019	0.016	1.402	1	0.236	0.981
Gender	1.888	0.615	9.416	1	0.002**	6.605
Mother as an entrepreneur	–1.167	0.891	1.715	1	0.190	0.311
Father as an entrepreneur	0.492	0.615	0.642	1	0.423	1.636
Constant	–7.379	2.155	11.724	1	0.001	0.001

Note: $* p < 0.05, ** p < 0.01, *** p < 0.001.$

DISCUSSION

Implications

Our results show that entrepreneurial intentions measured during studies do explain higher education students' entrepreneurial behaviour after graduation, and thus support the existence of entrepreneurial intention–behaviour linkage. The result also suggests that measuring change in entrepreneurial intentions does have value in gauging the effectiveness of, for example, entrepreneurship education or other pro-entrepreneurship interventions. However, in line with previous research findings (Ingram et al., 2000; Kautonen et al., 2013), we found no direct effect on behaviour from attitudes and subjective norm. This argues that while promoting positive attitudes towards entrepreneurship in both students and the general population may have other positive effects, it can do little to increase graduate start-up behaviour.

In our results the role of perceived behavioural control in actual entrepreneurial behaviour is, however, more important than that of actual intentions. This suggests that even the students who, during studies, have no intention to start a business, may do so if they feel confident of their abilities and a suitable opportunity occurs. All in all the significance of PBC for behaviour highlights the importance of students' perceptions of their own capabilities. Entrepreneurship educators should, in designing their curricula and methods, consider whether they are offering their students sufficient opportunities to gain confidence in their own abilities. Possibly the objective can be served by pedagogies emphasizing experimentation and experiential learning (i.e., active and real-world pedagogies, e.g., Fayolle, 2013).

It is interesting that few students with a high intention level during studies had become entrepreneurs after graduation. It may be that young people have rosy ideas about entrepreneurship when they enter higher education institutions but after graduation, they learn more what successful creation of new businesses actually requires. Once the graduates have more concrete ideas about the requirements related to an entrepreneurial career, their perceptions about their own abilities to succeed in entrepreneurial endeavour (i.e., entrepreneurial self-esteem) might become more realistic. Another possible explanation could be the economic situation in Finland, which has been developing negatively during the last years. It might be that the overall climate for starting up a new business is pessimistic.

Adam and Fayolle (2015) also suggest that implementation intention and commitment may have a role in entrepreneurial process. Implementation intention may moderate the intention–behaviour link and commitment is linked both to intention and action. This can explain why some students with high intention scores become entrepreneurs and others do not.

Gender has significant value in predicting entrepreneurial career choice: men are far more likely to become entrepreneurs than women. Gender has an effect not only on development of intentions (Joensuu et al., 2013) but also on behaviour. Yet entrepreneurship programmes can have an impact on women's entrepreneurial potential (e.g., European Commission, 2012). One possible conclusion is that insufficient attention is paid in higher education to possible gender differences in learning styles. Some earlier studies have found differences in learning style between men and women (Gallos, 1993; Kaenzig et al., 2007), suggesting that women are not as happy with group work or active-based pedagogies as men are. Entrepreneurship educators should also consider whether they unknowingly bias their presentation of entrepreneurship, for example, by the use of male case examples.

Although students' entrepreneurial intentions have been widely studied, follow-up studies extending to actualization of individual entrepreneurial intentions are rare. Overall, the results highlight the importance of both developing individual perspectives in entrepreneurship education: different methods and objectives should be designed for different groups. Students can be categorized into groups to be protected, cultivated and developed. The group to protect is the students starting a business during studies; they should be offered skills and knowledge related to an entrepreneurial career. The group to be cultivated is the students with high intention scores; they should be offered programmes that enhance their belief in their ability to succeed as entrepreneurs. The group to be developed is the students with low intention scores; they require more attitudinally focused entrepreneurship education. Also, gender effects should be considered when designing entrepreneurship education.

CONCLUSION

Limitations and Further Research

We hope to have added richness to the ongoing discussion among academics and educators alike regarding entrepreneurial intentions and to have added a new perspective in examining the role of antecedents in actual start-up activities. Our study has, however, some limitations that should be addressed in future research.

We have taken the liberty of examining behaviour from a theoretical perspective intended for explaining intentions. We acknowledge that this is extending Ajzen's theory beyond its aims. Nevertheless, as the rationale for studying formation of entrepreneurial intentions ultimately relates to promotion of actual entrepreneurial behaviour, testing the role of the antecedents in existing data is a reasonable step. The theoretical grounding in antecedents of intentions can, however, be considered a limitation in our study.

From an empirical standpoint, our sample was limited to higher education students in one country. This limits the scope of generalization, as different environments lead not only to different levels of entrepreneurial intentions but also differences in realization of intentions (see e.g., Grilo and Irigoyen, 2006). The instrument has also been developed in Finland, which could conceivably have an effect on the results. Another limitation of the study is that we have been unable, due to the limited number of graduates engaged in entrepreneurship, to examine the differences between study years. It would be highly useful, for example, to establish whether intentions formed closer to graduation are more likely to be realized. Also, with a larger sample size, variances in realization of intentions in different kinds of entrepreneurship could be distinguished and measured, for example, part-time and full-time entrepreneurship, solo entrepreneurship and growth entrepreneurship (see also Kautonen et al., 2013). It is also possible, that because the data from the first wave has been collected from individuals in different phases of their education, this might somehow bias the results. Some students had a first wave measurement from the first study year and others from the last study year. Older students may have more work experience, which can affect the level of entrepreneurial intention.

A theoretically important issue to be investigated empirically is the permanence of antecedents of entrepreneurial intentions, in particular PBC. Do students' perceptions of their capabilities change after graduation – or after actually starting a business? Additionally, Fayolle (2013; see also Fayolle and Liñán, 2014) has suggested that implementation intention theory and the concept of commitment be included when analysing the link between intentions and behaviour.

NOTE

* This research project has been funded by European Regional Development Fund and the support is gratefully acknowledged.

REFERENCES

Adam, A. and A. Fayolle (2015), 'Bridging the entrepreneurial intention–behaviour gap: the role of commitment and implementation intention', *International Journal of Entrepreneurship and Small Business*, **25** (1), 36–54.

Aizzat, M., A. Noor Hazlina and E. Chew (2009), 'Examining a model of entrepreneurial intention among Malaysians using SEM procedure', *European Journal of Scientific Research*, **33** (2), 365–73.

Ajzen, I. (1991), 'The theory of planned behavior', *Organizational Behavior and Human Decision Processes*, **50** (2), 179–211.

Ajzen, I. and M. Fishbein (2004), 'Questions raised by reasoned action approach: comment on Odgen (2003)', *Health Psychology*, **23** (4), 431–4.

Ajzen, I., C. Csasch and M. Flood (2009), 'From intentions to behaviour: implementation intention, commitment, and conscientiousness', *Journal of Applied Social Psychology*, **39** (6), 1356–72.

Aronsson, M. (2004), 'Education matters – but does entrepreneurship education? An interview with David Birch', *Academy of Management Learning and Education*, **3** (3), 289–92.

Autio, E., R.H. Keeley, M. Klofsten and T. Ulfstedt (1997), 'Entrepreneurial intent among students: testing an intent model in Asia, Scandinavia, and USA', in D.L. Sexton and J.D. Kasarda (eds), *Frontiers of Entrepreneurial Research*, Wellesley, MA: Babson College Publications, pp. 133–47.

Autio, E., R.H. Keeley and G. Klofsen et al. (2001), 'Entrepreneurial intent among students in Scandinavia and in the USA', *Enterprise and Innovation Management Studies*, **2** (2), 145–60.

Bandura, A., N. Adams, A. Hardy and G. Howells (1980), 'Test of the generality of self-efficacy theory', *Cognitive Therapy and Research*, **4** (1), 39–66.

Blanchflower, D.G. and B.D. Meyer (1994), 'A longitudinal analysis of the young self-employed in Australia and the United States', *Small Business Economics*, **6** (1), 1–19.

Bosma, N., J. Hessels and V. Schutjens et al. (2012), 'Entrepreneurship and role models', *Journal of Economic Psychology*, **33** (2), 410–24.

Boyd, N. and G. Vozikis (1994), 'The influence of self-efficacy on the development of entrepreneurial intentions and actions', *Entrepreneurship Theory and Practice*, **18** (4), 63–77.

Carsrud, A. and M. Brännback (2011), 'Entrepreneurial motivations: what do we still need to know?', *Journal of Small Business Management*, **49** (1), 9–26.

Chen, Y. and Y. He (2011), 'The impact of strong ties on entrepreneurial intention: an empirical study based on the mediating role of self-efficacy', *Journal of Chinese Entrepreneurship*, **3** (2), 147–58.

Cialdini, R. and M. Trost (1998), 'Social influence: social norms, conformity, and compliance', in D. Gilbert, S. Fiske and G. Lindzey (eds), *The Handbook of Social Psychology, Volume 2*, 4th edition, New York: McGraw-Hill, pp. 151–92.

Crant, M. (1996), 'The proactive personality scale as a predictor of entrepreneurial intentions', *Journal of Small Business Management*, **34** (3), 42–9.

Drost, E. and J. McGuire (2011), 'Fostering entrepreneurship among Finnish business students: antecedents of entrepreneurial intent and implications for entrepreneurship education', *International Review of Entrepreneurship*, **9** (2), 83–112.

Engle, R.L., N. Dimitriadi and J.V. Gavidia et al. (2010), 'Entrepreneurial intent. A twelve-country evaluation of Ajzen's model of planned behaviour', *International Journal of Entrepreneurial Research*, **16** (1), 35–57.

Engle, R.L., C. Schlaegel and S. Delanoe (2011), 'The role of social influence, culture, and gender on entrepreneurial intent', *Journal of Small Business and Entrepreneurship*, **24** (4), 471–92.

Ertuna, Z. and E. Gurel (2011), 'The moderating role of higher education on entrepreneurship', *Education + Training*, **53** (5), 387–402.

European Commission (2012), *Effects and Impact of Entrepreneurship Programmes in Higher Education*, Brussels: DG for Enterprise and Industry, Entrepreneurship Unit.

Fayolle, A. (2013), 'Personal views on the future of entrepreneurship education', *Entrepreneurship and Regional Development*, **25** (7–8), 1–10.

Fayolle, A. and F. Liñán (2013), 'Entrepreneurial intentions: literature review and new research perspectives', a paper presented at the 3rd GIKA Annual Conference, 7–9 July 2013, Valencia.

Fayolle, A. and F. Liñán (2014), 'The future of research on entrepreneurial intentions', *Journal of Business Research*, **67** (5), 663–6.

Finisterra do Paco, A.-M., J. Ferreira and M. Raposo et al. (2011), 'Behaviours and entrepreneurial intention: empirical findings about secondary students', *Journal of International Entrepreneurship*, **9** (1), 20–38.

Gallos, J. (1993), 'Women's experiences and ways of knowing: implications for teaching and learning in the organizational behaviour classroom', *Journal of Management Education*, **17** (1), 7–26.

Grilo, I. and J.M. Irigoyen (2006), 'Entrepreneurship in the EU: to wish and not to be', *Small Business Economics*, **26** (4), 305–18.

Henley, A. (2005), 'From entrepreneurial aspiration to business start-up: evidence from British longitudinal study', School of Business and Economics, University of Wales Swansea, accessed 31 May 2016 at https://www.iser.essex.ac.uk/files/conferences/bhps/2005/docs/pdf/papers/henley.pdf.

Ingram, K., J. Cope, B. Harju and K. Wuench (2000), 'Applying to graduate school: a test of the theory of planned behavior', *Journal of Social Behavior and Personality*, **15** (2), 215–26.

Joensuu, S., A. Viljamaa, E. Varamäki and E. Tornikoski (2013), 'Development of entrepreneurial intention in higher education and the effect of gender – a latent growth curve analysis', *Education + Training*, **55** (8/9), 781–803.

Joensuu, S., E. Varamäki and A. Viljamaa et al. (2014), 'Yrittäjyysaikomukset, yrittäjyysaikomusten muutos ja näihin vaikuttavat tekijät koulutuksen aikana'

[Entrepreneurial intentions, their change and factors affecting these during studies], *Seinäjoen ammattikorkeakoulun julkaisusarja*, Research Report No. A16 [in Finnish].

Jung, D.I., S.B. Ehrlich, A.F. de Noble and K. Baik (2001), 'Entrepreneurial self-efficacy and its relationship to entrepreneurial action: a comparative study between the US and Korea', *Management International*, **6** (1), 41–53.

Kaenzig, R., E. Hyatt and S. Anderson (2007), 'Gender differences in college business educational experiences', *Journal of Education for Business*, **83** (2), 95–100.

Kangasharju, A. and S. Pekkala (2002), 'The role of education in self-employment success in Finland', *Growth and Change*, **33** (2), 216–37.

Kautonen, T., M. van Gelderen and M. Fink (2015), 'Robustness of the theory of planned behavior in predicting entrepreneurial intentions and actions', *Entrepreneurship Theory and Practice*, **39** (3), 655–74.

Kautonen, T., M. van Gelderen, and E. Tornikoski (2013), 'Predicting entrepreneurial behaviour: a test of the theory of planned behaviour', *Applied Economics*, **45** (6), 697–707.

Kickul, J., F. Wilson, D. Marlino and S. Barbosa (2008), 'Are misalignments of perceptions and self-efficacy causing gender gaps in entrepreneurial intentions among our nation's teens?', *Journal of Small Business and Enterprise Development*, **15** (2), 321–35.

Kolvereid, L. (1996), 'Prediction of employment status choice intentions', *Entrepreneurship Theory and Practice*, **21** (1), 47–57.

Kolvereid, L. and E. Isaksen (2006). 'New business start-up and subsequent entry into self-employment', *Journal of Business Venturing*, **21** (6), 866–85.

Kristiansen, S. and N. Indarti (2004), 'Entrepreneurial intention among Indonesian and Norwegian students', *Journal of Enterprising Culture*, **12** (1), 55–78.

Krueger, N.F. and A.L. Carsrud (1993), 'Entrepreneurial intentions: applying the theory of planned behavior', *Entrepreneurship and Regional Development*, **5** (4), 315–30.

Krueger, N., M. Reilly and A. Carsrud (2000), 'Competing models of entrepreneurial intentions', *Journal of Business Venturing*, **15** (2), 411–32.

Lanero, A., J. Vazquez, P. Gutierrez and M. Purificación Garcia (2011), 'The impact of entrepreneurship education in European universities: an intention-based approach analyzed in the Spanish area', *International Review on Public and Nonprofit Marketing*, **8** (5), 111–30.

Lee, L., P. Wong, M. Foo and A. Leung (2011), 'Entrepreneurial intentions: the influence of organizational and individual factors', *Journal of Business Venturing*, **6** (1), 124–36.

Liñán, F. (2004), 'Intention-based models of entrepreneurship education', *Small Business*, **2004** (3), 11–35.

Liñán, F. and Y.-W. Chen (2009), 'Development and cross-cultural application of a specific instrument to measure entrepreneurial intentions', *Entrepreneurship Theory and Practice*, **33** (3), 593–617.

Liñán, F. and A. Fayolle (2015), 'A systematic literature review on entrepreneurial intentions: citation, thematic analyses, and research agenda', *International Entrepreneurship and Management Journal*, **11** (4), 907–33.

Matlay, H. and C. Carey (2007), 'Entrepreneurship education in the UK: a longitudinal perspective', *Journal of Small Business and Enterprise Development*, **14** (2), 252–63.

Melin, K. (2001), 'Yrittäjyysintentiot ja niiden taustatekijät Virossa ja Suomessa. Vertailukohteina eräissä ammatillisissa oppilaitoksissa opiskelevat nuoret kummassakin maassa' [The entrepreneurial intentions and their background in Estonia and Finland], *Acta Wasaensia*, No. 93, Vaasan yliopisto [in Finnish].

Moi, T., Y. Adeline and M. Dyana (2011), 'Young adult responses to entrepreneurial intent', *Researchers World*, **2** (3), 37–52.

Nabi, G., R. Holden and A. Walmsley (2010), 'From student to entrepreneur: towards a model of graduate entrepreneurial career-making', *Journal of Education and Work*, **23** (5), 389–415.

Pihie, L. and A. Bagheri (2011), 'Malay secondary school students' entrepreneurial attitude orientation and entrepreneurial self-efficacy: a descriptive study', *Journal of Applied Sciences*, **11** (2), 316–22.

Pihie, L., A. Zaidatol and H. Hassan (2009), 'Choice of self-employment intention among secondary school students', *The Journal of International Social Research*, **9** (2), 539–49.

Pihkala, J. (2008), 'Ammattikorkeakoulutuksen aikaiset yrittäjyysintentioiden muutokset' [Changes in entrepreneurship intentions during polytechnic education], *Opetusministeriön julkaisuja*, **1**, Helsinki [in Finnish].

Prodan, I. and M. Drnovsek (2010), 'Conceptualizing academic-entrepreneurial intentions: an empirical test', *Technovation*, **30** (5/6), 332–47.

Pruett, M., R. Shinnar and B. Toney et al. (2009), 'Explaining entrepreneurial intentions of university students: a cross-cultural study', *International Journal of Entrepreneurial Behavior & Research*, **15** (6), 571–94.

Schlaegel, C. and M. Koenig (2014), 'Determinants of entrepreneurial intent: a meta-analytic test and integration of competing models', *Entrepreneurship Theory and Practice*, **38** (2), 291–332.

Segal, G., D. Borgia and J. Schoenfeld (2005), 'The motivation to become an entrepreneur', *International Journal of Entrepreneurial Behavior and Research*, **11** (1), 42–57.

Sequeira, J., S. Mueller and J. McGee (2007), 'The influence of social ties and self-efficacy in forming entrepreneurial intentions and motivating nascent behaviour', *Journal of Developmental Entrepreneurship*, **12** (3), 275–93.

Shapero, A. and L. Sokol (1982), 'The social dimensions of entrepreneurship', in C. Kent, D. Sexton and K. Vesper (eds), *The Encyclopedia of Entrepreneurship*, Englewood Cliffs, NJ: Prentice-Hall, pp. 72–90.

Shay, J. and S. Terjesen (2005), 'Entrepreneurial aspirations and intentions and intentions of business students: a gendered perspective', paper presented at the Babson Entrepreneurship Conference, Boston MA.

Sheeran, P. (2002), 'Intention–behaviour relations: a conceptual and empirical review', in W. Strobe and M. Hewstone (eds), *European Review of Social Psychology, Volume 12*, Chichester, UK: Wiley, pp. 1–30.

Siu, W. and E. Lo (2013), 'Cultural contingency in the cognitive model of entrepreneurial intention', *Entrepreneurship Theory and Practice*, **37** (2), 147–73.

Swan, W., C. Chang-Schneider and K. McClarity (2007), 'Do people's self-views matter?', *American Psychologist*, **62** (2), 84–94.

Townsend, D.M., L.W. Busenitz and J.D. Arthurs (2010), 'To start or not to start: outcome and ability expectations in the decision to start a new venture', *Journal of Business Venturing*, **25** (2), 192–202.

Urban, B. (2006), 'Entrepreneurship in the rainbow nation: effect of cultural values and ESE on intentions', *Journal of Developmental Entrepreneurship*, **11** (3), 171–86.

Uygun, R. and M. Kasimoglu (2013), 'The emergence of entrepreneurial intentions in indigenous entrepreneurs: the role of personal background on the antecedents of intentions', *International Journal of Business and Management*, **8** (5), 24–40.

Van Auken, H., F. Fry and P. Stephens (2006), 'The influence of role models on entrepreneurial intentions', *Journal of Developmental Entrepreneurship*, **11** (2), 157–67.

Van Gelderen, M. and P. Jansen (2006), 'Autonomy as a start-up motive', *Journal of Small Business and Enterprise Development*, **13** (1), 23–32.

Wang, C. and P. Wong (2004), 'Entrepreneurial interest of university students in Singapore', *Technovation*, **24** (2), 161–72.

Wilson, F., J. Kickul and D. Marlino (2007), 'Gender, entrepreneurial self-efficacy, and entrepreneurial career intentions: implications for entrepreneurship education', *Entrepreneurship Theory and Practice*, **31** (3), 387–406.

Wilson, F., D. Marlino and J. Kickul (2004), 'Our entrepreneurial future: examining the diverse attitudes and motivations of teens across gender and ethnic identity', *Journal of Development Entrepreneurship*, **9** (3), 177–97.

Yordanova, D. and M.-A. Tarrazon (2010), 'Gender differences in entrepreneurial intentions: evidence from Bulgaria', *Journal of Developmental Entrepreneurship*, **15** (3), 245–61.

Zampetakis, L., K. Kafetsios and N. Bouranta et al. (2009), 'On the relationship between emotional intelligence and entrepreneurial attitudes and intentions', *International Journal of Entrepreneurial Behavior & Research*, **15** (6), 595–618.

Zhang, Y., G. Duyesters and M. Cloodt (2014), 'The role of entrepreneurship education as a predictor of university students' entrepreneurial intention', *International Entrepreneurship Management Journal*, **10** (3), 623–41.

Zhao, H., S. Seibert and G. Hills (2005), 'The mediating role of self-efficacy in the development of entrepreneurial intentions', *Journal of Applied Psychology*, **90** (6), 1265–72.

APPENDIX

Table 8A.1　Variables and their items

Variables (All Measured on a Seven-point Likert Scale; Translated from Finnish)	Items
Entrepreneurial intention	How likely are you to start your own business and work as an entrepreneur after graduation or while still studying?
	If you were forced to choose between entrepreneurship and salaried work after graduation, which one would you choose?
	How strong is your intention to embark on entrepreneurship at some point of your professional career?
	How likely are you to embark on entrepreneurship after you have gathered a sufficient amount of work experience?
	If you were forced to choose between entrepreneurship and unemployment after graduation, which one would you choose?
Subjective norm	I believe that *my closest family members* think I should not/should strive to start my own business and to work as an entrepreneur after graduation
	How much attention do you pay to what your closest *family members* think if you strive to start your own business and to work as an entrepreneur after graduation?
	I believe that *my best friends* think I should not/should strive to start my own business and to work as an entrepreneur after graduation
	How much attention do you pay to what *your best friends* think if you strive to start your own business and to work as an entrepreneur after graduation?
	I believe that *my significant others* think I should not/should strive to start my own business and to work as an entrepreneur after graduation
	How much attention do you pay to what *your significant others* think if you strive to start your own business and to work as an entrepreneur after graduation?

Variables (All Measured on a Seven-point Likert Scale; Translated from Finnish)	Items
Perceived behavioural control	If I established a business and started to work as an entrepreneur after graduation, my chance of success would be (good/bad)
	If I really wanted to, I could easily start a business and work as an entrepreneur after graduation
	There are very few/numerous things that are beyond my own control but could prevent me from starting my own business and working as an entrepreneur after graduation
	For me, starting my own business and working as an entrepreneur after graduation is (very easy/very difficult)
	If I established my own business and started to work as an entrepreneur after graduation, my risk of failure would be (very small/very big)
Attitudes towards entrepreneurship	To what extent do the following attributes correspond to your perceptions of entrepreneurship (i.e., establishing a business and working as an entrepreneur):
	Interesting
	Esteemed
	Worth pursuing
	Boring
	Fascinating
	Despised
	Good income level
Start-up behaviour	Are you currently starting your own business? (E.g., you are working on a business idea or other plans) (yes/no)?

Table 8A.2   Correlations among studied variables

Variable		Intentions	Subjective Norm	Perceived Behavioural Control	Attitudes	Gender	Mother as an Entrepreneur	Father as an Entrepreneur
Intentions	Pearson correlation	1						
	Sig. (2-tailed)							
	N							
Subjective Norm	Pearson correlation	0.146**	1					
	Sig. (2-tailed)	0.000						
	N	3498						
Perceived Behavioural Control	Pearson correlation	0.518**	−0.001	1				
	Sig. (2-tailed)	0.000	0.938					
	N	3570	3498					
Attitudes	Pearson correlation	0.562**	0.134**	0.389**	1			
	Sig. (2-tailed)	0.000	0.000	0.000				
	N	3565	3495	3563				

Gender	Pearson correlation	0.165**	−0.106**	0.146**	0.032	1	
	Sig. (2-tailed)	0.000	0.000	0.000	0.060		
	N	3560	3488	3558	3555		
Mother as an Entrepreneur	Pearson correlation	0.204**	0.047**	0.106**	0.126**	−0.013	1
	Sig. (2-tailed)	0.000	0.006	0.000	0.000	0.447	
	N	3488	3417	3486	3483	3479	
Father as an Entrepreneur	Pearson correlation	0.269**	0.044*	0.147**	0.186**	−0.016	0.324**
	Sig. (2-tailed)	0.000	0.011	0.000	0.000	0.354	0.000
	N	3472	3400	3470	3467	3463	3463

Note: $* p < 0.05$, $** p < 0.01$, $*** p < 0.001$.

9. 'Made in Liverpool': exploring the contribution of a university–industry research partnership to innovation and entrepreneurship

Sam Horner and Benito Giordano

INTRODUCTION

In recent years, promoting a combination of research, entrepreneurship, innovation and technology transfer has become an important public policy objective at all levels of government in Europe, the USA, as well as in most developing economies (OECD, 2008, 2010, 2013). The premise is that these elements are the key ingredients for promoting economic competitiveness in the global 'knowledge economy' (OECD, 2010). The dominant policy paradigm is that innovation and entrepreneurship can provide the foundations for new businesses, new jobs and potentially new industries, which should contribute towards enhanced employment opportunities and productivity growth (Audretsch and Feldman, 1996; Cooke et al., 1998; Lundvall et al., 2002; Cooke and Leydesdorff, 2006; Lundvall, 2007; OECD, 2008, 2010; Cooke, 2008; European Commission, 2010; Perren and Sapsed, 2013).

One of the core elements of a range of territorial innovation policies is premised upon the explicit role that university–industry linkages can play as drivers of local and regional economic development (Chesbrough, 2003; OECD, 2008, 2010; Ylinenpää, 2009; European Commission, 2010). Interestingly, whilst several contributions have explored the potential role that universities may play in open innovation (Perkmann and Walsh, 2007), the predominant concern is the generation and commercialization of intellectual property (IP) through formalized technology transfer mechanisms such as patents and licences.

Focusing on the development of the Centre for Materials Discovery (CMD) at the University of Liverpool (UoL), the contribution of this chapter is to explore the broader role that universities can play in the context of open innovation, beyond the generation of codified knowledge for commercialization. The CMD has developed over the last decade as a result of a unique partnership between Unilever PLC and the UoL. This partnership, based upon joint scientific interests, has attracted significant funding from UK and European sources and involves a range of stakeholders in the creation of an ongoing collaboration to nurture innovation (ERDF, 2009; Barr et al., 2013). Exploring the UoL–Unilever case, therefore, illustrates the ways in which a university–industry partnership can play a crucial role in enhancing open-innovation efforts and capabilities at the city-regional level.

The rest of this chapter is structured as follows. The first section explores some of the literature relating to open-innovation, university–industry collaboration and research partnerships. The literature on proximity dimensions of innovation is also reviewed. This is followed by a brief discussion of the methodological approach that was used to carry out the research. The third section goes on to discuss the main findings generated from the CMD case study. The last section provides some concluding remarks.

EXPLORING OPEN INNOVATION

Open innovation (OI) stems from the premise that valuable ideas may be sourced from within or outside the firm (Chesbrough, 2003). The OI paradigm advocates a 'new logic of innovation' whereby organizations structure themselves to make use of external knowledge and technology (ibid.). Although sometimes misconstrued as the simple 'outsourcing of R&D activities', the OI paradigm in fact advocates that firms 'should use external ideas as well as internal ideas as they seek to advance their technology' (Chesbrough et al., 2006, p. 1). The most widely adopted definition of OI reflects the 'use of purposive inflows and outflows of knowledge to accelerate internal innovation and expand markets for external use of innovation' (Chesbrough et al., 2006, p. 1; West et al., 2014).

The analytical unit employed in the majority of open-innovation research is the firm level. Firm-level studies of OI carry a specific focus on how innovations are transferred across organizational boundaries to create value and revenue streams (Wikhamn and Wikhamn, 2013). OI studies that adopt a firm-level perspective explore the important factors or antecedents of OI implementation. Antecedents of successful OI implementation include open business strategies and models (Chesbrough and Appleyard, 2007), corporate and private venture capital (Van de

Vrande et al., 2011), advanced technologies (Dodgson et al., 2006), conducive corporate cultures and top management support (Huston and Sakkab, 2008; Wikhamn and Wikhamn, 2013). Other firm-level studies have explored the contextual differences that may impact the implementation of OI practices. For example, studies have explored how the adoption of OI varies between high-tech and low-tech organizational contexts as well as product and service contexts (Chesbrough and Crowther, 2006; Chesbrough, 2011; Wikhamn and Wikhamn, 2013).

Although firm-level studies are more prevalent within OI research, emergent perspectives that offer analysis at an 'ecosystem' level offer more scope for enhancing our understanding of open innovation. Ecosystem-level studies focus more on the innovation activities that happen outside of the firm boundaries but within the broader business ecosystem (Moore, 1993; Wikhamn and Wikhamn, 2013). Much of the work within this stream of literature explores facets of user innovation, primarily within open source contexts (Wikhamn and Wikhamn, 2013). Although there is some dispute over the position of user innovation within the OI literature, the ecosystem-level perspective also considers the roles played by other ecosystem participants. This includes studies that consider the roles that suppliers play within OI implementation (Brem and Tidd, 2012) as well as the important role played by universities in shared value creation (Perkmann and Walsh, 2007; Wikhamn and Wikhamn, 2013). The potentially significant role that universities may play within open-innovation contexts will now be explored in greater depth.

The Role of University–Industry Collaboration

University–industry (U–I) linkages and their impact on innovation have been considered from various perspectives, including management perspectives, economics of innovation perspectives and science studies perspectives (Mowery et al., 2004; Agrawal, 2006; Perkmann and Walsh, 2007). There has also been increased policy emphasis on universities to deliver economic development via interaction with industrial partners (Rothaermel et al., 2007; European Commission, 2010; Petruzzelli, 2011; Kalar and Antoncic, 2015).

Specifically, universities have been encouraged to become more entrepreneurial through engaging in patenting, licensing and spin-out activities (D'Este and Patel, 2007; Perkmann et al., 2013). Furthermore, research on U–I interaction has been predominantly focused on such commercialization activities, primarily because they are more empirically accessible (Perkmann and Walsh, 2007; Perkmann et al., 2013). For example, researchers are able to utilize generally accessible patent databases, which can be used to examine patenting activities of universities (Lissoni et al., 2008; Perkmann et al., 2013). The number of university spin-out firms can be observed as well as directorships held by university academics, all of which can be used to assess commercialization activities of universities (Perkmann et al., 2013).

It has recently been argued, however, that the research and policy emphasis on commercialization activities has resulted in a rather narrow understanding of U–I linkages, as well as an underappreciation of the potential contribution of U–I linkages to industrial innovation and knowledge-based economic development (D'Este and Patel, 2007; Bruneel et al., 2010; D'Este and Perkmann, 2011; Perkmann et al., 2013). Rather, it is suggested that a broader consideration of the so-called 'engagement' activities of universities may be useful for providing a deeper understanding of the contributions of U–I linkages in the context of open innovation (Perkmann and Walsh, 2007; Perkmann et al., 2013).

In short, it is argued that university–industry interactions with a higher degree of relational involvement are a potentially more important form of promoting industrial innovation than those forms of interaction characterized by low relational involvement (Perkmann and Walsh, 2007; Perkmann et al., 2013). This chapter is particularly concerned with the form of interaction with the highest degree of relational involvement, research partnerships.

Developing Collaborative Innovation Research Partnerships

The purpose of this section is to integrate several perspectives on research partnerships, which are widely studied within mainstream management and innovation literatures but much less so within the context of U–I collaboration. The contribution of this chapter, therefore, is to contribute to this 'gap' by exploring the development of the UoL–Unilever university–industry research partnership and highlight the potential implications of such a configuration for innovation and entrepreneurship.

Research partnerships are broadly defined as 'innovation-based relationships that involve, in some capacity, a significant effort in research and development' (Hagedoorn et al., 2000 p. 567). Within the context of U–I collaboration, they have been characterized as formal collaborative arrangements between organizations with the objective to cooperate on research and development activities (Perkmann and Walsh, 2007). The temporal duration of research partnerships remains undefined, although it has been conceded that partnerships can range from short-term individual projects to long-term multifaceted collaborative efforts (Perkmann and Walsh, 2007; Perkmann et al., 2013). Research partnerships have also been analysed in terms of the degree of formality associated with collaborative interaction (Hagedoorn et al., 2000; Perkmann et al., 2013). Conventional interorganizational collaboration literature suggests that research partnerships may consist of formal and informal interactions (Hagedoorn et al., 2000). Notably, the understanding of informal collaborative research partnerships remains underdeveloped due to the difficulties of empirically tracing informality. Consequently, the antecedents, mechanisms and outcomes of informal research partnerships remain somewhat undefined. Formal interorganizational research partnerships may consist of equity-based and non-equity-based interactions, which have been labelled 'research corporations' and 'research joint ventures' (ibid.). Equity-based research partnerships entail the establishment of a corporate entity via which joint R&D efforts are pursued. Non-equity research partnerships are underpinned by contractual mechanisms that facilitate the pooling of resources. Research consortia, R&D pacts and research contracts are common forms of 'research joint ventures'.

Hagedoorn et al. (2000) comprehensively outline the research partnership construct in a review that is primarily based upon interactions that occur between privately owned organizations. Recently it has been argued that U–I partnerships are conceptually and analytically distinct from normative interorganizational partnerships (Perkmann et al., 2013; Ankrah and Al-Tabbaa, 2015). Within the U–I context the conceptualization of research partnerships is more narrowly focused on non-equity collaborative mechanisms (Perkmann and Walsh, 2007). This is because equity-based collaborative interactions between university and industry partners are subject to intense academic investigation within the field of academic entrepreneurship (Shane, 2004), which has developed along theoretical and empirical trajectories that are underpinned by entrepreneurship theory (Perkmann et al., 2013). Consequently, research partnerships in a U–I context can consist of individual, project-level collaborations or larger organizational-level strategic collaborations. An example of the former may be the industry sponsorship of a PhD student, whereas the latter may include the co-creation of joint research facilities. It has been argued recently that studies of U–I 'engagement' remain under-represented and under-theorized within the extant university–industry literature (Perkmann et al., 2013). This is despite recent policy reviews that highlight the importance of 'strategic partnerships' between academic and industrial organizations for innovation and entrepreneurship (Dowling, 2015).

R&D partnerships are also characterized as important configurations that facilitate the implementation of open innovation (Du et al., 2014; Piller and West, 2014). It is highlighted that R&D partnerships enable organizations to access and leverage external complementary resources and capabilities (Eisenhardt and Schoonhoven, 1996; Grant and Baden-Fuller, 2004; Du et al., 2014), which lowers the costs and risks associated with innovation (Belderbos et al., 2004; Chesbrough et al., 2014). Firms may engage with science-based partners or market-based partners in open-innovation efforts (Du et al., 2014). Within the context of open innovation, science-based partners provide access to state-of-the-art tacit and codified knowledge, facilitating the incorporation of the latest scientific knowledge into innovation efforts (Fabrizio, 2009). It is also highlighted that science-based partnerships can provide industrial R&D teams with a detailed understanding of the technological context in which innovation solutions can be formulated (Du et al., 2014). Despite recent attention to science-based open-innovation partnerships, the overwhelming focus within open innovation remains on the interactions amongst privately owned firms (Wikhamn and Wikhamn, 2013).

The next section explores the role of 'proximity' in facilitating innovation processes. Once again, there are various dimensions to this, which are relevant to the development of U–I relationships, but that hitherto remain rather unexplored in the literature.

Proximity Dimensions of Innovation

First, 'geographic' proximity is a significant dimension. Considerable academic and policy focus has been placed on the success of 'exemplar' cases of specialized industrial agglomerations and clusters such as Silicon Valley in the USA or Cambridge in the UK (Saxenian, 1994; Doloreux and Parto, 2005; Tödtling and Trippl, 2005; Grimaldi et al., 2011). It is argued that a concentration of similar firms in certain localities ensures that knowledge is transferred more easily, which in turn improves the level of awareness about the actions of competitors, enhancing rivalry and stimulating greater commitment to differentiation and innovation (Porter, 2000; Bathelt et al., 2004).

Some authors suggest that economic benefits alone do not fully capture the influence that geographic proximity has on innovation (Bathelt et al., 2004). Accordingly, to fully appreciate the impact geography has on innovation, the socio-institutional settings and interfirm collaboration processes, which are heavily influenced by geographical proximity, need to be acknowledged (Maskell and Malmberg, 1999; Bathelt, 2002;

Bathelt et al., 2004; Boschma, 2005). This is particularly pertinent to the UoL–Unilever case, as will be discussed subsequently in this chapter.

Second, another element of 'proximity' relates to the point that co-located firms and partner organizations benefit from a knowledge, information and communication *ecology*, or so-called 'local buzz' (Bathelt et al., 2004), which arises from frequent face-to-face contact between actors in the same locality (Gertler, 1995, 2003; Bathelt et al., 2004). To elaborate, a 'local buzz' can benefit firms and stakeholders located in a specific locality as it enhances the potential for knowledge exchange and interactive learning, both of which are crucial for innovation (Gertler, 2003; Bathelt et al., 2004). Moreover, a 'local buzz' also leads to the establishment of a shared knowledge base; participants can work together to (re-)configure their resources to produce new knowledge (Maskell and Malmberg, 1999; Bathelt et al., 2004). Despite the advantages of geographic co-location, it is recognized that a 'local buzz' may not always manifest itself, due to differing social structures and hostile previous interaction between respective actors and stakeholders (Bathelt, 2002, 2005).

The 'local buzz' argument is fundamentally about the sharing of tacit knowledge, which is arguably a crucial requirement for innovation (Gertler, 2003; Asheim et al., 2007). Given that tacit knowledge is difficult to codify and articulate, it is probably most effectively shared through demonstration and practice (Nonaka and Takeuchi, 1995; Gertler, 2003). There is also an important argument that states tacit knowledge may be context-specific and spatially 'sticky' (Gertler, 2003). As codified knowledge is arguably much more widespread and accessible, unique capabilities and products may depend on the creation and application of tacit knowledge (Maskell and Malmberg, 1999; Gertler, 2003). This means that geographic proximity will have a significant influence on innovation as tacit knowledge is most effectively disseminated through interpersonal interactions (Gertler, 2003; Bathelt, 2005). This argument has been supported by empirical studies, which have indicated that knowledge externalities tend to be geographically bounded (Jaffe et al., 1993; Audretsch and Feldman, 1996; Boschma, 2005; D'Este et al., 2013).

Here it is important to note that geographic proximity has been considered particularly influential in the effective transfer of knowledge and technology between universities and industry (Abramovsky et al., 2007; D'Este et al., 2013). This is because such collaborations are characterized by bi-directional knowledge flows, basic research and enduring social relationships between partners (Ponds et al., 2007;

D'Este et al., 2013), all of which are facilitated by face-to-face communication (D'Este et al., 2013). Again, this is an important point to explore in the UoL–Unilever case.

Third, it is increasingly recognized that geographic propinquity alone is neither necessary nor sufficient to stimulate and sustain innovation (Bathelt et al., 2004; Boschma, 2005). This suggestion is based on the recognition that too great an emphasis on local interaction makes firms insular and regional innovation systems become closed and inflexible, resulting in 'lock-in' (Boschma, 2005). Lock-in refers to situations whereby firms and regions are dependent on established technologies, knowledge bases and routines and therefore find it difficult to recognize and assimilate new knowledge (Boschma, 2005; Tödtling and Trippl, 2005). Extra-local linkages between discrete regional clusters are essential for sustained interactive learning and innovation (Bathelt et al., 2004; Gertler, 2008). These trans-local connections are perceived as important to innovation as they provide new knowledge from different but related contexts, as well as information about potential new markets, which enhances the dynamism of a 'local buzz' (Bathelt et al., 2004).

This alternative perspective suggests that as geographic proximity becomes less influential in interactive knowledge transfer and innovation, other dimensions of proximity may become more important (Gertler, 2003; Boschma, 2005). Some authors highlight the importance of cognitive proximity to promote interactive learning and innovation (Boschma, 2005). Generally, when firms search for new knowledge they seek to extend their existing knowledge bases (ibid.). It is argued that actors require similar knowledge bases, or cognitive proximity, in order to be able to communicate, understand and apply new knowledge successfully (Boschma and Lambooy, 1999; Boschma, 2005). It is also suggested that there must be a balance between cognitive distance and cognitive proximity; actors that are too cognitively proximate will not benefit from differentiated knowledge, whereas actors that are too cognitively distant may not be able to understand and apply new knowledge (Boschma and Frenken, 2010). The technological innovation system approach (TIS) promoted by Carlsson and Stankiewicz (1991) suggested that innovation systems can be delineated by specific knowledge fields as opposed to geographical boundaries (Carlsson et al., 2002).

Fourth, social proximity is another dimension that has been identified in nurturing innovation (Boschma, 2005; Boschma and Frenken, 2010). Social proximity refers to relationships between individual agents. Agents are considered socially proximate when relationships are based on trust, friendship and shared experiences (Boschma, 2005). It has been argued that social proximity may substitute for geographical proximity in knowledge exchange, as trusting relationships between agents with shared experience can facilitate the transfer of tacit knowledge (Boschma, 2005; Gertler, 2008).

Furthermore, social proximity can result in the establishment of geographically dispersed communities of practice that consist of individuals who share the same organizational and personal interests (Lave and Wenger, 1991; Gertler, 2008). Breschi and Lissoni (2001) highlight the importance of social proximity to knowledge transfer by demonstrating that social connectedness between inventors plays a more significant role in knowledge spillovers than geographical proximity. In addition, Gertler (2008) suggested that while geographical proximity may play a role in fostering mutual understanding between innovation actors, innovation processes can be successfully spatially distributed when there is a strong social connectedness.

By considering these contrasting perspectives, the importance of the different forms of 'proximity' to developing open-innovation partnerships can be more thoroughly evaluated (Boschma, 2005; Boschma and Wenting, 2007). The rest of the chapter focuses on the UoL–Unilever case to examine the ways in which the collaboration has evolved in the last decade or so. In the next section we discuss the methodological approach adopted for carrying out the empirical research.

METHODOLOGICAL APPROACH

This research adopts a social constructivist perspective and seeks to provide insight into the *genesis* of the UoL–Unilever research partnership with the aim of extending our understanding of such collaboration to enhancing innovation and entrepreneurship. A single case study design is employed, as this facilitates a detailed exploration of context and relevant events, which can yield deeper insights (Stake, 1995, 2005; Siggelkow, 2007). The case study explores the nature and extent of interactions between Unilever and the UoL (as well as other relevant stakeholders) that have led to the emergence of the Centre for Materials Chemistry (CMD) based at the UoL campus within the Liverpool city-region.

The selection of the CMD case was informed by the concept of theoretical sampling (Eisenhardt and Graebner, 2007). The CMD represents a unique industry–academic research partnership between the UoL and Unilever, which has not been replicated by any other UK university (ERDF, 2009; Barr et al., 2013; Liverpool Local Enterprise Partnership, 2013). The collaboration dates back some years given the proximity of Unilever's original base at Port Sunlight on the River Mersey estuary.

The mix of domestic and EU funding has been used to generate state-of-the-art laboratories and involves the co-location of Unilever and UoL researchers (ERDF, 2009; Barr et al., 2013).

This research draws exclusively upon qualitative data primarily because the aim is to generate a comprehensive understanding of a phenomenon in a particular context. Therefore it was decided that the 'richness' (Bryman and Bell, 2011) that qualitative data provides would be most useful to serve the purpose of this study. The primary source of data is in-depth, semi-structured interviews carried out with the four most important individuals who were instrumental in establishing the CMD. These individuals were identified through consultation with a senior R&D manager in Unilever who was able to ensure access. The advice of the senior manager was deemed reliable as he was active within Unilever's R&D department at the time that the CMD was established. Although a comparably low number of interviews were carried out, the data is considered appropriate and sufficient because of the instrumental role that the selected interviewees had in the development of the partnership between Unilever and the UoL. Interviewees included founding partners of the CMD and current relationship managers from both organizations.

The initial interview guide was crafted progressively building on findings from a detailed in-depth pilot interview with a key informant that highlighted some of the pertinent issues in the development of the CMD. The final interview guide focused on three broad themes: (1) a general description of the CMD; (2) the development of the CMD; and (3) the contribution of the CMD to broader open-innovation efforts within the Liverpool city-region.

The interviewees were asked the same set of open questions to enable them to share their personal narrative of the establishment of the CMD. As a result of their various backgrounds and organizational roles, the interviewees highlighted different aspects of the establishment of the CMD, which enabled the construction of a holistic narrative account. All the in-depth interviews were undertaken by the first author and took place between June and September 2014; each lasted between 45 and 120 minutes. Data also included detailed documentary evidence including internal reports from the UoL and Unilever (such as corporate presentations) as well as Northwest Regional Development Agency (NWDA) funding proposals and European Regional Development Fund (ERDF) performance reports that contained detailed information on the contribution of the CMD to the development of the city-regional economy.

Data from interviews and documentary sources were used to construct a narrative account of the establishment of the CMD, which illustrated how interactions and knowledge transfer contributed towards the development of the open-innovation partnership. Following the construction of this narrative, data were coded to identify the most salient factors that were instrumental in the establishment of the CMD. Codes were devised retroductively, in that they were based on a review of the open-innovation literature as well as careful consideration of the data itself. All coding was completed by the lead author, although codes were discussed amongst the research team until consensus was reached. Coding resulted in four key themes that were instrumental in the establishment of the CMD: (1) geographic proximity between actors; (2) social proximity between individual agents; (3) public policy support; (4) the strategic emphasis on open innovation by Unilever, the 'orchestrator' firm (Nambisan and Sawhney, 2007). Data were also arranged into tables in order to highlight how different actors perceived the important factors in the establishment of the CMD. The next section discusses the empirical findings in detail.

MAIN FINDINGS

The CMD is the shared technological platform whose main purpose is to utilize 'high-throughput' (HT) technologies to enhance the process of materials discovery. These HT technologies include robotic synthesis platforms, liquid formulation and handling platforms as well as analytical technologies such as spectroscopic plate readers. The CMD contains what has been termed, generic radical technology (Maine and Garnsey, 2006) as the technology has potentially useful applications across a broad range of economic sectors as well as the potential to dramatically enhance the process of new materials discovery. The concentration of HT technologies in the CMD required significant capital expenditure, even for a global multinational organization such as Unilever. As a result, CMD funding was generated by interaction between several partners: Unilever, UoL, the (NWDA (now defunct) and the European Commission (via the ERDF) (ERDF, 2009; Barr et al., 2013).

In terms of the key stakeholders, Unilever are a multinational fast-moving consumer goods (FMCG) organization with annual revenues of approximately €50 billion. Open innovation is a strategic priority at Unilever. The organization was quick to adopt the principles of open innovation and still actively seeks to develop innovations from such open sources (Unilever PLC, 2013). The UoL is a research university with a research income of over £70 million (University of Liverpool, 2014). Over 50 per cent of research outputs from the chemistry department are classified as world-leading according to the latest available data.[1] All regional development agencies, including the NWDA, were abolished by the coalition government elected in June 2010 and replaced by Local Enterprise Partnerships (LEPs) (Bentley et al., 2010).

Partnership Emergence

In the early 2000s, Unilever began to embrace the principles of open innovation whereby R&D managers were encouraged to look for solutions to problems from sources outside the firm (Unilever PLC, 2013). During this time the issue of how synthetic chemistry was conducted at Unilever was subject to serious debate; the firm was seeking radical new ways to conduct synthetic chemistry in order to accelerate the pace of R&D. The favoured approach adopted by Unilever was the HT screening approach, which accelerates the process of materials discovery as it enables the production and analysis of large numbers of materials in parallel.

As a result Unilever sought to outsource synthetic chemistry research to HT screening organizations based in the USA, although the utility of this approach was limited, as highlighted by the head of one of Unilever's synthetic chemistry research groups:

> Large amounts of money were paid by Unilever to a company that had no real understanding of Unilever's needs, no history of what worked and didn't work in the past, that just screened looking for answers and threw things back over the fence to Unilever when it thought it had found something.

At that time, a manager in the Unilever measurement science group attempted to implement a collaborative partnership with another university in the Northwest region. The project focused on shared research outcomes and required a significant investment from Unilever. Ultimately the project failed to deliver, as the geographic distance between Unilever's R&D labs and the university meant staff found it difficult to meet regularly. The alignment around research outcomes also became difficult to maintain, which contributed towards the failure of the project.

Subsequently, the head of one of Unilever's synthetic chemistry groups sought to address innovation needs by engaging with the UoL, which was local to the company. He began talking to a research chemist at the UoL with whom he had ongoing collaborative projects. In fact, this was the catalytic event that led serendipitously to the establishment of the CMD. The two scientists – one from Unilever and one from the UoL – met regularly to discuss shared scientific issues and problems including the limitations of the high-throughput screening approach to materials discovery that Unilever had adopted. Such discussions ultimately led to the development of a new approach for the application of high-throughput technology for synthetic chemistry. This involved using applied conventional chemistry, which also enabled the production of substantial volumes of new materials, but speeding up the whole process by utilizing high-throughput technologies. This is fundamentally different to the screening approach that produces hundreds of materials in insufficient quantities that cannot be chemically tested. Collectively the two scientists believed that an increase in the speed of experimentation, which produced better and more insightful results, was much more beneficial than simply increasing the number of experiments from which the results were of limited utility. This quote from the Unilever research scientist illustrates the point:

> And what we said was that we would like to build a platform that did HT research, not HT screening, which was what [SX] was doing, apply conventional chemistry but quicker, making multiple grams of materials you could analyse. You knew what the material was and then you could do rapid analysis on how well it worked.

Following this, the two research scientists made an application to the (then) Department of Trade and Industry (DTI) for funding to locate the HT Technology Centre at the UoL. The initial bid was unsuccessful on the grounds that the amount of funding requested was not enough to cover the cost of the project. Subsequently, an updated funding application was developed that reconceptualized the centre as an open access facility that provided a *capability* to do advanced robotic synthesis enabled by a full-time staff of experimental officers. The alignment around a technological capability, open to any organization, as opposed to a focus on research outcomes was the critical success factor.

The two research scientists sought to achieve buy-in from senior managers within their respective organizations; the Head of the Chemistry Department at the UoL was a keen supporter of the project as it increased floor space for chemistry research. This was followed by endorsement from the UoL Pro Vice-Chancellor, which also made it easier to get buy-in from Unilever senior executives. This quote from the Unilever research scientist explains why his pitch was successful within Unilever:

> [...] a complementing activity close by that we [Unilever] become the prime customer of and probably design from the ground up, a willing partner in that creation and a partner that was keen to engage, access to funds which

Unilever couldn't get access to normally ... A capital base that wasn't ours, that didn't depreciate, we didn't own it, we just used it and not a single penny until it was built ... but also without losing the skills and training and the input from Unilever scientists.

After the industry and academic partners had an 'in principle' agreement on the project, funding was sought from the NWDA and ERDF. The proposal for public funding support was successful and the project commenced in June 2005; the centre opened in April 2007. The cost of the CMD exceeded £8 million of which 24 per cent was provided by the NWDA, 24 per cent from ERDF, 27 per cent by the UoL and 25 per cent by Unilever, which also contributed to the provision of software and training (ERDF, 2009; Barr et al., 2013).

Contribution to City-regional Innovation and Entrepreneurship

The CMD contributed to enhancing regional innovation and entre-preneurship in two main ways. First, it deliberately engaged with local small and medium-sized enterprises (SMEs). Second, it provided a model for triple helix collaboration that became trusted by both Unilever and the UoL. This is evidenced by the growing number of subsequent collabor-ative projects between these two organizations that are based on the successful CMD model.

In terms of SME engagement, the CMD assisted 30 small firms over the course of the ERDF funding period (2000 to 2006), through the provision of services including contract research, fixed-term working arrangements, fixed-term research staff, training workshops and know-ledge transfer partnerships (ERDF, 2009). Small firms invited to the CMD were typically introduced to the HT technology and were encour-aged to explore the potential applications of this technology. One small firm providing contract chemical synthesis used the CMD to train in HT technology. This training allowed the firm to speed up its processes, which meant that it could accept contracts that were previously unobtain-able. Another firm worked with the CMD to identify the applications of HT technology to their existing R&D. This firm was successful in securing public funding, which allowed them continued access to the CMD, enabling them to enhance their R&D activities. BE Energy, another local small firm, worked with the CMD to develop application of HT technology in its existing R&D portfolio. This firm also engaged with other organizations to prepare a successful proposal for public funding to undertake a 24-month research programme in the CMD, which significantly enhanced their R&D operations. Some start-up firms decided to locate in the UoL's incubator in order to gain access to the CMD (ibid.).

The CMD outperformed the expectations of the founding organizations. Unilever had three 'quick hits' with innovations developed at the CMD going to market rapidly. As of December 2013, the CMD had enabled Unilever to enhance the speed of its materials research by a factor of ten. It had also doubled the patent output per researcher and had delivered a total of five innovations to market, with another two global innovations approaching market readiness. The UoL was also able to accelerate the pace of research significantly, resulting in 17 publications in top-tier scientific journals from 2002 to 2013 based on research at the CMD. The success of the CMD ensured that the project has survived beyond its five-year initial plan, with Unilever committing to the facility until 2016 (ibid.).

The success of the CMD provided a model for industry–academia collaboration that was increasingly utilized by the UoL and Unilever and other projects have followed. For example, the Ultra-Processing and Mixing Facility is an open access facility, funded by Unilever and the UoL, providing unique capabilities in mixing and processing chemicals. Furthermore, in 2014 the Integrated High-Throughput Formulation Centre was opened. This project was based on the CMD model, whereby funding was derived from the UoL, Unilever and the UK government's Regional Growth Fund (RGF). This facility is also an open access facility that provides a capability in high-throughput formulation.

Most recently, the largest collaborative project between the two partners, called the Materials Innovation Factory (MIF) was agreed in 2014. This is an extension of the CMD and the MIF will accommodate 250 research staff and will incorporate a much broader array of technology, increasing its utility to organizations in various industries. Investment of £33 million was secured through Unilever, the UoL and the Higher Education Funding Council for England.[2]

In terms of key factors in the development of the open-innovation partnership, the individuals involved within Unilever and the UoL were significant in driving the development of the CMD. It was shared concerns about the existing application of HT technology that instigated the development of the CMD. Furthermore, the key individuals took responsibility for driving the project 'upwards' to senior management in their respective organizations. The CMD, however, was not set up strategically at a senior management level, but rather an organic project that was conceptualized, presented, pursued and developed by individual scientists operating at a middle-manager level. These individuals could see the potential for development of an open-innovation ecosystem. This was highlighted by one interviewee who suggested:

> [...] they agreed on a vision and worked on it so the four years they were working on it they were both trying to convince seniority at different levels in both institutions that this was the way to go forward and that it was the right thing.

Interviewees suggested that geographic proximity between Unilever and the UoL was 'essential' to the establishment of the CMD, for several different reasons. First, geographic proximity enabled regular face-to-face contact between the key individuals that conceptualized the CMD. It also ensured that contact between senior managers was straightforward and easy to maintain. Geographic proximity between the two partners ensured that any potential issues could be addressed quickly and facilitated mutual trust.

Second, the HT platforms that the CMD contained required the physical presence of research staff. The geographic proximity between the UoL and Unilever meant that it was much easier for knowledge transfer between managers in the latter organization to mobilize their research staff to engage with the CMD. Put simply, had the CMD been located elsewhere, this task could have been much more difficult and would have posed a serious threat to the viability of such a platform.

Third, the project area was eligible for significant EU funding as part of the then Merseyside Objective 1 programme.[3] This ensured that there was a large 'pot' of potential European funding to access. Moreover, funding from public organizations was 'critical to the success' of the CMD. The business plan highlights that NWDA funding in particular was crucial, as this ensured a match from the ERDF. The report also details that the funding from public organizations was crucial as there was a paucity of alternative funding options (ERDF, 2009). The most viable alternative option was a joint investment from Unilever and the UoL, although this would have meant the facility was considerably smaller and hence would have been of much less interest to Unilever. Public funding also meant that the UoL became more committed to the facility and this was highlighted by one senior UoL manager who suggested:

> I just needed some leverage on some funds and so as soon as we got the NWDA and ERDF funding we lined up the funding package, it was then quite straightforward for me to talk to the Dean and get him involved in the discussions.

In short, public funding provided the level of capital investment desired by Unilever, at a much reduced risk, and it also solidified the collaboration with the UoL, which was the main project sponsor.

The fourth factor critical to the establishment of the CMD was the support of Unilever. This helped to secure the public funds that were contingent on so-called 'match funding' from the private sector. Unilever were not only influential in securing the public funding but they also played a significant role in the design of the CMD, by adopting the role of a 'lead user' (Von Hippel, 1988). This fact was highlighted by one interviewee who was responsible for the management of the CMD:

> [...] we had an anchored-tenant. So our industrial match, we met straight away, so we weren't chasing around to get cash in, so we were secure in that ... If Unilever went away we could lose ERDF and NWDA support, it was like a house of cards ... It was a bit of a risk but we knew we could bring in the money.

CONCLUSIONS

Several points emerge from the CMD case that are worthy of note in terms of further understanding the formation of science-based open-innovation partnerships (Du et al., 2014).

First, the CMD case study narrative outlined here illustrates that both 'geography' and 'physical space' (Bathelt et al., 2004; Boschma, 2005) played a significant role in the formation and functioning of the open-innovation partnership. This is interesting because whilst 'place' is recognized as an important factor in other concepts, hitherto the open-innovation literature has largely failed to fully appreciate the role that 'geography' can play.

Geographic proximity was important as it facilitated the transfer and exchange of tacit knowledge; it also facilitated interpersonal trusting relationships and it enabled engagement with the technological platform. As scientists from Unilever and the UoL were co-located at the CMD, the exchange of tacit knowledge became commonplace (Barr et al., 2013). For example, scientists shared knowledge about how best to configure the HT technologies for certain purposes.

Furthermore, close geographic proximity between Unilever and UoL also meant that key personnel could be called upon when needed. This meant that any concerns could be addressed quickly, minimizing the risk of project failure. As the HT technological platform required physical user engagement, close geographic proximity had a direct effect on the user's ability to engage with the platform. It is suggested that the geographic proximity between Unilever's Port Sunlight facility and the CMD meant that research staff from Unilever were more willing to engage actively with the UoL and the CMD.

Third, evidence from the CMD suggests that EU and domestic funding can play a critical role in promoting the appropriate conditions for the establishment of such research partnerships. Other theoretical approaches such as the triple helix and regional innovation systems emphasize the role of institutional context and public policy in facilitating and instigating relationships between industry and academia (Autio, 1998; Etzkowitz et al., 2000; Cooke, 2001; Etzkowitz, 2003). The role of institutional context, however, is largely overlooked in the open-innovation literature. As a consequence of the public support, the other organizations involved in the establishment of the CMD arguably became more committed to the project, as the financial investment decreased the inherent risk of failure. Furthermore, support from public organizations was critical as the conditions attached to the EU funding ensured that smaller firms became engaged with the technological platform, contributing towards sustained open-innovation activities in the Liverpool city-region.

Furthermore, the creation of a common technology platform or 'capability' was a crucial success factor in the CMD, upon which the main stakeholders could cooperate and share knowledge. This was arguably much more beneficial than focusing on joint research outputs between Unilever and the UoL. Consequently, it is pertinent to suggest that policy-makers should consider much more a focus on 'platform policies' as opposed to more traditional cluster policies (Cooke, 2012). Cluster policy attempts to support a specialized concentration of knowledge and expertise within a specific geographic area (Porter, 2000; Cooke, 2012). Platform policies, on the other hand, aim to support more complex arrangements of organizations that operate in fields of 'related variety' (Cooke, 2012, p. 1419).

Similarly, local and regional agencies can play an active role in encouraging diverse firms to cooperate on specific technological platforms by, for example, coordinating events that share information on a novel technological capability (Abreu, 2011; Cooke, 2012). Alternatively, public agencies may wish to consider directly funding initiatives for the development of platform technologies, which have a wide range of applications across various industries and clusters (Cooke, 2012), as was the case with the CMD and the HT technology in Liverpool. These types of 'platform policies' may be particularly useful in stimulating local and regional economic development in areas that are economically challenged due to the decline of traditional industry clusters (ibid.).

Fourth, another important finding generated by this research is the importance of individual agency to the establishment and functioning of a dynamic open-innovation partnership. Ylinenpää (2009) highlights that, although the systems approaches conceive innovation as a social and interactive process (Edquist, 1997, 2005; Cooke, 2001; Lundvall et al., 2002; Lundvall, 2007), they fail to fully understand the roles played by individual actors, as well as serendipity, within the interactive innovation process. The UoL–Unilever case illustrates that individuals actually play a critical role in the interactive innovation process. It was the creation of trusting relationships between individuals from both organizations that helped to drive collaboration and knowledge transfer. Furthermore, it was the common concerns shared between individual scientists that led to the development of novel applications of the HT technology. Put simply, social proximity (Boschma, 2005; Boschma and Frenken, 2010) was one of the key drivers in the development of the CMD.

Fifth, prevailing theoretical perspectives within academic entre-preneurship suggest that the main contribution of universities to entre-preneurial endeavours occurs through a formal transfer of intellectual property (Perkmann et al., 2013). On the other hand, the CMD case suggests that universities may contribute to entrepreneurial efforts by providing tacit know-how, technological capabilities and 'open access' facilities that otherwise would have remained inaccessible.

For example, Polymer Ltd utilized the CMD technological platform so it could develop products that were relevant to Unilever. However, the generic nature of the technological facilities meant that not all small firms that utilized them were related to the core interests of Unilever. BE Energy's work with the CMD had little relevance to Unilever. They did, however, benefit from the tacit 'know-how' that was embedded in the CMD due to the presence of Unilever researchers, which allowed them to conduct more advanced R&D. BE Energy also benefitted in other ways from engagement with the CMD; they began to work closely with other partners such as the UoL. Dimension Heat Ltd benefitted in a similar way, in that engagement with the platform allowed them to become more familiar with other partners, which helped facilitate future science-based open-innovation partnerships and knowledge transfer.

Overall, the main benefit to small firms in this case was the access to the technological platform and knowledge transfer from Unilever and the UoL. To illustrate this point, the 30 small firms that engaged with the CMD benefitted primarily by receiving advice on the application of HT technology (ERDF, 2009). This was knowledge that the respective small firms would not have been able to access had they not engaged with the technological platform. In addition, this case study illustrates that small firms may benefit from engagement in open-innovation partnerships as the technological platform can act as an interface for triple helix relationships (Etzkowitz et al., 2000; Etzkowitz, 2003). These triple helix relationships may enhance the innovative capacity of small firms by enabling them to leverage external knowledge resources (Ranga et al., 2008). These relationships are often difficult for small firms to establish due to the communication barriers that exist between small firms, government agencies and universities (ibid.).

Last, the findings from the CMD case highlight that open-innovation partnerships contribute to a wide array of interactions that may be far more beneficial for nurturing innovation and entrepreneurship – for example, the provision of novel technological capabilities, collaborative and contract research, consultancy support and access to human capital. The focus hitherto in both the open-innovation and university–industry collaboration literatures is on the transfer and commercialization of formal intellectual property rights. However, this research illustrates that other forms of collaboration, such as the CMD, do provide very useful mechanisms to encourage research and development, innovation and entrepreneurship. There is a need, therefore, for more research to be carried out on the development of strategic partnerships (Dowling, 2015) between academic and industrial organizations.

NOTES

1. According to Research Excellence Framework 2014, accessed 1 June 2016 at http://results.ref.ac.uk/Results/BySubmission/2161.
2. See University of Liverpool (undated), 'Materials Innovation Factory', accessed 1 June 2016 at https://www.liverpool.ac.uk/materials-innovation-factory/.
3. Objective 1 status was allocated to regions whose GDP was below 75 per cent of average EU GDP.

REFERENCES

Abramovsky, L., R. Harrison and H. Simpson. (2007), 'University research and the location of business R&D', *Economic Journal*, **117** (519), 114–41.
Abreu, M. (2011), 'Absorptive capacity in a regional context', in B. Cooke, R. Asheim and R. Boschma et al. (eds), *The Handbook of Regional Innovation and Growth*, Cheltenham, UK and Northampton, MA, USA: Edward Elgar Publishing, pp. 211–21.
Agrawal, A. (2006), 'Engaging the inventor: exploring licensing strategies for university inventions and the role of latent knowledge', *Strategic Management Journal*, **27** (1), 63–79.

Ankrah, S. and O. Al-Tabbaa (2015), 'Universities–industry collaboration: a systematic review', *Scandinavian Journal of Management*, **31** (3), 387–408.

Asheim, B., L. Coenen, J. Moodysson and J. Vang (2007), 'Constructing knowledge-based regional advantage: implications for regional innovation policy', *International Journal of Entrepreneurship and Innovation Management*, **7** (2), 140–55.

Audretsch, D.B. and M.P. Feldman (1996), 'R&D spillovers and the geography of innovation and production', *American Economic Review*, **86** (3), 630–40.

Autio, E. (1998), 'Evaluation of RTD in regional systems of innovation', *European Planning Studies*, **6** (2), 131–40.

Barr, C., L. Barry, E. Thompson and J. Sharp (2013), 'Industry relationship framework, University of Liverpool', unpublished report, Liverpool: University of Liverpool Faculty of Science and Engineering.

Bathelt, H. (2002), 'The re-emergence of a media industry cluster in Leipzig', *European Planning Studies*, **10** (5), 583–612.

Bathelt, H. (2005), 'Cluster relations in the media industry: exploring the "distanced neighbour" paradox in Leipzig', *Regional Studies*, **39** (1), 105–27.

Bathelt, H., A. Malmberg and P. Maskell (2004), 'Clusters and knowledge: local buzz, global pipelines and the process of knowledge creation', *Progress in Human Geography*, **28** (1), 31–56.

Belderbos, R., M. Carree and B. Lockshin (2004), 'Cooperative R&D and firm performance', *Research Policy*, **33** (10), 1477–92.

Bentley, G., D. Bailey and J. Shutt (2010), 'From RDAs to LEPs: a new localism? Case examples of West Midlands and Yorkshire', *Local Economy*, **25** (7), 535–57.

Boschma, R.A. (2005), 'Proximity and innovation: a critical assessment', *Regional Studies*, **39** (1), 61–74.

Boschma, R.A. and K. Frenken (2010), 'The spatial evolution of innovation networks: a proximity perspective', in R. Boschma and R. Martin (eds), *The Handbook of Evolutionary Economic Geography*, Cheltenham, UK and Northampton, MA, USA: Edward Elgar Publishing, pp. 120–38.

Boschma, R.A. and J.G. Lambooy (1999), 'Evolutionary economics and economic geography', *Journal of Evolutionary Economics*, **9** (4), 411–29.

Boschma, R.A. and R. Wenting (2007), 'The spatial evolution of the British automobile industry: does location matter?' *Industrial and Corporate Change*, **16** (2), 213–38.

Brem, A. and J. Tidd (eds) (2012), *Perspectives on Supplier Innovation: Theories, Concepts and Empirical Insights on Open Innovation and the Integration of Suppliers, Series on Technology Management, Volume 18*, London: Imperial College Press.

Breschi, S. and F. Lissoni (2001), 'Knowledge spillovers and local innovation systems: a critical survey', *Industrial and Corporate Change*, **10** (4), 975–1005.

Bruneel, J., P. D'Este and A. Salter (2010), 'Investigating the factors that diminish the barriers to university–industry collaboration', *Research Policy*, **39** (7), 858–68.

Bryman, A. and E. Bell (eds) (2011), *Business Research Methods*, Oxford: Oxford University Press.

Carlsson, B. and R. Stankiewicz (1991), 'On the nature, function and composition of technological systems', *Journal of Evolutionary Economics*, **1** (2), 93–118.

Carlsson, B., S. Jacobsson, M. Holmen and A. Rickne (2002), 'Innovation systems: analytical and methodological issues', *Research Policy*, **31** (2), 233–45.

Chesbrough, H.W. (2003), *Open Innovation: The New Imperative for Creating and Profiting from Technology*, Boston, MA: Harvard Business School Press.

Chesbrough, H. (2011), 'Bringing open innovation to services', *MIT Sloan Management Review*, **52** (2), 85–90.

Chesbrough, H.W. and M.M. Appleyard (2007), 'Open innovation and strategy', *California Management Review*, **50** (1), 57–76.

Chesbrough, H and A.K. Crowther (2006), 'Beyond high tech: early adopters of open innovation in other industries', *R&D Management*, **36** (3), 229–36.

Chesbrough, H.W., W. Vanhaverbeke and J. West (2006), *Open Innovation: Researching a New Paradigm*, Oxford: Oxford University Press.

Chesbrough, H., W. Vanhaverbeke and J. West (eds) (2014), *New Frontiers in Open Innovation*, Oxford: Oxford University Press.

Cooke, P. (2001), 'Regional innovation systems, clusters, and the knowledge economy', *Industrial and Corporate Change*, **10** (4), 945–74.

Cooke, P. (2008), 'The evolution of biotechnology in bioregions and their globalisation', *International Journal of Biotechnology*, **10** (5), 476–95.

Cooke, P. (2012), 'From clusters to platform policies in regional development', *European Planning Studies*, **20** (8), 1415–24.

Cooke, P. and L. Leydesdorff (2006), 'Regional development in the knowledge-based economy: the construction of advantage', *Journal of Technology Transfer*, **31** (1), 5–15.

Cooke, P., M.G. Uranga and G. Etxebarria (1998), 'Regional systems of innovation: an evolutionary perspective', *Environment and Planning A*, **30** (9), 1563–84.

D'Este, P. and P. Patel (2007), 'University–industry linkages in the UK: what are the factors underlying the variety of interactions with industry?', *Research Policy*, **36** (9), 1295–313.

D'Este, P. and M. Perkmann (2011), 'Why do academics engage with industry? The entrepreneurial university and individual motivations', *Journal of Technology Transfer*, **36** (3), 316–39.

D'Este, P., F. Guy and S. Iammarino (2013), 'Shaping the formation of university–industry research collaborations: what type of proximity does really matter?', *Journal of Economic Geography*, **13** (4), 537–58.

Dodgson, M., D. Gann and A. Salter (2006), 'The role of technology in the shift towards open innovation: the case of Procter & Gamble', *R&D Management*, **36** (3), 333–46.

Doloreux, D. and S. Parto (2005), 'Regional innovation systems: current discourse and unresolved issues', *Technology in Society*, **27** (2), 133–53.

Dowling, A. (2015), *The Dowling Review of Business–University Research Collaborations*, London: Department for Business Innovation and Skills.

Du, J., B. Leten and W. Vanhaverbeke (2014), 'Managing open innovation projects with science-based and market-based partners', *Research Policy*, **43** (5), 828–40.

Edquist, C. (ed.) (1997), *Systems of Innovation: Technologies, Institutions and Organizations*, London: Pinter.

Edquist, C. (2005), 'Systems of innovation: perspectives and challenges', in J. Fagerberg, D.C. Mowery and R.R. Nelson (eds), *The Oxford Handbook of Innovation*, Oxford: Oxford University Press, pp. 181–208.

Eisenhardt, K.M. and M.E. Graebner (2007), 'Theory building from cases: opportunities and challenges', *Academy of Management Journal*, **50** (1), 25–32.

Eisenhardt, K.M. and C.B. Schoonhoven (1996), 'Resource-based view of strategic alliance formation: strategic and social effects in entrepreneurial firms', *Organization Science*, **7** (2), 136–50.

Etzkowitz, H. (2003), 'Innovation in innovation: the triple helix of university–industry–government relations', *Social Science Information*, **42** (3), 293–337.

Etzkowitz, H., A. Webster and C. Gebhardt et al. (2000), 'The future of the university and the university of the future: evolution of ivory tower to entrepreneurial paradigm', *Research Policy*, **29** (2), 313–30.

European Commission (2010), *Europe 2020 – A Strategy for Smart, Sustainable and Inclusive Growth*, Brussels: European Commission.

European Regional Development Fund (ERDF) (2009), *The Final Report for the ERDF Funded Project: 'Centre for High Throughput Materials Discovery' (ERDF/ 040617)*, Liverpool: European Regional Development Fund.

Fabrizio, K.R. (2009), 'Absorptive capacity and the search for innovation', *Research Policy*, **38** (2), 255–67.

Gertler, M.S. (1995) '"Being there"': proximity, organization, and culture in the development and adoption of advanced manufacturing technologies', *Economic Geography*, **71** (1), 1–26.

Gertler, M.S. (2003), 'Tacit knowledge and the economic geography of context, or the undefinable tacitness of being (there)', *Journal of Economic Geography*, **3** (1), 75–99.

Gertler, M.S. (2008), 'Buzz without being there? Communities of practice in context' in A. Amin and J. Roberts (eds), *Community, Economic Creativity and Organization*, Oxford: Oxford University Press, pp. 203–27.

Grant, R.M. and C. Baden-Fuller (2004), 'A knowledge accessing theory of strategic alliances', *Journal of Management Studies*, **41** (1), 61–84.

Grimaldi, R., M. Kenney, D.S. Siegel and M. Wright (2011), '30 years after Bayh-Dole: reassessing academic entrepreneurship', *Research Policy*, **40** (8), 1045–57.

Hagedoorn, J., A.N. Link and N.S. Vonortas (2000), 'Research partnerships', *Research Policy*, **29** (4), 567–86.

Huston, L. and N. Sakkab (2006), 'Connect and develop: inside Procter & Gamble's new model for innovation', *Harvard Business Review*, **84** (3), 58–67.

Jaffe, A.B., M. Trajtenberg and R. Henderson (1993), 'Geographic localization of knowledge spillovers as evidenced by patent citations', *Quarterly Journal of Economics*, **108** (3), 577–98.

Kalar, B. and B. Antoncic (2015), 'The entrepreneurial university, academic activities and technology and knowledge transfer in four European countries', *Technovation*, **36** (1), 1–11.

Lave, J. and E. Wenger (1991), *Situated Learning: Legitimate Peripheral Participation*, Cambridge, UK: Cambridge University Press.

Lissoni, F., P. Llerena, M. McKelvey and B. Sanditov (2008), 'Academic patenting in Europe: new evidence from the KEINS database', *Research Evaluation*, **17** (2), 87–102.

Liverpool Local Enterprise Partnership (2013), *Innovation within the Liverpool City Region*, Liverpool: Liverpool Local Enterprise Partnership.

Lundvall, B. (2007), 'National innovation systems – analytical concept and development tool', *Industry and Innovation*, **14** (1), 95–119.

Lundvall, B., B. Johnson, E.S. Anderson and B. Dalum (2002), 'National systems of production, innovation and competence building', *Research Policy*, **31** (2), 213–31.

Maine, E. and E. Garnsey (2006), 'Commercializing generic technology: the case of advanced materials ventures', *Research Policy*, **35** (3), 375–93.

Maskell, P. and A. Malmberg (1999), 'Localised learning and industrial competitiveness', *Cambridge Journal of Economics*, **23** (2), 167–85.

Moore, J.F. (1993), 'Predators and prey: a new ecology of competition', *Harvard Business Review*, **71** (3), 75–86.

Mowery, D.C., R.R. Nelson, B.N. Sampat and A.A. Ziedonis (2004), *Ivory Tower and Industrial Innovation: University–Industry Technology Transfer Before and After the Bayh-Dole Act*, Stanford, CA: Stanford University Press.

Nambisan, S. and M. Sawhney (2007), *The Global Brain: Your Roadmap for Innovating Faster and Smarter in a Networked World*, Upper Saddle River, NJ: Wharton School Publishing.

Nonaka, I. and H. Takeuchi (1995), *The Knowledge Creating Company: How Japanese Companies Create the Dynamics of Innovation*, Oxford: Oxford University Press.

Organisation for Economic Co-operation and Development (OECD) (2008), *Open Innovation in Global Networks*, Paris: OECD.

Organisation for Economic Co-operation and Development (OECD) (2010), *Ministerial Report on the OECD Innovation Strategy: Fostering Innovation to Strengthen Growth and Address Global and Social Challenges*: Paris: OECD.

Organisation for Economic Co-operation and Development (OECD) (2013), 'Main science and technology indicators; science, technology and R&D statistics', Paris: OECD.

Perkmann, M. and K. Walsh (2007), 'University–industry relationships and open innovation: towards a research agenda', *International Journal of Management Reviews*, **9** (4), 259–80.

Perkmann, M., V. Tartari and M. McKelvey et al. (2013), 'Academic engagement and commercialisation: a review of the literature on university–industry relations', *Research Policy*, **42** (2) 423–42.

Perren, L. and J. Sapsed (2013), 'Innovation as politics: the rise and reshaping of innovation in UK parliamentary discourse 1960–2005', *Research Policy*, **42** (10), 1815–28.

Petruzzelli, A.M. (2011), 'The impact of technological relatedness, prior ties, and geographical distance on university–industry collaborations: a joint-patent analysis', *Technovation*, **31** (7), 309–19.

Piller, F. and J. West (2014), 'Firms, users and innovation: an interactive model of coupled open innovation', in H. Chesbrough, W. Vanhaverbeke and J. West (eds), *New Frontiers in Open Innovation*, London: Oxford University Press, pp. 29–49.

Ponds, R., F. van Oort and K. Frenken (2007), 'The geographical and institutional proximity of research collaboration', *Papers in Regional Science*, **86** (3), 423–43.

Porter, M.E. (2000), 'Location, competition, and economic development: local clusters in a global economy', *Economic Development Quarterly*, **14** (1), 15–34.

Ranga, L.M., J. Miedema and R. Jorna (2008), 'Enhancing the innovative capacity of small firms through triple helix interactions: challenges and opportunities', *Technology Analysis and Strategic Management*, **20** (6), 697–716.

Rothaermel, F.T., S.D. Agung and L. Jiang (2007), 'University entrepreneurship: a taxonomy of the literature', *Industrial and Corporate Change*, **16** (4), 691–791.

Saxenian, A. (1994), *Regional Advantage: Culture and Competition in Silicon Valley and Route 128*, Boston, MA: Harvard University Press.

Shane, S.A. (2004), *Academic Entrepreneurship: University Spin-offs and Wealth Creation*, Cheltenham, UK and Northampton, MA, USA: Edward Elgar Publishing.

Siggelkow, N. (2007), 'Persuasion with case studies', *Academy of Management Journal*, **50** (1), 20–24.

Stake, R.E. (1995), *The Art of Case Study Research*, Thousand Oaks, CA: Sage Publications.

Stake, R.E. (2005), 'Qualitative case studies' in N. Denzin and Y.S. Lincoln (eds), *The Sage Handbook of Qualitative Research*, London: Sage Publications, pp. 443–66.

Tödtling, F. and M. Trippl (2005), 'One size fits all? Towards a differentiated regional innovation policy approach', *Research Policy*, **34** (8), 1203–19.

Unilever PLC (2013), *Annual Report and Accounts 2013*, London: Unilever PLC.

University of Liverpool (2014), 'About', accessed 1 June 2016 at https://www.liverpool.ac.uk/about/.

Van de Vrande, V., W. Vanhaverbeke and G. Duysters (2011), 'Additivity and complementarity in external technology sourcing: the added value of corporate venture capital investments', *IEEE Transactions on Engineering Management*, **58** (3), 483–96.

Von Hippel, E. (1988), *The Sources of Innovation*, London: Oxford University Press.

West, J., A. Salter, W. Vanhaverbeke and H. Chesbrough (2014), 'Open innovation: the next decade', *Research Policy*, **43** (5), 805–11.

Wikhamn, B. and W. Wikhamn (2013), 'Structuring of the open innovation field', *Journal of Technology Management and Innovation*, **8** (3), 173–85.

Ylinenpää, H. (2009), 'Entrepreneurship and innovation systems: towards a development of the ERIS/IRIS concept', *European Planning Studies*, **17** (8), 1153–70.

Index

academic entrepreneurship
  in 1990s Finland 122, 124
  in 1990s Russia 123–4
  equity-based collaborative
    interactions within 172
  as important contemporary research
    theme 3
  theoretical perspective within 186
  see also scientrepreneurs, role
    identity construction
Adam, A. 148, 157
agency theory 42, 44
Ahuja, G. 96–7, 110
Ajzen, I. 146–50, 153, 158
alliances, asymmetrical
  concepts and research questions 94–5
  conceptual frame of reference 95–8
  cross-case analysis
    influence of proximity 104–8
    limitations and future research
      111–12
    size asymmetry 102–4
    study conclusions and implications
      110–11
    study discussion 108–10
  methodology
    case presentation 100–102
    data analysis 99–100
    research design and data collection
      99
Alvarez, S.A. 96, 110
ambiguous legitimacy 22
Amit, R. 41, 77
amplified immediacy 12–13, 20–21
Anderson, B.B. 8–9
Andersson, S. 78, 80
Arthurs, J.D. 32, 44
Asheim, B.T. 108, 174

asymmetrical alliances *see* alliances,
  asymmetrical
attitudes
  towards behaviour, as determinant of
    intention 148–9
  towards entrepreneurship
    creating index of 153
    as having little effect on
      entrepreneurial behaviour
      150, 155–6
Audretsch, D.B. 168, 174
Autio, E. 72, 74, 88, 148–9, 185
Avdeitchikova, S. 49, 53

B2B markets to B2C markets 57–60
Balland, P.-A. 94, 97
Barr, C. 169, 176–8, 181, 184
Bathelt, H. 173–5, 184
BE Energy 181, 186
Becker, G.S. 52–3
behaviour, entrepreneurial *see*
  intention–behaviour link of
  graduates
behaviour theory 40, 44
Belderbos, R. 96, 173
Belleflamme, P. 31–4, 36–41
Berglund, K. 6–7
Bornstein, D. 8–9
Boschma, R.A. 95, 97–8, 174–6, 184,
  186
Bosse, D.A. 96, 110
Bourdieu, P. 10–11, 13
Brabham, D.C. 32–3
Busenitz, L.W. 32, 44
business angels (BAs)
  case narrative
    from B2B markets to B2C markets
      57–60

towards strategic cooperation
   60–63
case study
   analysis and discussion 63–5
   findings 65–6
   defining 49–51
   event-driven processual approach
      54–5
   factors precluding investment in
      emerging growth companies 35
   impact of crowdfunding acts 38
   literature review 50–54
   methodology 55–7
   non-financial contributions 52–4
   prior research on 49–50
   as traditional investors 30, 35
   unable to apply due diligence process
      40

Carsrud, A. 146–7
Centre for Materials Discovery (CMD)
   access to, as main benefit of small
      firms 186–7
   contribution to city-regional
      innovation and entrepreneurship
      181–4
   development of 168–9
   establishment of
      catalytic event leading to 179–81
      themes instrumental in 178
   funding 178–9, 181, 185
   highlighting contribution of open
      innovation partnerships 187
   highlighting universities'
      contribution to entrepreneurial
      efforts 186
   importance of geography and
      physical space 184–5
   individuals instrumental in
      establishing 177
   location 176
   platform technologies 185
   purpose of 178
   selection informed by theoretical
      sampling 176–7
   as shared technological platform 178,
      185–6
   social proximity as driver of 186

Certo, S.T. 41–2
Chao, Y.-C. 94, 112
Chesbrough, H.W. 168–70, 173
Chia, R.C.H. 10–11, 14
Chreim, S. 119, 130
city-regional innovation 181–4
collaborative innovation research
      partnerships, developing 171–3
collaborative network approach 10
collective
   effort 24
   as subject/actor 17
commercialization of intellectual
      property rights 168, 170–71, 187
commercialization of research 3, 117,
      119, 123, 125, 127–8, 131, 133–5
common industry experience 105,
      110–11
common technology platform *see*
      Centre for Materials Discovery
      (CMD)
Connelly, B.L. 32, 40, 44
ContentShare 55–66
control, in equity crowdfunding 42–3
Cooke, P. 168, 185–6
crowdfunders
   areas for future research 40
   perspective of 36–7
crowdfunding
   aims of 31
   classification into models 33–4
   conceptualization of 32–3
   equity model 34–5
   historical use of 33
   research interest in 30–31
   saturation of donation model 34
   see also equity crowdfunding
Cumming, D. 31, 35, 38–9, 41, 43
'cunning intelligence' 12

Dees, J.G. 8–9
Department of Trade and Industry (DTI)
      6, 180
D'Este, P. 97, 170–71, 174–5
Dezhina, I. 123–4
Dowling, A. 172, 187
Du, J. 173, 184
dynamic involvement 13, 21

ecosystem-level studies 170
Eisenhardt, K.M. 15–16, 25, 99, 173, 176
Engle, R.L. 149, 151
entrepreneurial behaviour *see* intention–behaviour link of graduates; start-up behaviour
entrepreneurial intentions
  attitude towards behaviour 148–9
  categorizations of previous studies 147
  intention–behaviour relationship 149–50, 156–7
  limitations and future research 157–8
  meaning of 146
  perceived behavioural control 149–51, 153, 155–6
  research methodology 151–4
  results and implications 154–7
  role of gender and entrepreneurial role models in 150–51, 153–5, 157
  subjective norm 148–51, 153, 155–6
entrepreneurial role models 150–51, 153–5
entrepreneurs
  and equity crowdfunding
    areas for future research 40–41
    perspective 37–8
  perspective on business angels 53, 56–66
  science-based *see* scientrepreneurs, role identity construction
entrepreneurship
  contributions to 181–4
  educators 156–7
  social 8–10
equity crowdfunding
  benefits and risks 36
  crowdfunder perspective 36–7
  founder perspective 37–8
  government perspective 38–9
  as innovative method of securitization 31
  research agenda for future studies
    asymmetric information, investment readiness and networks 41–2

crowdfunders 40
  entrepreneurs 40–41
  ownership and control 42–3
  regulatory environment 43
  research limitations 44
  research methods 31–2
  risk management 39–43
  vs traditional financing methods 34–5
Eriksson, P. 55–7
Etzkowitz, H. 117, 122, 125, 185, 187
European Commission 150, 157, 168, 170, 178
European Regional Development Fund (ERDF) 169, 176–8, 181, 183–4, 186
event-driven processual approach
  aim of 55
  analysis and discussion 63–5
  case narrative 57–63
  different research designs and methodologies 54–5
  intensive case study strategy 55–7
  main interest of 54
  study conclusions 65–6
'exploding,' risk of 10
'Explosion' project 14–15, 17–18, 20
external financing
  accessing
    difficulties in 30
    informal 30, 33
    traditional methods of 30, 35–6
  business angels as crucial source of 50–51
  of research activities, academic institution as shell for 132
  scientists competing for 117

Fayolle, A. 6, 146–8, 150, 156–8
Feldman, M.P. 168, 174
Fernandez, H. 6, 8
financial capital 9, 24–5
financial viability, urgency for 23–4
Finland
  1990s academic entrepreneurship 122, 124, 130
  as context for science-based entrepreneurship 121–5
  economic situation in 156

entrepreneurship increasingly
        accepted 131
instrument developed in 151, 158
meaning of being a scientist in 125–6
scientist becoming entrepreneurs
        126–8, 133–4
universities in entrepreneurship
        121–2, 124–5, 127, 132, 134,
        138–40
firm-level studies 169–70
franchising
    as commercial expansion strategy 8
    franchisor–franchisee study 13–25
    as method of accelerating diffusion of
        learning and growth 9
    social 8–9, 14, 24
    as strategy to control risk of
        'exploding' 10
Freear, J. 49, 53
Frenken, K. 175, 186
funding
    academic research
        in Finland 122, 124, 130–31
        in Russia 124, 130
    and business angels 53, 57, 59–61
    for university–industry collaboration
        169, 178–85
    see also crowdfunding; equity
        crowdfunding; external
        financing

Gassmann, O. 70–71, 89
gender, role of
    as categorical variable 154
    in entrepreneurial behaviour 150–51
    as independent variable 153
    in literature 147
    value in predicting start-up behaviour
        155, 157
geographical proximity
    academic and policy focus on 173
    benefits of, in university–industry
        study 183–5
    case study approach 99–100
    definitions and characteristics 98
    degree of, in study firms 101
    impact on innovation 173–4
    importance for small firms 94–5

influence of 104, 106–8
influence on transfer of knowledge
        and technology 174–5
limitations 175, 179
and 'local buzz' 174
non-spatial proximity compensating
        for lack of 111
study findings 108–9
George, G. 70, 72–3, 76
Gertler, M.S. 174–6
Ghoshal, S. 52–3
Giddens, A. 11, 17
Gimeno, J. 118, 126
government, and equity crowdfunding
        38–9, 43–4
graduate study *see* intention–behaviour
        link of graduates
Graebner, M.E. 99, 176
Gulati, R. 72, 97, 110

Hagedoorn, J. 171–2
Hakala, J. 117, 119, 125
Hamel, G. 94, 96
Hansen, T. 109, 111
'hard' task-centred activities
    of business angels 53
    as category of non-financial
        contributions 50
Harrison, R.T. 41, 50–51, 53
Henley, A. 146, 149
Henriksen, J.T. 95, 97
Hoang, H. 97, 118, 126
Holmlund, M. 108, 110
Holt, R. 10–11
Howe, J. 30, 32
HT (high-throughput) technologies
        178–86
Huberman, A.M. 99–100
human capital
    case demonstrating 55–66
    definition 52

individual agency 175–6, 186
individuals
    in open innovation partnerships 177,
        182–3, 186
    as subject/actor 17, 20
informal financing methods 30, 33

information asymmetry 41–2
Ingram, K. 149, 156
innovation, proximity dimensions of
    173–6
institutional context
    in open innovation 185
    role in scientrepreneurs study 130–33
institutional rules of action 18
intellectual property rights,
    commercialization of 168,
    170–71, 187
intention–behaviour link of graduates
    context and objectives of study 146–7
    implications of study 156–7
    limitations and future research 157–8
    literature review and hypotheses
        development
        entrepreneurial intentions 148–9
        intention–behaviour relationship
            149–50
        role of gender and entrepreneurial
            role models 150–51
    research methodology
        data collection process 151–3
        testing procedures 154
        variables 153, 164–7
    results 154–5
internationalization
    early
        areas for future research 88, 89–90
        definition 73
        discussion 86–7
        measures 76
        and resource flexibility 73–4
        results 80, 82, 84
        variables 76–9
    impact of resources
        data and methods 75–9
        limitations and future research
            87–8
        previous research 70–71
        results 80–85
        study discussion and conclusions
            86–90
        theory and hypotheses 72–5
    performance of new ventures
        areas for future research 88
        discussion 86–7

measures 76
    and resource flexibility 74–5
    results 84
    study implications 89–90
    variables 76–9
Internet
    crowdfunding via 31, 35–8, 40, 42
    sales, as control variable 71, 78–83,
        85
investment readiness 41–2

Jain, S. 117–19, 128, 133
Jarzabkowski, P. 12, 18
Joensuu, S. 146, 151, 157
Johan, S. 35, 38–9, 41, 43
Johannisson, B. 11–15, 17, 19, 25

Kaufmann Firm Survey (KFS) 71, 75–6
Kaukonen, E. 121–3
Kautonen, T. 42, 149–50, 156, 158
Keupp, M.M. 70–71, 89
Kiseleva, V.V. 123–4
Knoben, J. 94–5, 97–8
Kock, S. 108, 110
Koenig, M. 148–9
Kolvereid, L. 150–51
Kovalainen, A. 55–6
Krueger, N.F. 146, 148–9

Lane, P.J. 95, 98
Langley, A. 49, 54
Larralde, B. 33–4, 37
learning advantages of newness (LAN)
    72
legitimacy
    ambiguous legitimacy 22
    in asymmetrical alliances 97, 111
    awareness of social identity 18
    of entrepreneurship 131
    and social goals 9
Lehner, O.M. 31, 33–7, 40, 43
Letaifa, S.B. 95, 98, 108–9
Levinsohn, D.S. 15, 25
Li, D. 77, 97
liabilities of newness 73
liabilities of smallness 103, 108,
    110–11
Libaers, D. 119, 133

Lin, W.T. 72–3
Liñán, F. 146–7, 149–50, 158
Lissoni, F. 171, 176
Liverpool *see* university–industry
    collaboration
local adaptation 24
'local buzz' 174–5
lock-in 175
Loucks, D. 31, 35–6
Lubatkin, M. 95, 98
Lundvall, B. 168, 186
Lyon, F. 6, 8

Macht, S.A. 49–50, 52–4, 64
Macken Högsby 13–25
Macken Växjö 13–25
Mair, J. 6, 9
Malmberg, A. 173–4
Marti, I. 6, 9
Maskell, P. 173–4
Mason, C.M. 41, 50–51, 53, 63, 65
Matlay, H. 6, 146
Mattes, J. 109, 111
Meister, C. 95, 98
mentoring role 52–3
Merseyside *see* university–industry
    collaboration
Miles, M.B. 99–100
Mollick, E. 31–4, 38, 42–3
mutual dependence 110–11

Nahapiet, J. 52–3
Nelson, R.R. 17, 19
new logic of innovation 169
Nieminen, M. 121–2
non-financial contributions
    case highlighting 55–66
    literature review 52–4
Nonaka, I. 10, 174
Northwest Regional Development
    Agency (NWDA) 177–9, 181,
    183–4
Norwegian oil and gas industry *see*
    alliances, asymmetrical

OECD 76, 168
Oerlemans, L.A.G. 94–5, 97–8
open access facilities 180, 182, 186

open innovation (OI)
    case illustrating evolution of 176–87
    contribution of crowds 30–31
    developing collaborative innovation
        research partnerships 171–3
    ecosystem-level studies 170
    firm-level studies 169–70
    paradigm 169
    proximity dimensions 173–6
    role of university–industry
        collaboration 170–71
Ordanini, A. 31, 33, 35–8
organizational proximity
    case study approach 99–100
    definitions and characteristics 98
    degree of
        between alliance partners 97
        method of categorizing 100
    functions 95
    influence of 104–8
    study findings 109–11
ownership, and equity crowdfunding
    42–3

Patel, P. 170–71
Pentland, B.T. 49, 54
perceived behavioural control (PBC)
    creating index of 153
    as determinant of intention 149
    and gender effect on entrepreneurial
        intentions 151
    role in actual entrepreneurial
        behaviour 156
    start-up behaviour
        having direct effect on 149–50
        having value in predicting 155
Pérez, L. 96, 109
Perkmann, M. 168, 170–72, 186
personal relationships 105, 110–11
personal rules of action 18
Pless, N. 8–9
Polanyi, M. 14, 18
Politis, D. 49, 51–3, 63, 65–6, 117, 119
Polymer Ltd 186
Porter, M.E. 173, 185
practice theory 7, 10–12
processual character of social enterprise
    6

processual phenomenon,
    entrepreneuring as 7, 16
processual practices 12–13, 19–24
professional management approach 10
proximity
    dimensions of innovation 173–6
    literature, study results contributing
        to 111
    non-spatial 100, 110–12
    perspective
        benefits 97
        gaining central position in research
            streams 94, 97
        see also geographical proximity;
            organizational proximity; social
            proximity; technological
            proximity
Pruett, M. 148, 150

Rabeau, Y. 95, 98, 108–9
Rallet, A. 95, 98, 100, 109
regional innovation systems 25, 175,
    185
regulatory environment for equity
    crowdfunding 43
RENT Conference XXVIII 4–5
resource acquisition role
    case demonstrating 55–65
    as role through which non-financial
        contributions are delivered 52–3
resource flexibility
    conceptualization of 70, 75–6
    data and methods
        control variables 78
        dependent variables 76–7
        independent variable 77–8
        sample 75–6
        variable definitions 79
    gap in literature on role of 71–2
    limitations and future research 87–8
    results 80–85
    study discussion and conclusions
        86–90
    theory and hypotheses
        and early internationalization 73–4
        and performance of international
            new ventures 74–5
        slack resources 72–3

Reynolds, P.D. 123, 130
Riedl, J. 33, 36–8
risk
    in equity crowdfunding 39–43
    of 'exploding' 10
    taking, and resource flexibility 72–3
Robinson, K.C. 76–7
role identity construction *see*
    scientrepreneurs, role identity
    construction
Russia
    1990s academic entrepreneurship
        123–4, 132, 134
    as context for science-based
        entrepreneurship 121–5
    discussing identity through work
        content 129
    meaning of being a scientist in 125–6
    on role determinants 134
    scientist becoming entrepreneurs
        118, 123, 126–8, 130–31, 134
    self-identification as scientist 132
    universities in entrepreneurship
        122–3, 125, 132, 138–40
    use of snowballing method of
        research 120

Sætre, A.S. 49, 53, 63
Salamonsen, K. 95, 97
Sapienza, H. 71–3, 75, 88
Sarasvathy, S.D. 18–19, 74, 117, 119
Schatzki, T.R. 10–11, 18
Schewienbacher, A. 33–4, 37
Schlaegel, C. 148–9
Schwartz, A.A. 32–5, 38–42
scientists
    becoming entrepreneurs
        compatibility between identities
            128–30, 134
        in Finland 126–8, 133–4
        role conflict 118–19
        in Russia 118, 123, 126–8, 130–31,
            134
    contemporary expectations of 117
    involvement in commercial activities
        adopting hybrid role identity 119,
            133

all-encompassing sample 135,
   138–40
analysis supporting research on
   133
views on 117
role of, in Finland and Russia 125–6
self-identification as 132
scientrepreneurs, role identity
   construction
compatibility between identities as
   scientist and entrepreneur
   128–30
context and objectives of study
   117–18
data and methods 120–21
   examples of interview codes
      140–45
   profiles of scientrepreneurs
      138–40
Finland and Russia as contexts for
   science-based entrepreneurship
   121–5
meaning of being a scientist in
   Finland and Russia 125–6
meaning of scientist as entrepreneur
   126–8
role of institutional context in shaping
   role identities 130–33
study conclusions
   limitations and future research 135
   research implications 133–4
theoretical framing 118–20
Segal, G. 148–9
self-enforced heterogeneity 22–3
self-identity 18–19
Sequeira, J. 146–7, 149–50
Shane, S. 30, 50, 117, 119
Shapero, A. 148–9
Shiller, R.J. 30–31, 34, 43
Sigar, K. 31, 36
slack resources 70, 72–3, 87, 89
'smallness challenge' study *see*
   alliances, asymmetrical
social bricolage 12, 19–20
social capital
   case demonstrating 55–65
   definition 52
   and social enterprises 24–5

substitution with financial capital 9
social enterprise
   compared with commercial
      enterprise 6–7, 9–10
   defining 6
   practicing entrepreneuring as
      processual phenomenon 7, 16
   processual character of 6
   work integrating 7, 9–10, 12, 17
social entrepreneuring
   field research
      background and design 13–14
      implications for further research
         25
      methodology 14–16
      processual practices 19–24
      structural practices 16–19
      study conclusions 24–5
   practice theory 10–12
   previous research 12–13
   social enterprises 6–7
   social entrepreneurship 8–10
social franchising *see* franchising
social identity 18–19
social networks
   mobilizing equity crowdfunding
      36
   and provision of information 38,
      42
   use in accessing start-up finance
      30
social proximity
   as driver in CMD development 186
   and innovation 175–6
social relationships 105, 111
'soft' people-centred activities
   of business angels 53
   case demonstrating 55–64
   as category of non-financial
      contributions 50
Sokol, L. 148–9
Sorensen, I.E. 31–2, 36
Sørheim, R. 51–3
sounding board/strategic role
   case demonstrating 55–65
   as role through which non-financial
      contributions are delivered 52
Stam, E. 73–4

start-up behaviour
  after graduation, as dependent
    variable 153
  attitudes and subjective norm having
    no direct effect on 156
  gender as factor influencing 151, 155
  perceived behavioural control
    having direct effect on 149
  value in predicting 155
  statistical significance of intentions
    explaining 154
Steyaert, C. 6–7, 16, 54
structural practices 16–19
Stuart, T.E. 96, 110, 119
supervision and monitoring role
  case demonstrating 55–65
  as role through which non-financial
    contributions are delivered 52

tacit knowledge 14, 173–4, 176, 184,
    186
Takeuchi, H. 10, 174
Tarrazon, M.-A. 150–51
technological capabilities 180, 182,
    185–7
technological proximity
  case study approach 99–100
  definitions and characteristics 98
  degree of
    between alliance partners 97
    method of categorizing 100
  functions 95
  influence of 105–8
  study findings 110–11
technology, shared understanding of
    105, 110–11
theory of planned behaviour (TPB)
    147–50
Tödtling, F. 173, 175
Torre, A. 94–5, 98, 100, 109
traditional financing methods 30, 35–6
triple helix 181, 185, 187
Trippl, M. 173, 175

Unilever PLC 169, 171, 176–87
universities in entrepreneurship
  in Finland 121–2, 124–5, 127, 132,
    134, 138–40

in Russia 122–3, 125, 132, 138–40
university–industry collaboration
  context and objectives of study 168–9
  developing research partnerships
    171–3
  firm-level and ecosystem-level
    studies 169–70
  funding 169, 178–85
  individual agency 175–6, 186
  individuals 177, 182–3, 186
  institutional context 185
  main findings
    contexts 178–9
    contribution to city-regional
      innovation and
      entrepreneurship 181–4
    partnership emergence 179–81
  methodological approach 176–8
  open access facilities 180, 182, 186
  proximity dimensions 173–6
  role of 170–71
  study conclusions 184–7
  tacit knowledge 173–4, 176, 184,
    186
  technological capabilities 180, 182,
    185–7
University of Liverpool (UoL) 168–9,
    171, 176–87
urgency for financial viability 23–4

Van de Ven, A.H. 14, 54
Venkataraman, S. 42, 117, 119
venture capitalists
  equity model enabling 34
  factors precluding investment in
    emerging growth companies 35
  impact of crowdfunding acts 38
  as traditional investors 30, 35
  unable to apply due diligence process
    40
Villanueva, J. 97, 110

Walsh, K. 168, 170–72
Wang, T. 119, 133
Weigmann, K. 31, 38
Wenger, E. 18, 176
Werker, C. 95, 98
West, J. 169, 173

Wieck, E. 31, 33
Wikhamn, B. 169–70, 173
Wikhamn, W. 169–70, 173
Wilson, D.C. 12, 18
Wilson, F. 149–50
work integrating enterprises 7, 9–10,
    12, 17

Yang, H. 94, 96, 108, 110
Ylinenpää, H. 168, 186
Yordanova, D. 150–51

Zaheer, S. 74, 94
Zahra, S.A. 8, 36, 70, 73, 76
Zhang, Y. 146, 150